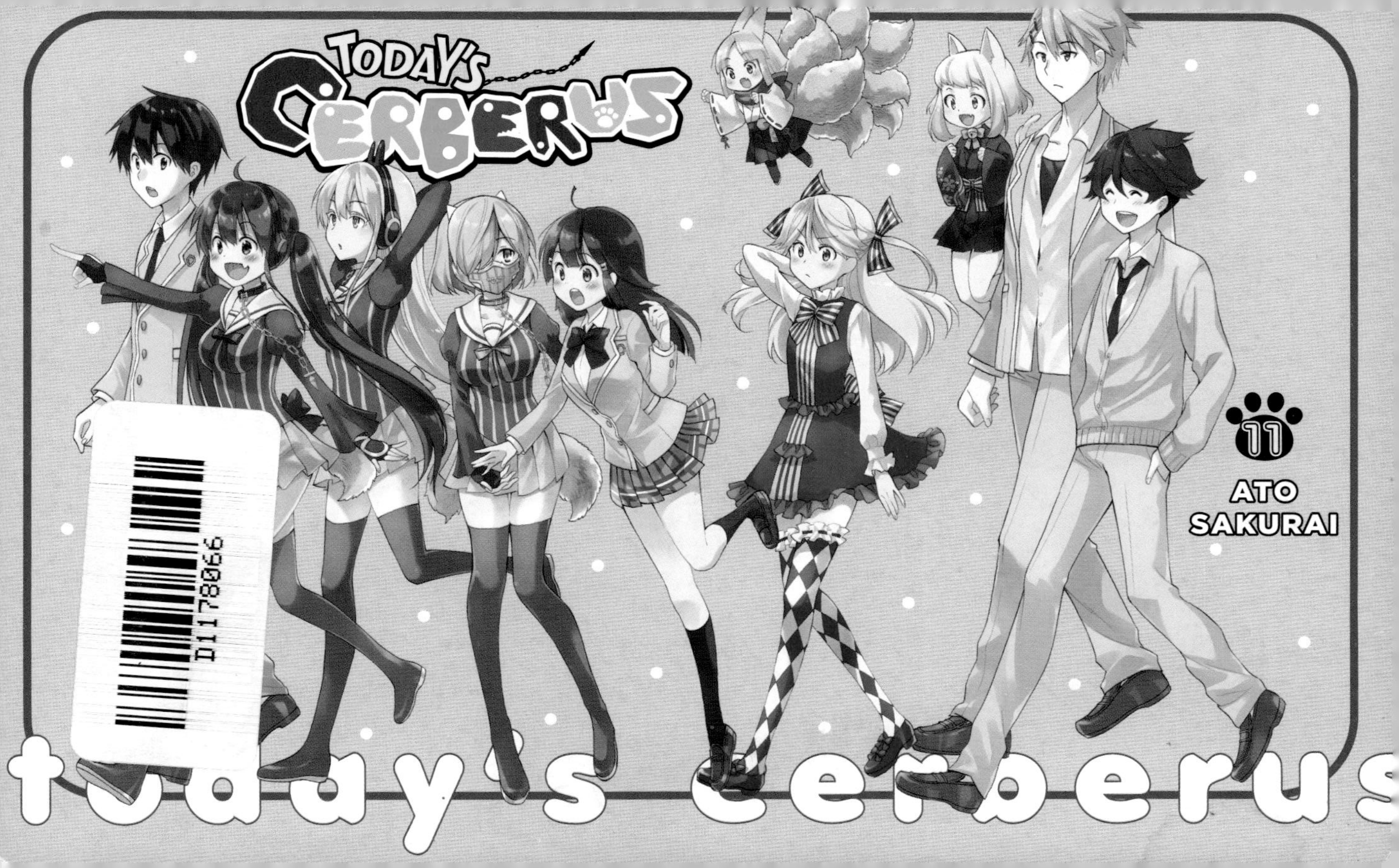
TODAY'S CERBERUS
11
ATO SAKURAI
today's cerberus

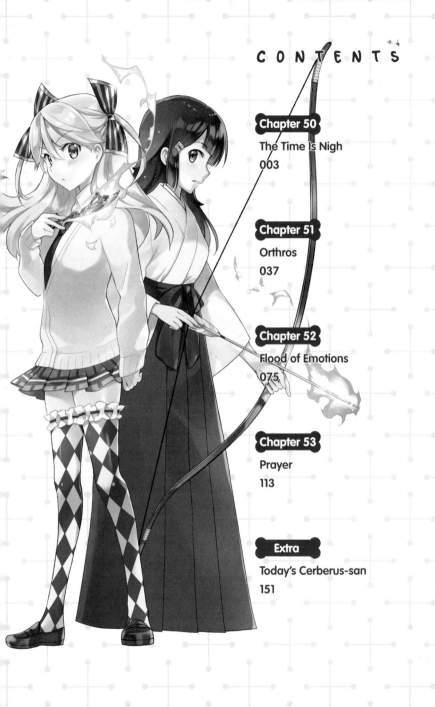

CONTENTS

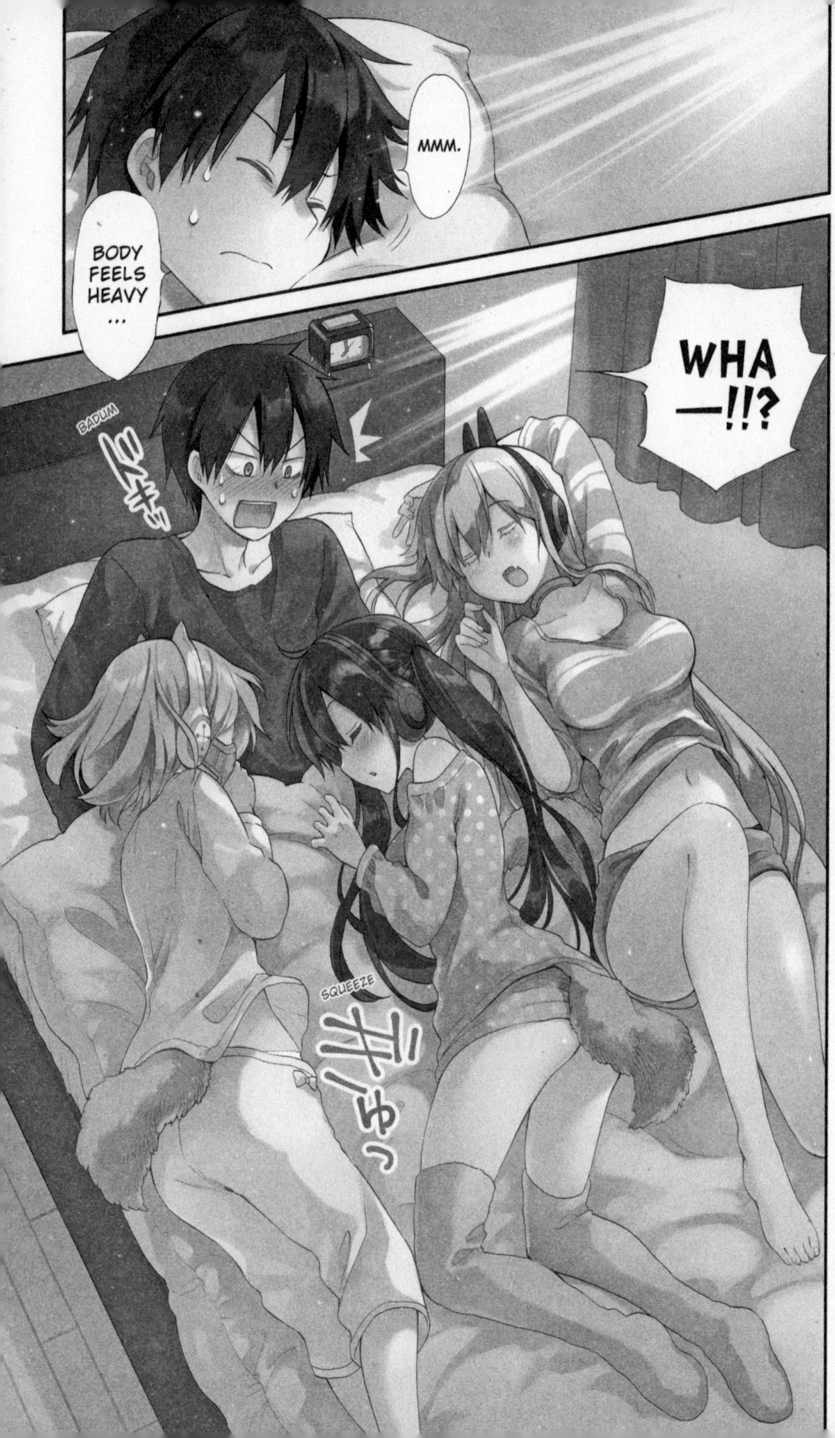
MMM.
BODY FEELS HEAVY ...
WHA—!!?
BADUM
SQUEEZE

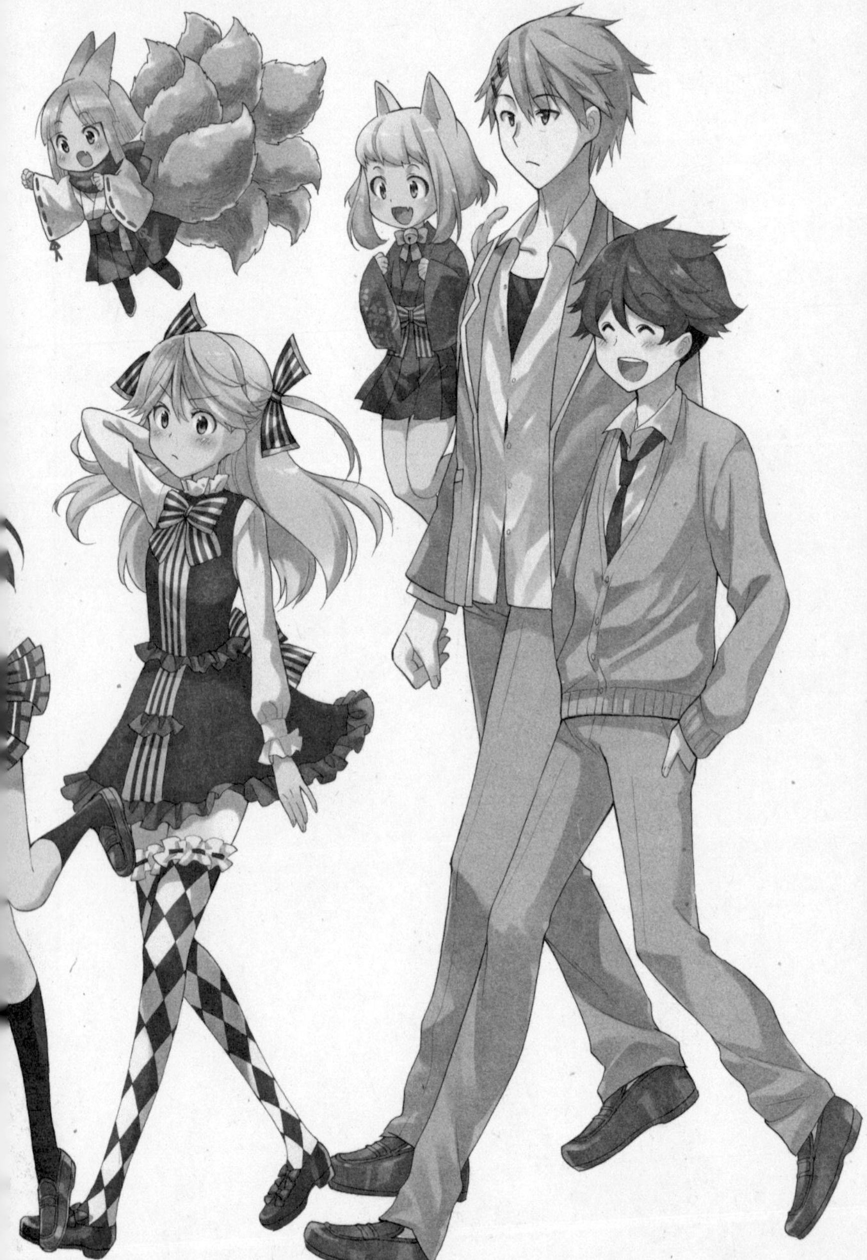

CHAPTER 50: THE TIME IS NIGH

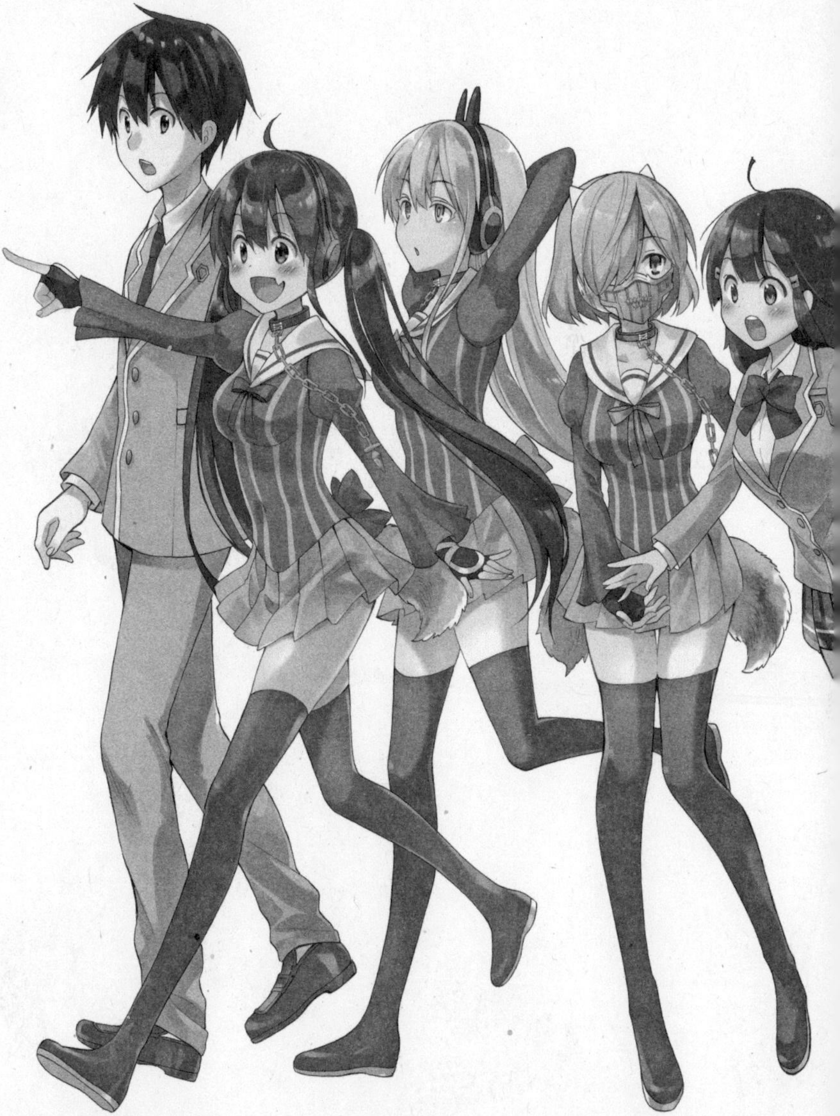

TODAY'S CERBERUS 🐾

SQUIRM
SQUIRM

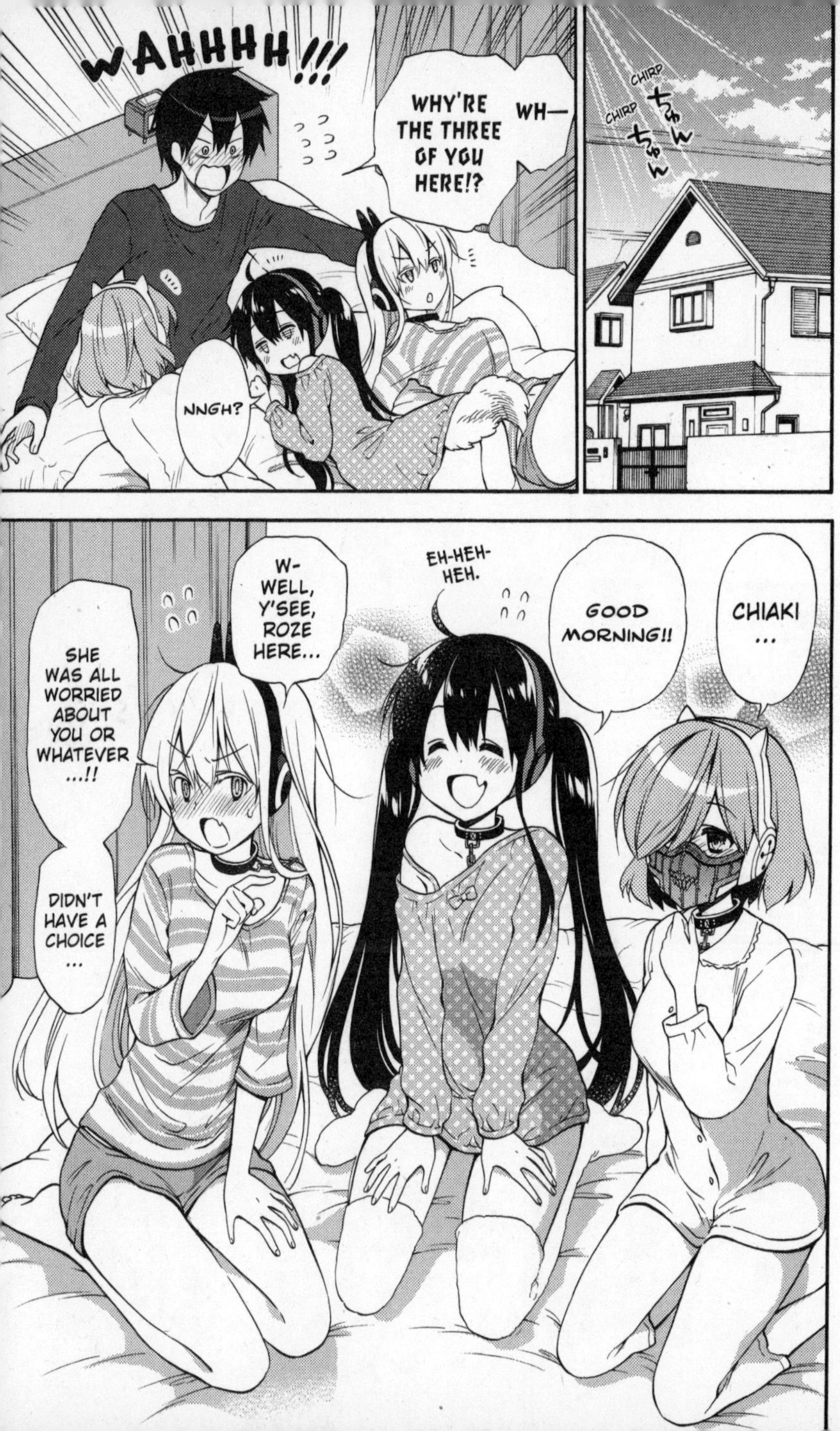
CHIRP
ちゅん
CHIRP
ちゅん
WH—
WHY'RE THE THREE OF YOU HERE!?
WAHHHH!!!
NNGH?
CHIAKI...
GOOD MORNING!!
EH-HEH-HEH.
W-WELL, Y'SEE, ROZE HERE...
SHE WAS ALL WORRIED ABOUT YOU OR WHATEVER...!!
DIDN'T HAVE A CHOICE...

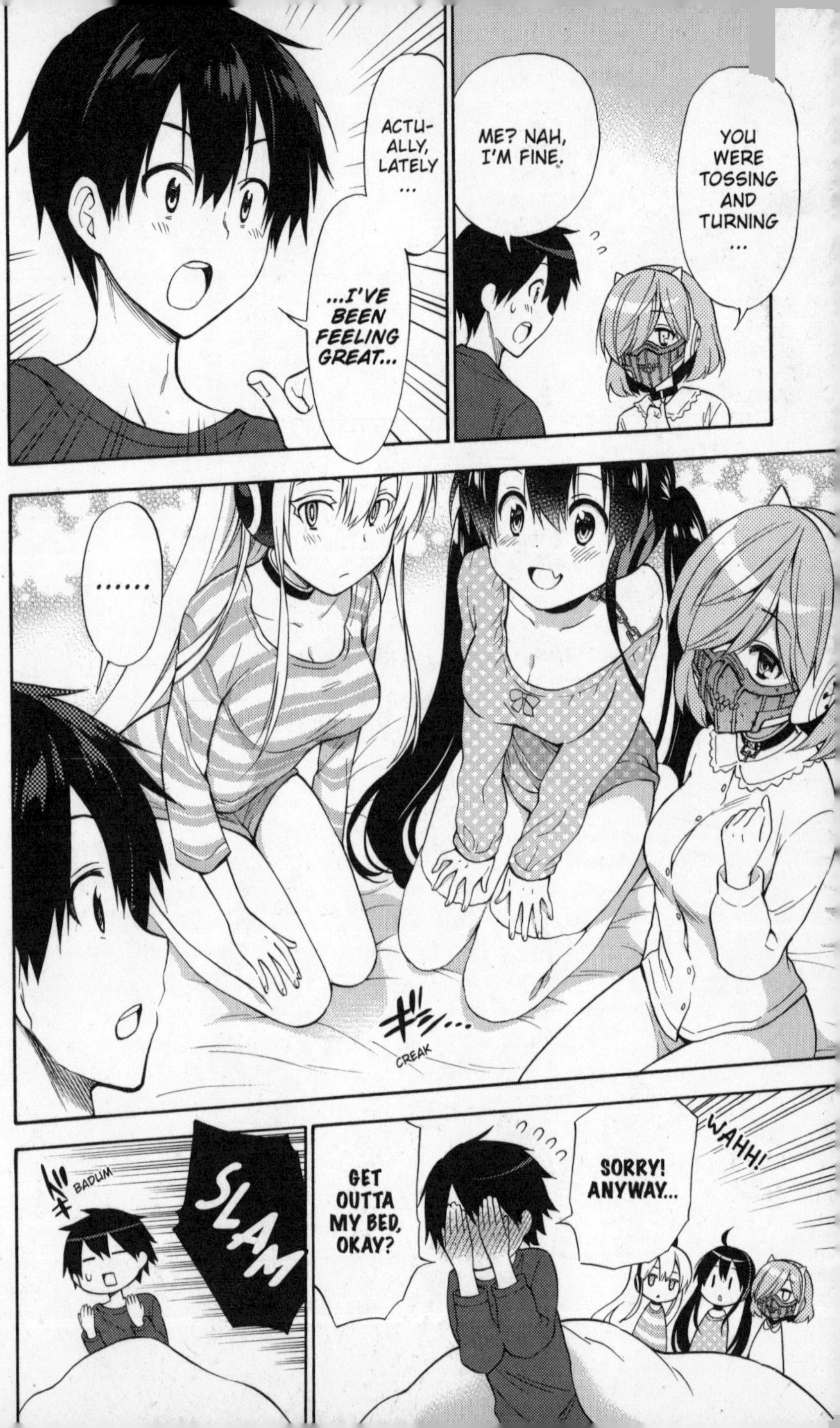
YOU WERE TOSSING AND TURNING...
ME? NAH, I'M FINE.
ACTU-ALLY, LATELY...
...I'VE BEEN FEELING GREAT...
......
CREAK
WAHH!
SORRY! ANYWAY...
GET OUTTA MY BED, OKAY?
SLAM
BADUM

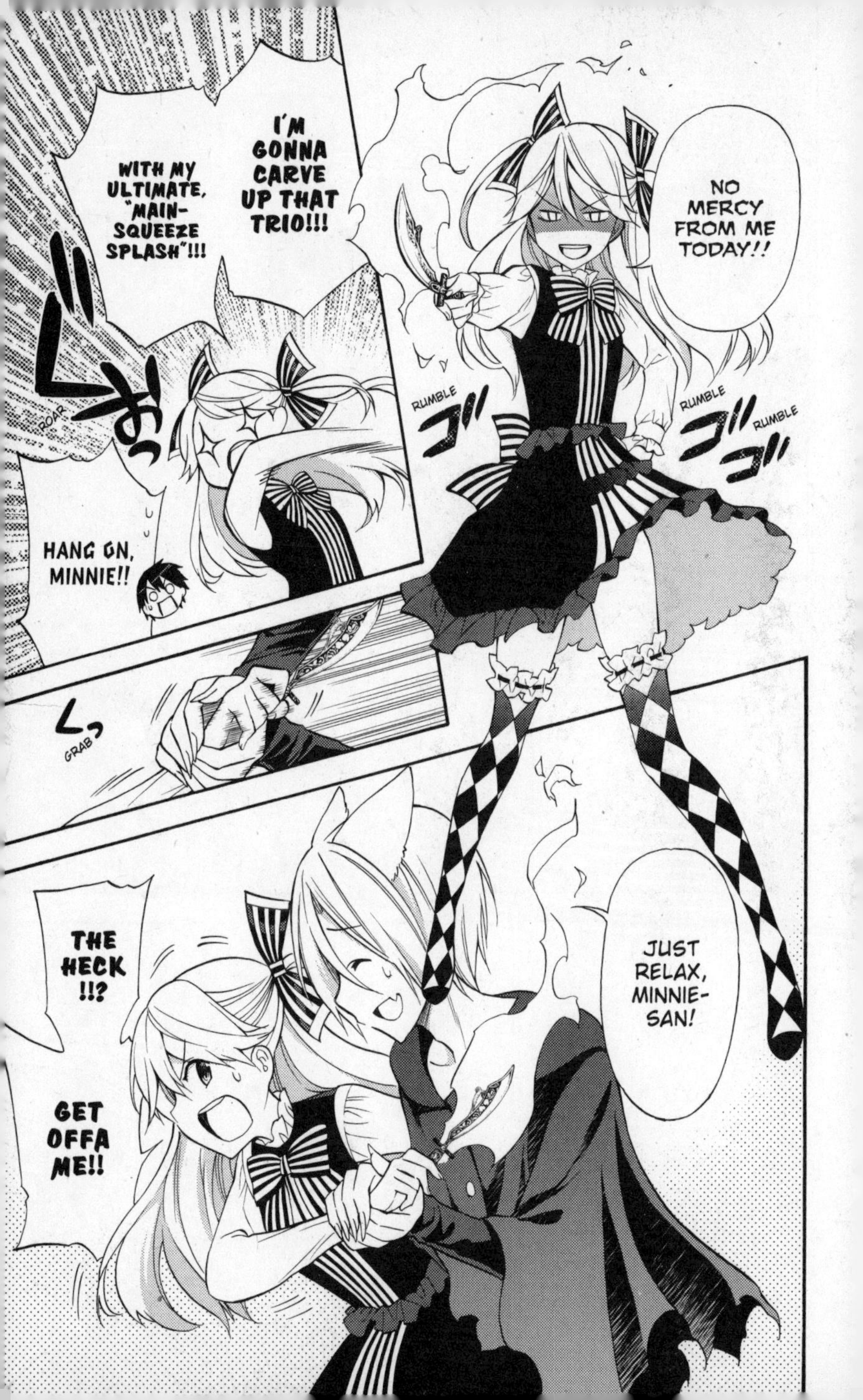

NO MERCY FROM ME TODAY!!
RUMBLE ゴ
RUMBLE ゴ
RUMBLE ゴ
I'M GONNA CARVE UP THAT TRIO!!!
WITH MY ULTIMATE, "MAIN-SQUEEZE SPLASH"!!!
ぐおっ ROAR
HANG ON, MINNIE!!
ぐっ GRAB
JUST RELAX, MINNIE-SAN!
THE HECK!!?
GET OFFA ME!!

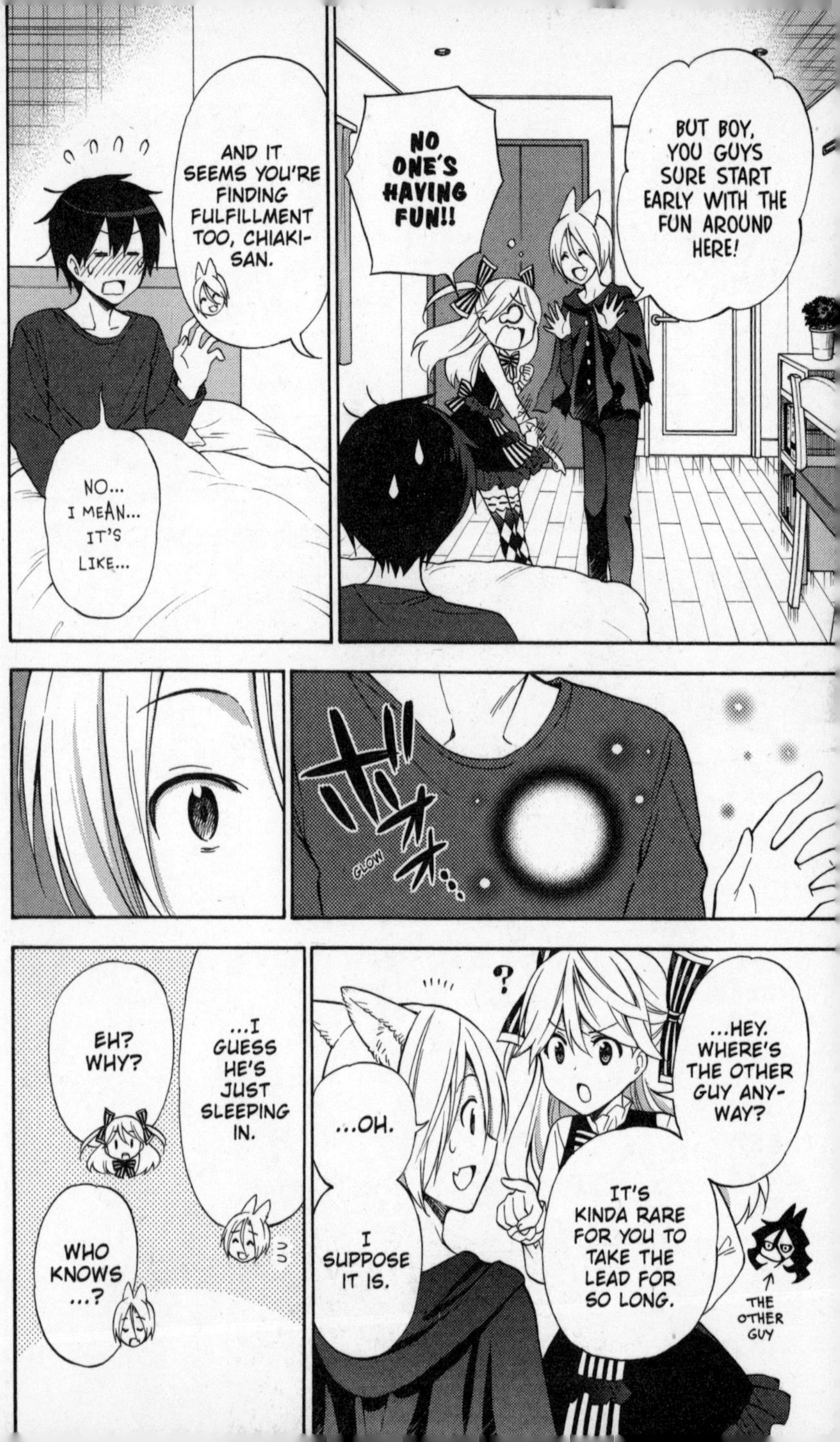
BUT BOY, YOU GUYS SURE START EARLY WITH THE FUN AROUND HERE!
NO ONE'S HAVING FUN!!
AND IT SEEMS YOU'RE FINDING FULFILLMENT TOO, CHIAKI-SAN.
NO... I MEAN... IT'S LIKE...
GLOW
...HEY. WHERE'S THE OTHER GUY ANYWAY?
...OH.
IT'S KINDA RARE FOR YOU TO TAKE THE LEAD FOR SO LONG.
I SUPPOSE IT IS.
THE OTHER GUY
...I GUESS HE'S JUST SLEEPING IN.
EH? WHY?
WHO KNOWS ...?

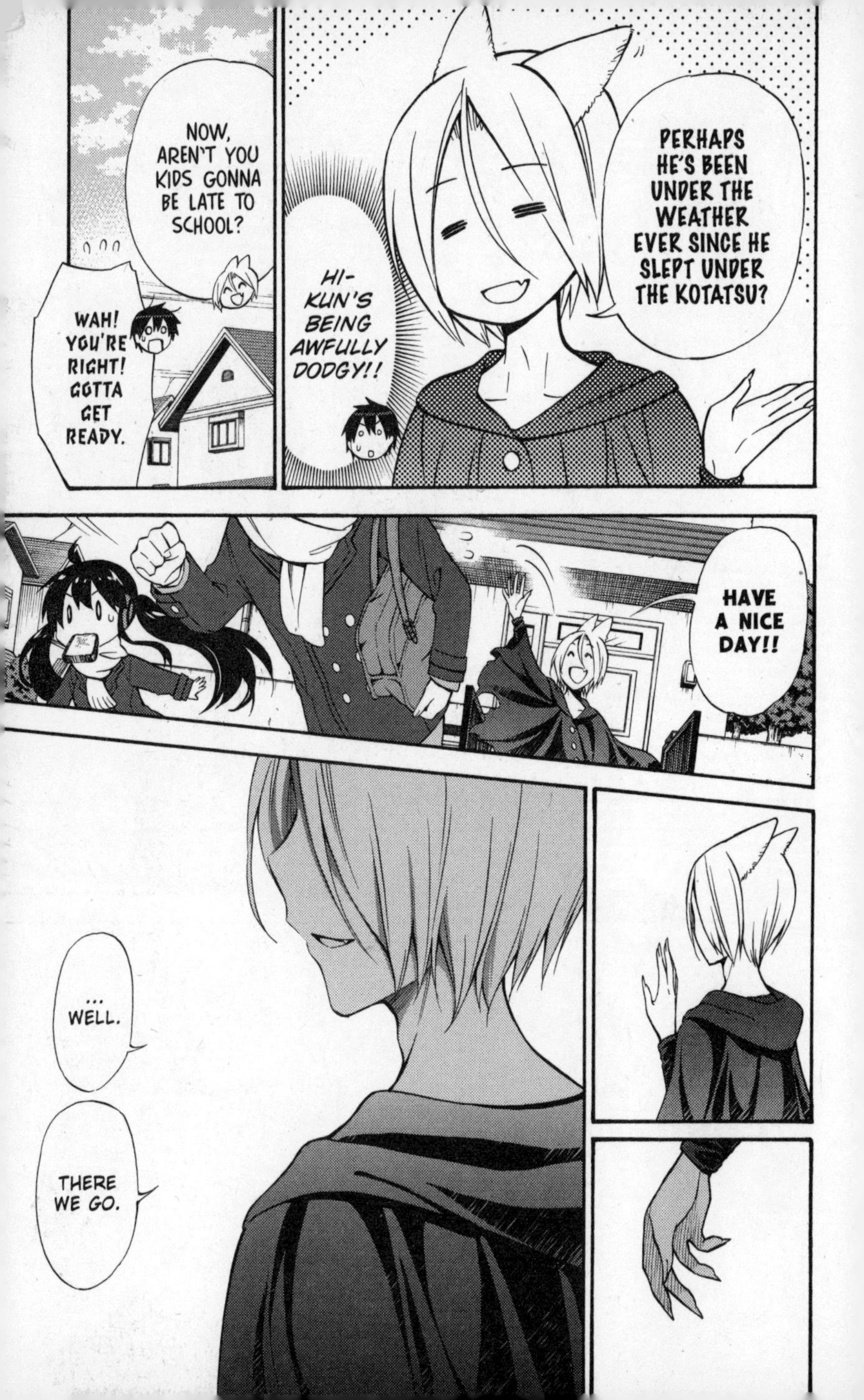
PERHAPS HE'S BEEN UNDER THE WEATHER EVER SINCE HE SLEPT UNDER THE KOTATSU?
HI-KUN'S BEING AWFULLY DODGY!!
NOW, AREN'T YOU KIDS GONNA BE LATE TO SCHOOL?
WAH! YOU'RE RIGHT! GOTTA GET READY.
HAVE A NICE DAY!!
... WELL.
THERE WE GO.

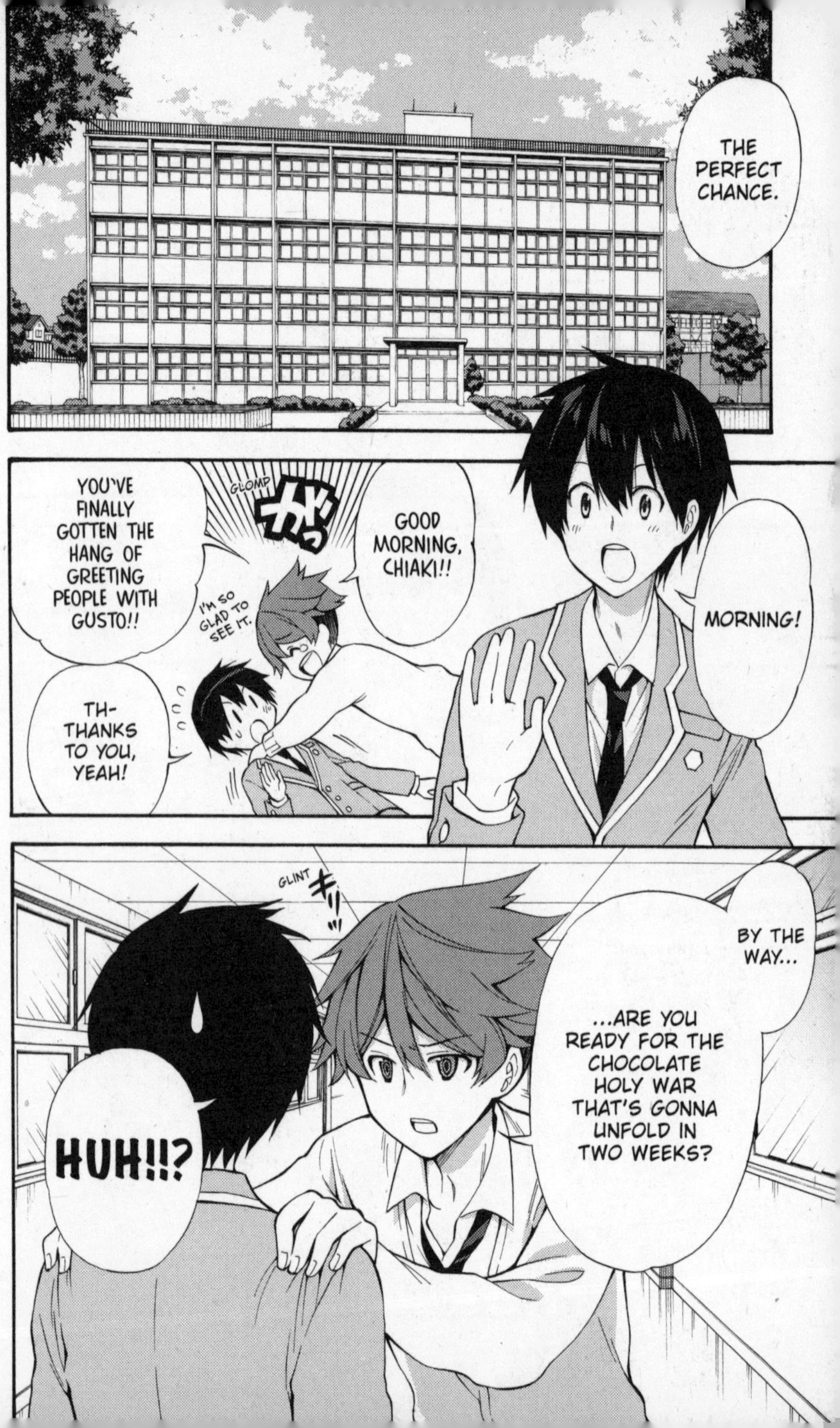
THE PERFECT CHANCE.
MORNING!
GOOD MORNING, CHIAKI!!
GLOMP
YOU'VE FINALLY GOTTEN THE HANG OF GREETING PEOPLE WITH GUSTO!!
I'M SO GLAD TO SEE IT.
TH- THANKS TO YOU, YEAH!
GLINT
BY THE WAY...
...ARE YOU READY FOR THE CHOCOLATE HOLY WAR THAT'S GONNA UNFOLD IN TWO WEEKS?
HUH!!?

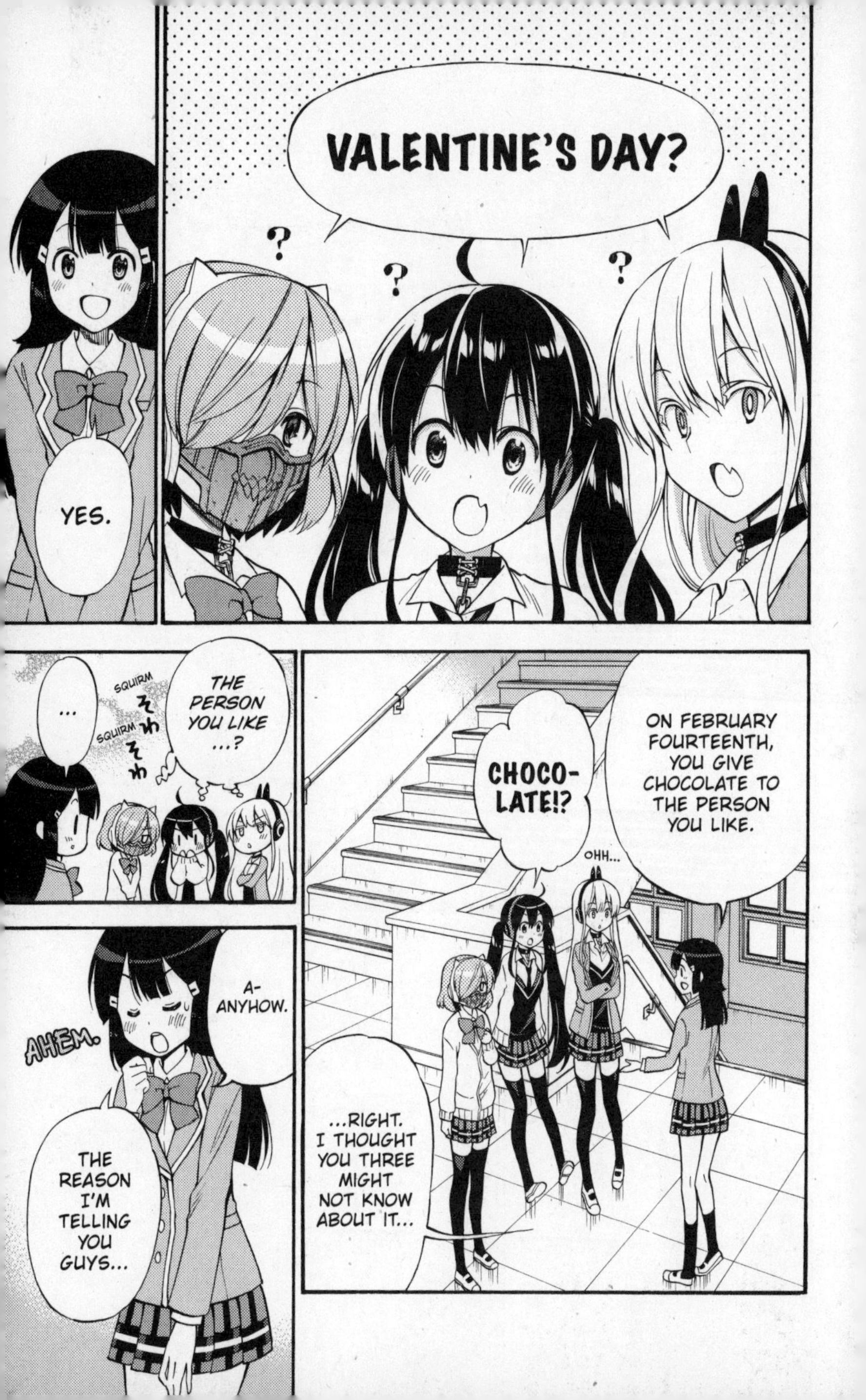
VALENTINE'S DAY?
YES.
ON FEBRUARY FOURTEENTH, YOU GIVE CHOCOLATE TO THE PERSON YOU LIKE.
CHOCO-LATE!?
OHH...
...RIGHT. I THOUGHT YOU THREE MIGHT NOT KNOW ABOUT IT...
THE PERSON YOU LIKE ...?
SQUIRM
SQUIRM
...
A- ANYHOW.
AHEM.
THE REASON I'M TELLING YOU GUYS...

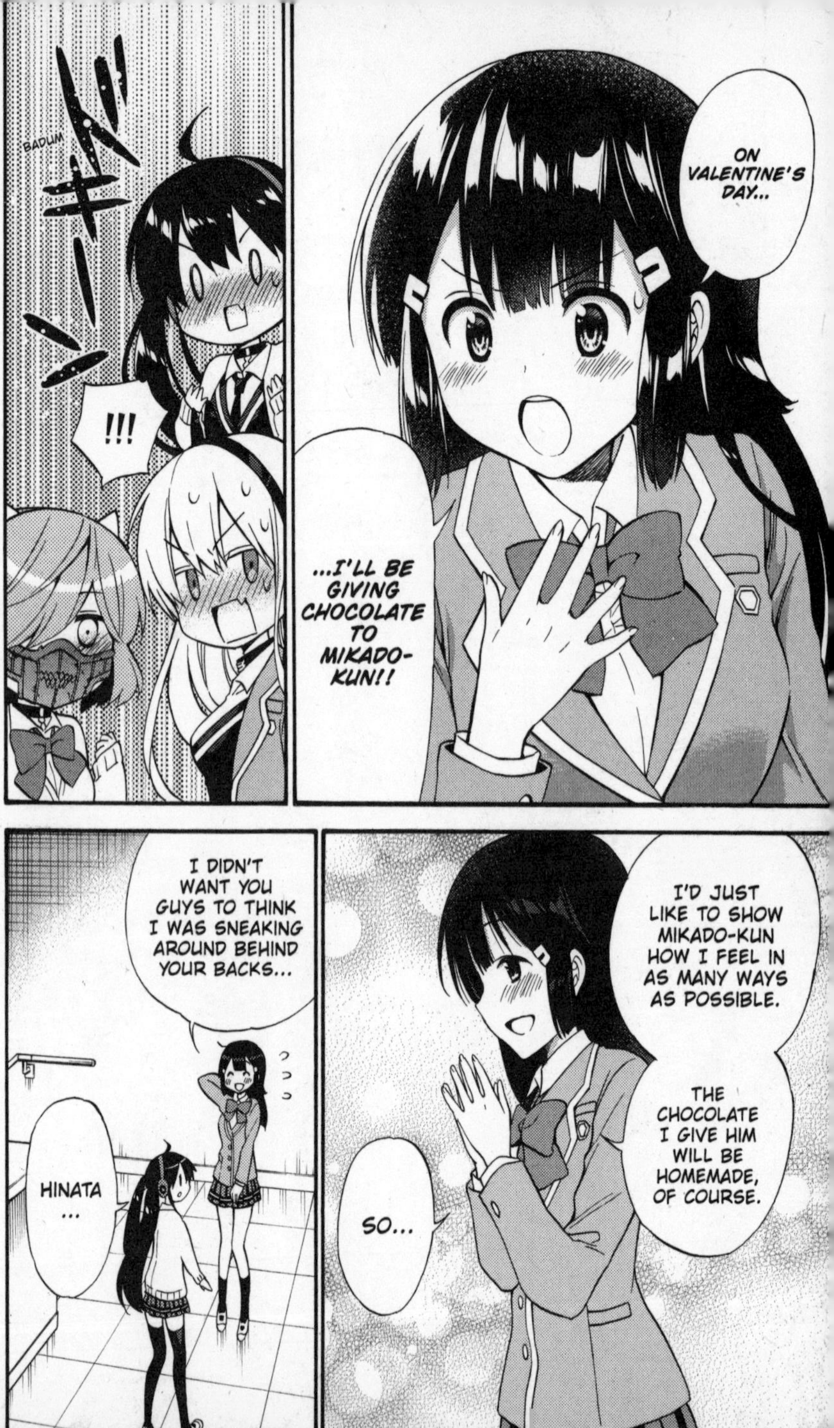
ON VALENTINE'S DAY...
...I'LL BE GIVING CHOCOLATE TO MIKADO-KUN!!
BADUM
!!!
I'D JUST LIKE TO SHOW MIKADO-KUN HOW I FEEL IN AS MANY WAYS AS POSSIBLE.
THE CHOCOLATE I GIVE HIM WILL BE HOMEMADE, OF COURSE.
SO...
I DIDN'T WANT YOU GUYS TO THINK I WAS SNEAKING AROUND BEHIND YOUR BACKS...
HINATA ...

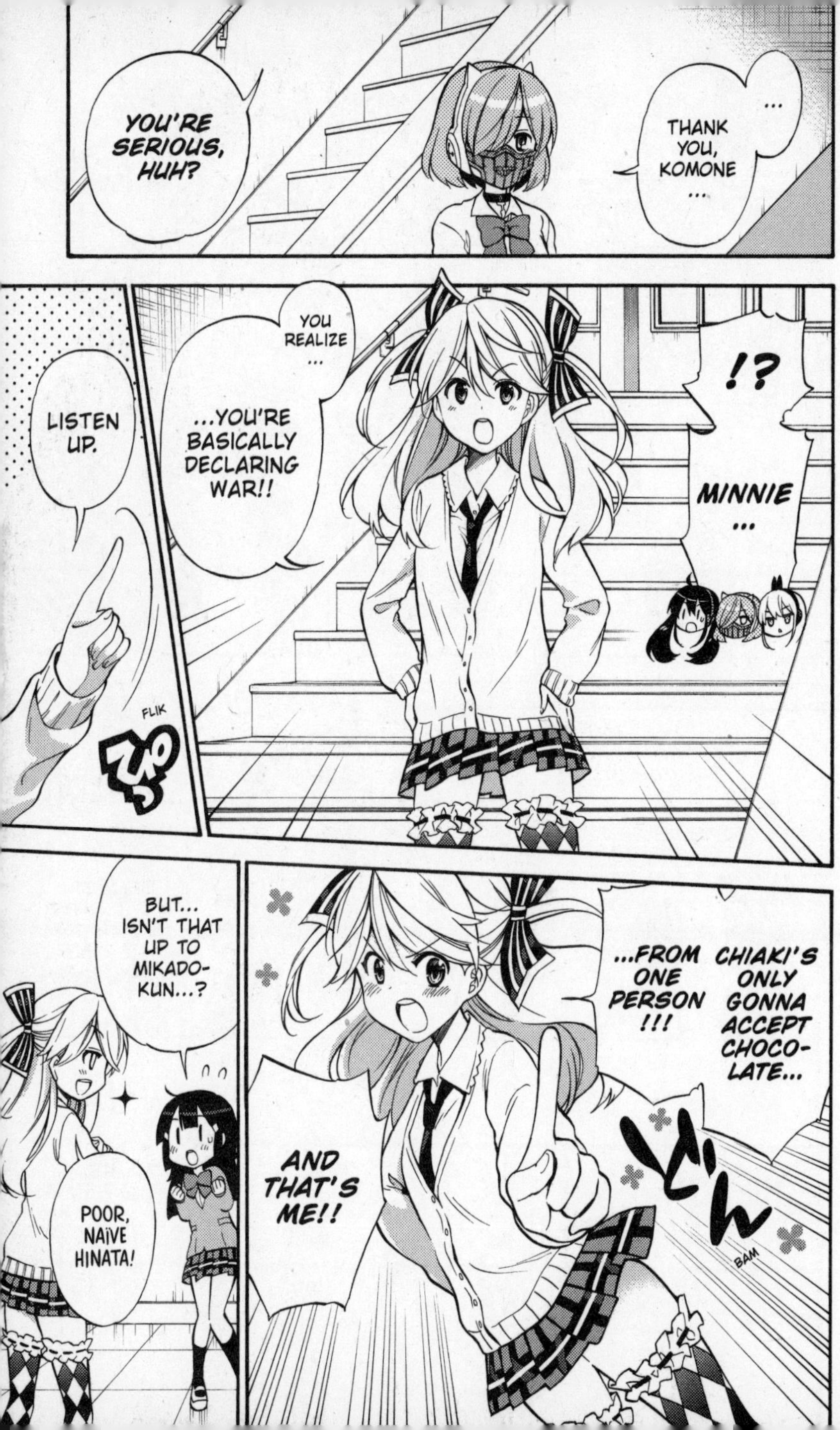
... THANK YOU, KOMONE ...
YOU'RE SERIOUS, HUH?
!?
MINNIE ...
YOU REALIZE ...
...YOU'RE BASICALLY DECLARING WAR!!
LISTEN UP.
FLIK
CHIAKI'S ONLY GONNA ACCEPT CHOCO-LATE...
...FROM ONE PERSON!!!
AND THAT'S ME!!
BAM
BUT... ISN'T THAT UP TO MIKADO-KUN...?
POOR, NAÏVE HINATA!

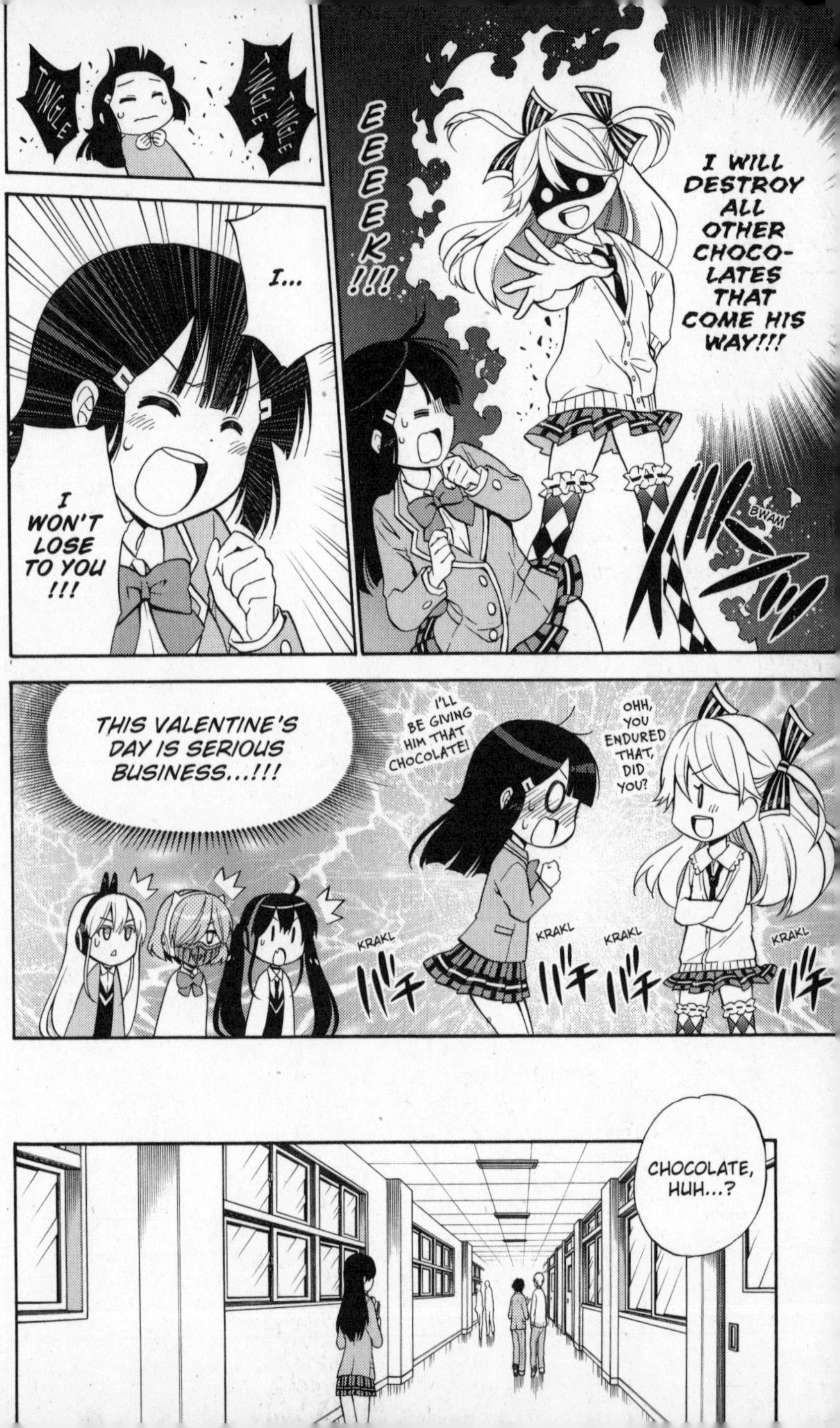
I WILL DESTROY ALL OTHER CHOCOLATES THAT COME HIS WAY!!!
EEEEEK!!!
BWAM
TINGLE
TINGLE TINGLE
I...
I WON'T LOSE TO YOU!!!
OHH, YOU ENDURED THAT, DID YOU?
I'LL BE GIVING HIM THAT CHOCOLATE!
THIS VALENTINE'S DAY IS SERIOUS BUSINESS...!!!
KRAKL
KRAKL
KRAKL
KRAKL
CHOCOLATE, HUH...?

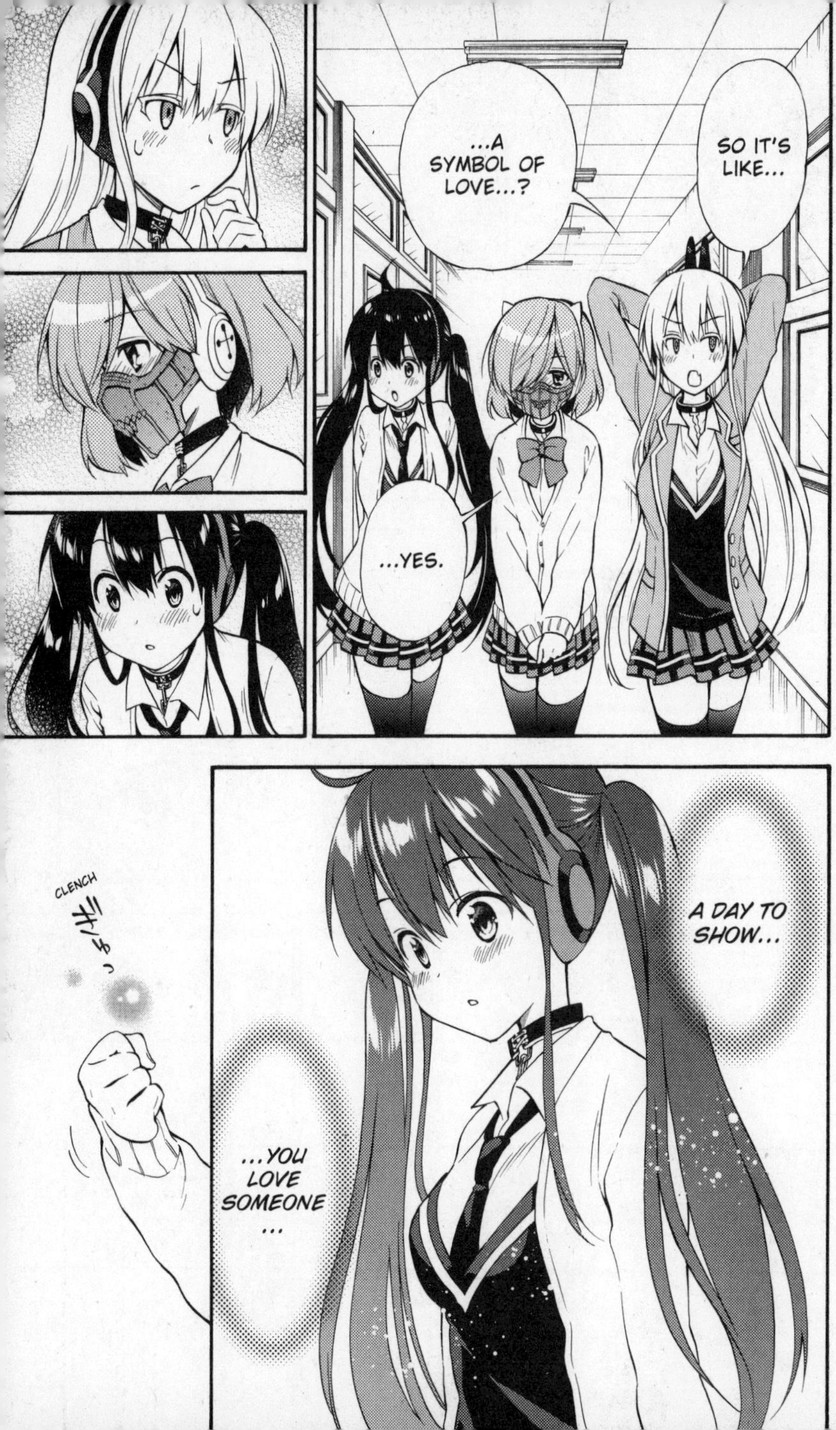
SO IT'S LIKE...
...A SYMBOL OF LOVE...?
...YES.
A DAY TO SHOW...
CLENCH
ぎゅっ
...YOU LOVE SOMEONE ...

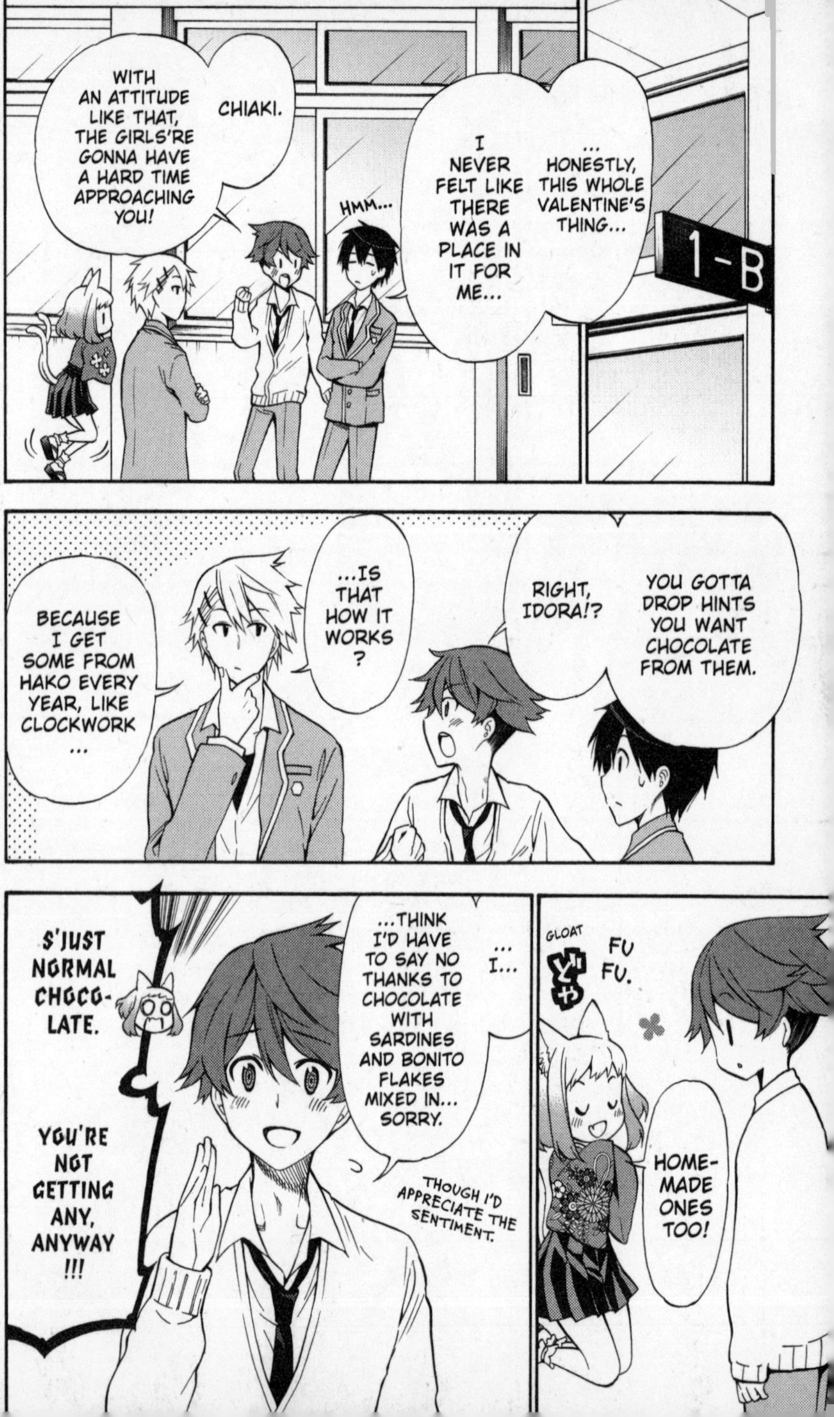
...HONESTLY, THIS WHOLE VALENTINE'S THING... I NEVER FELT LIKE THERE WAS A PLACE IN IT FOR ME...
HMM...
CHIAKI.
WITH AN ATTITUDE LIKE THAT, THE GIRLS'RE GONNA HAVE A HARD TIME APPROACHING YOU!
YOU GOTTA DROP HINTS YOU WANT CHOCOLATE FROM THEM.
RIGHT, IDORA!?
...IS THAT HOW IT WORKS?
BECAUSE I GET SOME FROM HAKO EVERY YEAR, LIKE CLOCKWORK...
GLOAT
FU FU.
HOME-MADE ONES TOO!
...I...
...THINK I'D HAVE TO SAY NO THANKS TO CHOCOLATE WITH SARDINES AND BONITO FLAKES MIXED IN... SORRY.
THOUGH I'D APPRECIATE THE SENTIMENT.
S'JUST NORMAL CHOCO-LATE.
YOU'RE NOT GETTING ANY, ANYWAY!!!

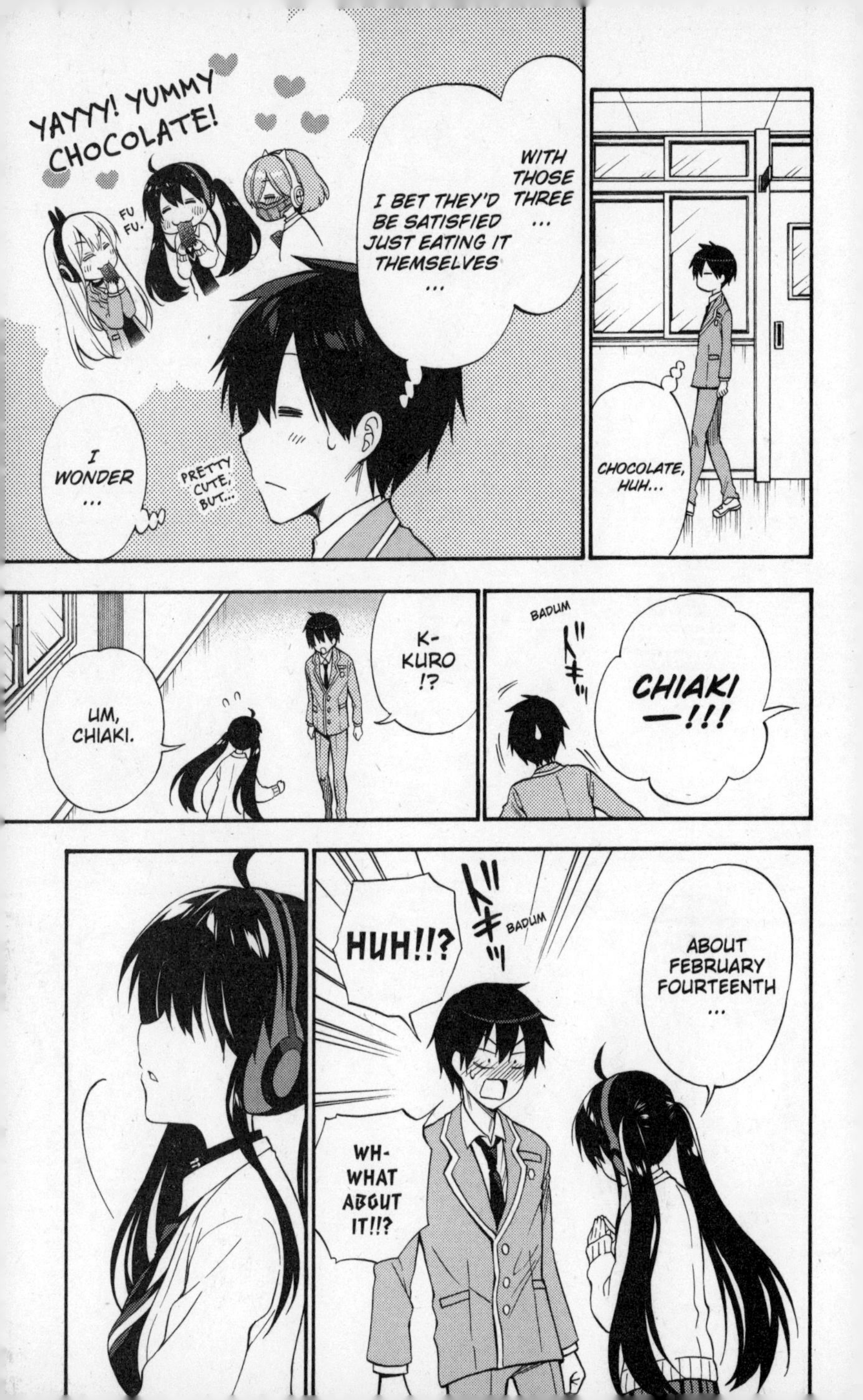
CHOCOLATE, HUH...
WITH THOSE THREE ...
I BET THEY'D BE SATISFIED JUST EATING IT THEMSELVES ...
YAYYY! YUMMY CHOCOLATE!
FU FU.
PRETTY CUTE, BUT...
I WONDER ...
BADUM
CHIAKI —!!!
K-KURO !?
UM, CHIAKI.
ABOUT FEBRUARY FOURTEENTH ...
BADUM
HUH!!?
WH- WHAT ABOUT IT!!?

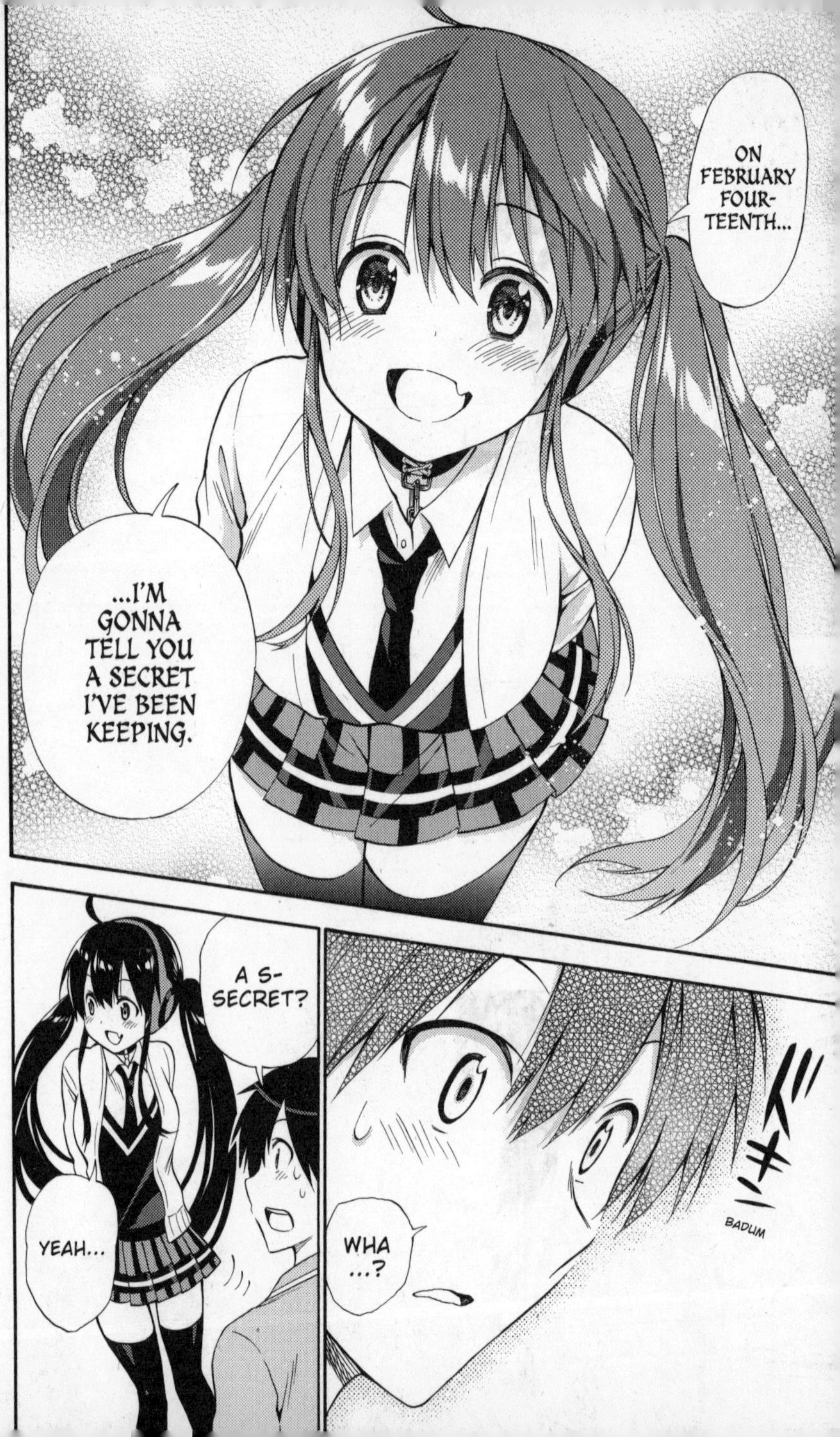
ON FEBRUARY FOUR-TEENTH...
...I'M GONNA TELL YOU A SECRET I'VE BEEN KEEPING.
BADUM
WHA ...?
A S-SECRET?
YEAH...

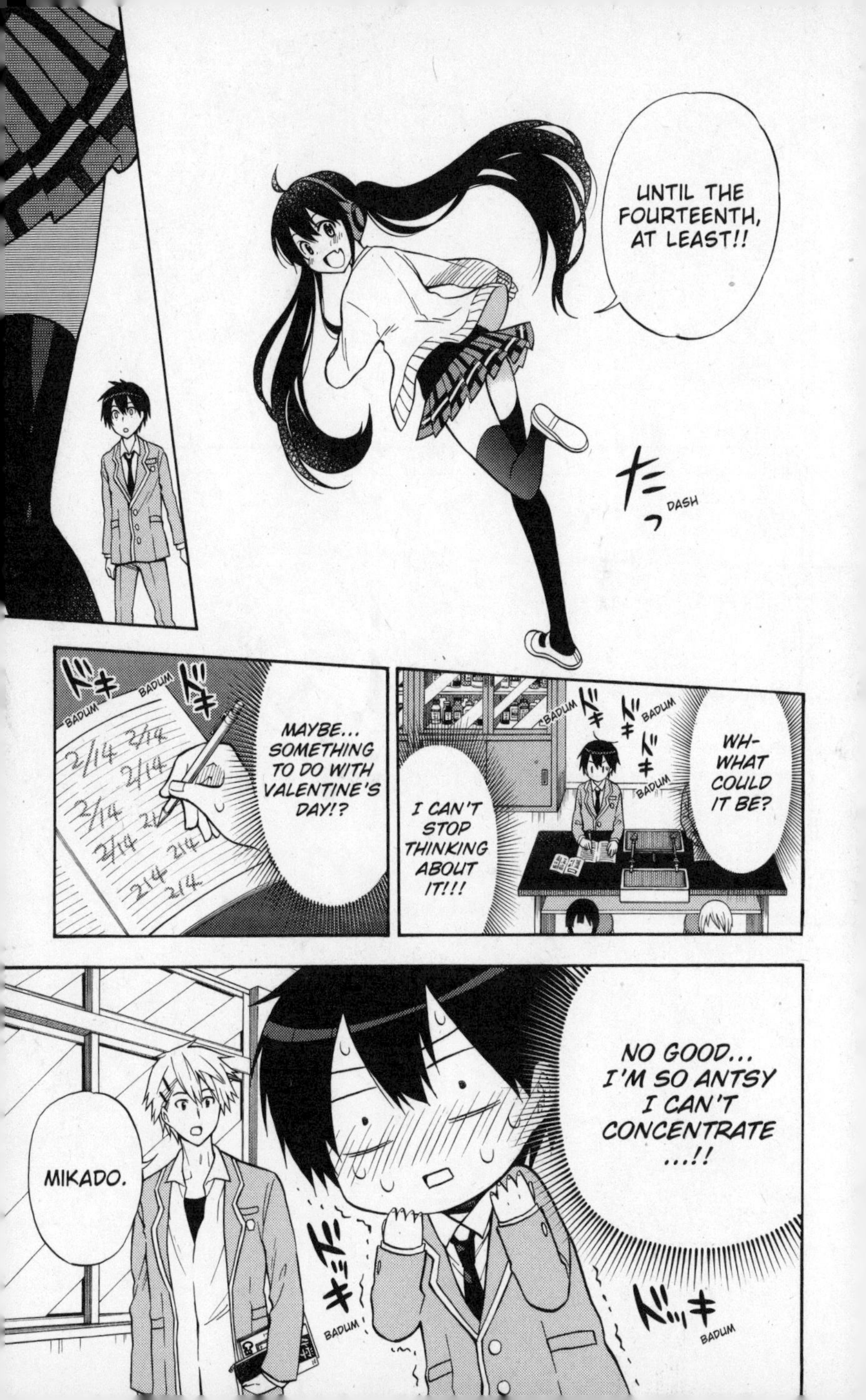
UNTIL THE FOURTEENTH, AT LEAST!!
DASH
BADUM BADUM BADUM
WH- WHAT COULD IT BE?
I CAN'T STOP THINKING ABOUT IT!!!
BADUM BADUM
MAYBE... SOMETHING TO DO WITH VALENTINE'S DAY!?
NO GOOD... I'M SO ANTSY I CAN'T CONCENTRATE ...!!
BADUM BADUM
MIKADO.

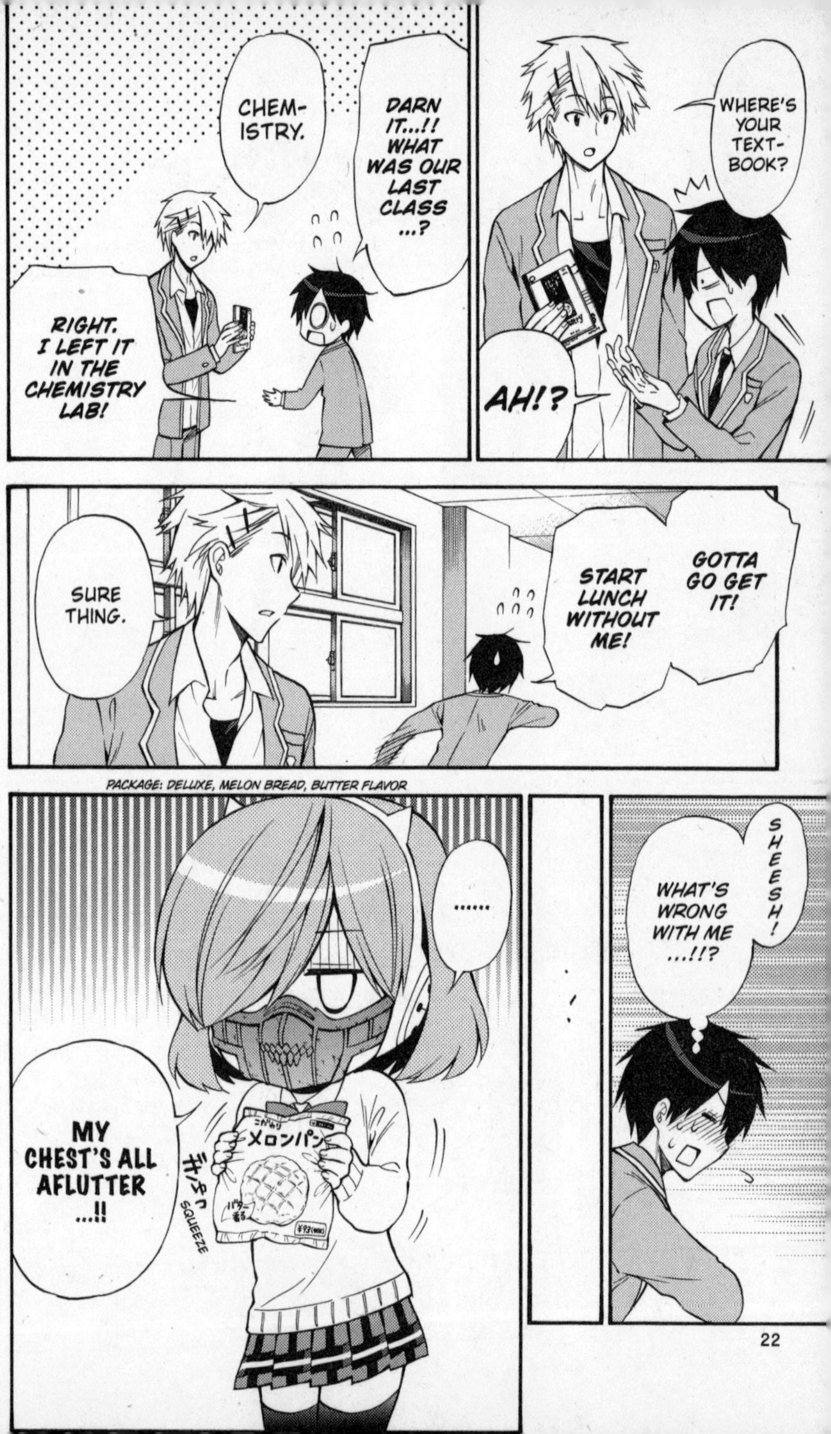
WHERE'S YOUR TEXT-BOOK?
AH!?
DARN IT...!! WHAT WAS OUR LAST CLASS ...?
CHEM-ISTRY.
RIGHT. I LEFT IT IN THE CHEMISTRY LAB!
GOTTA GO GET IT!
START LUNCH WITHOUT ME!
SURE THING.
PACKAGE: DELUXE, MELON BREAD, BUTTER FLAVOR
SHEESH!
WHAT'S WRONG WITH ME ...!!?
...!
......
メロンパン
ギュッ
SQUEEZE
MY CHEST'S ALL AFLUTTER ...!!

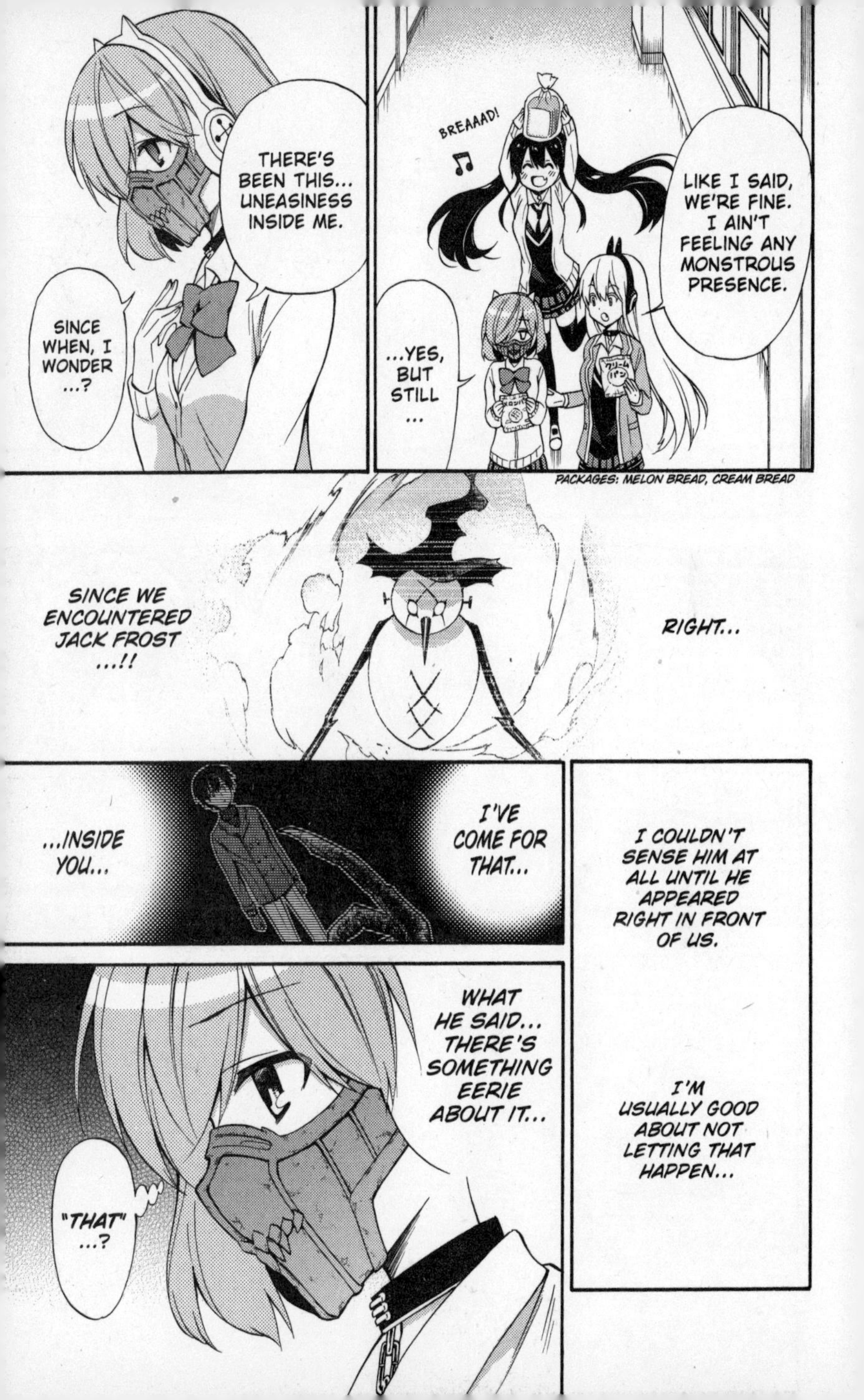
BREAAAD!
LIKE I SAID, WE'RE FINE. I AIN'T FEELING ANY MONSTROUS PRESENCE.
...YES, BUT STILL ...
PACKAGES: MELON BREAD, CREAM BREAD
THERE'S BEEN THIS... UNEASINESS INSIDE ME.
SINCE WHEN, I WONDER ...?
RIGHT...
SINCE WE ENCOUNTERED JACK FROST ...!!
I COULDN'T SENSE HIM AT ALL UNTIL HE APPEARED RIGHT IN FRONT OF US.
I'M USUALLY GOOD ABOUT NOT LETTING THAT HAPPEN...
I'VE COME FOR THAT...
...INSIDE YOU...
WHAT HE SAID... THERE'S SOMETHING EERIE ABOUT IT...
"THAT" ...?

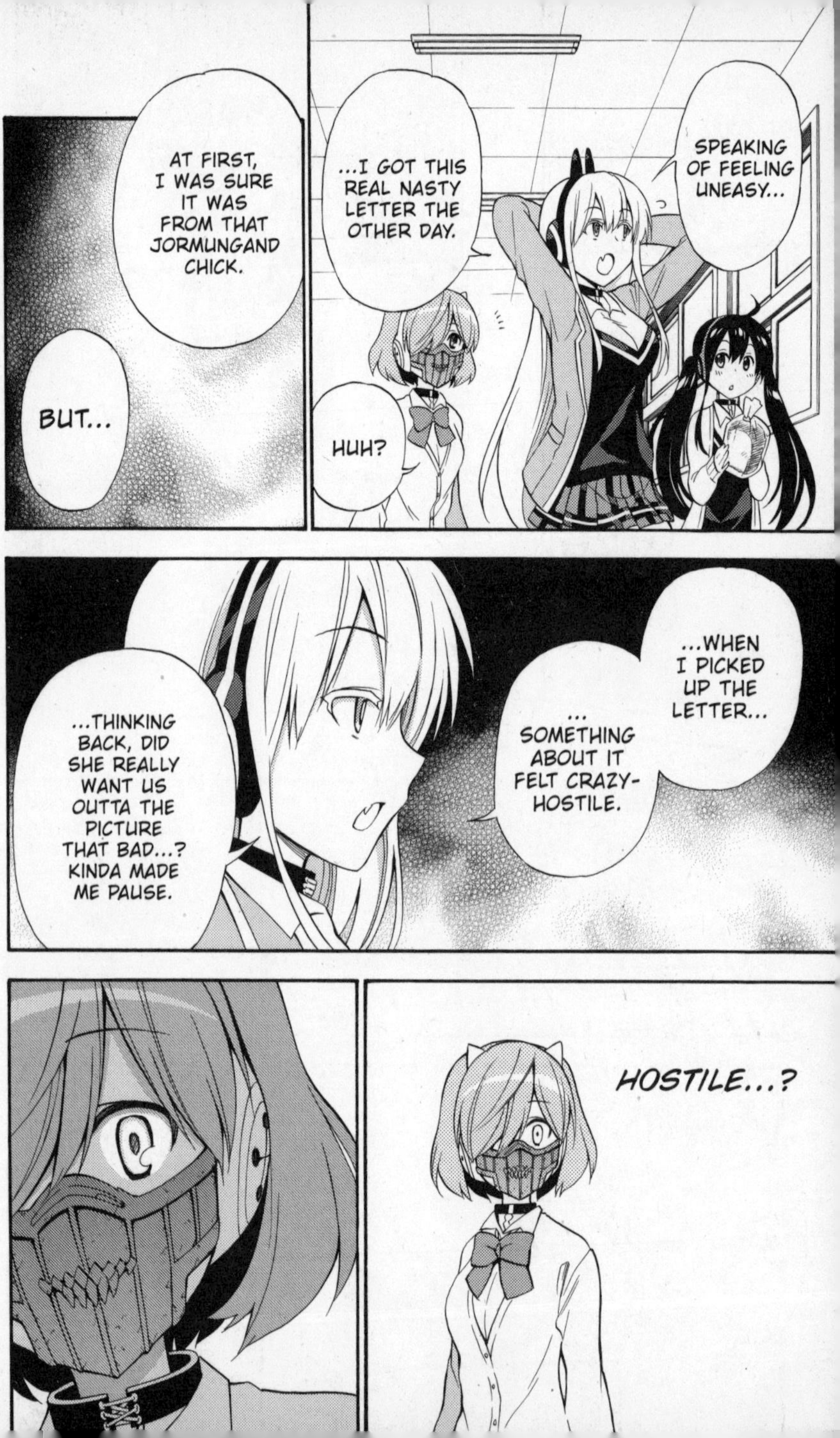
SPEAKING OF FEELING UNEASY...
...I GOT THIS REAL NASTY LETTER THE OTHER DAY.
HUH?
AT FIRST, I WAS SURE IT WAS FROM THAT JORMUNGAND CHICK.
BUT...
...WHEN I PICKED UP THE LETTER...
... SOMETHING ABOUT IT FELT CRAZY-HOSTILE.
...THINKING BACK, DID SHE REALLY WANT US OUTTA THE PICTURE THAT BAD...? KINDA MADE ME PAUSE.
HOSTILE...?

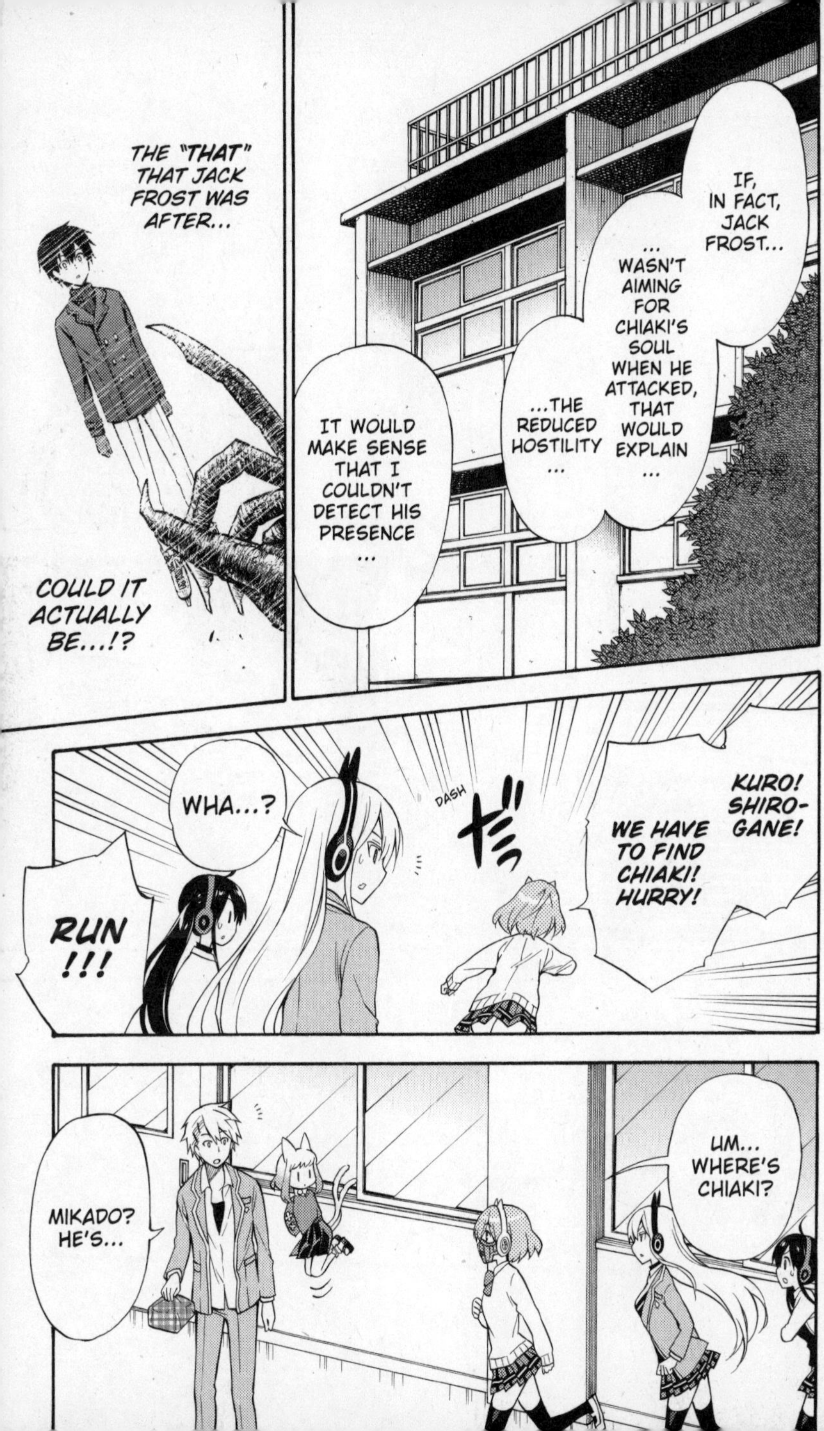
IF, IN FACT, JACK FROST...
... WASN'T AIMING FOR CHIAKI'S SOUL WHEN HE ATTACKED, THAT WOULD EXPLAIN ...
...THE REDUCED HOSTILITY ...
IT WOULD MAKE SENSE THAT I COULDN'T DETECT HIS PRESENCE ...
THE "THAT" THAT JACK FROST WAS AFTER...
COULD IT ACTUALLY BE...!?
KURO! SHIRO-GANE!
WE HAVE TO FIND CHIAKI! HURRY!
DASH
WHA...?
RUN !!!
UM... WHERE'S CHIAKI?
MIKADO? HE'S...

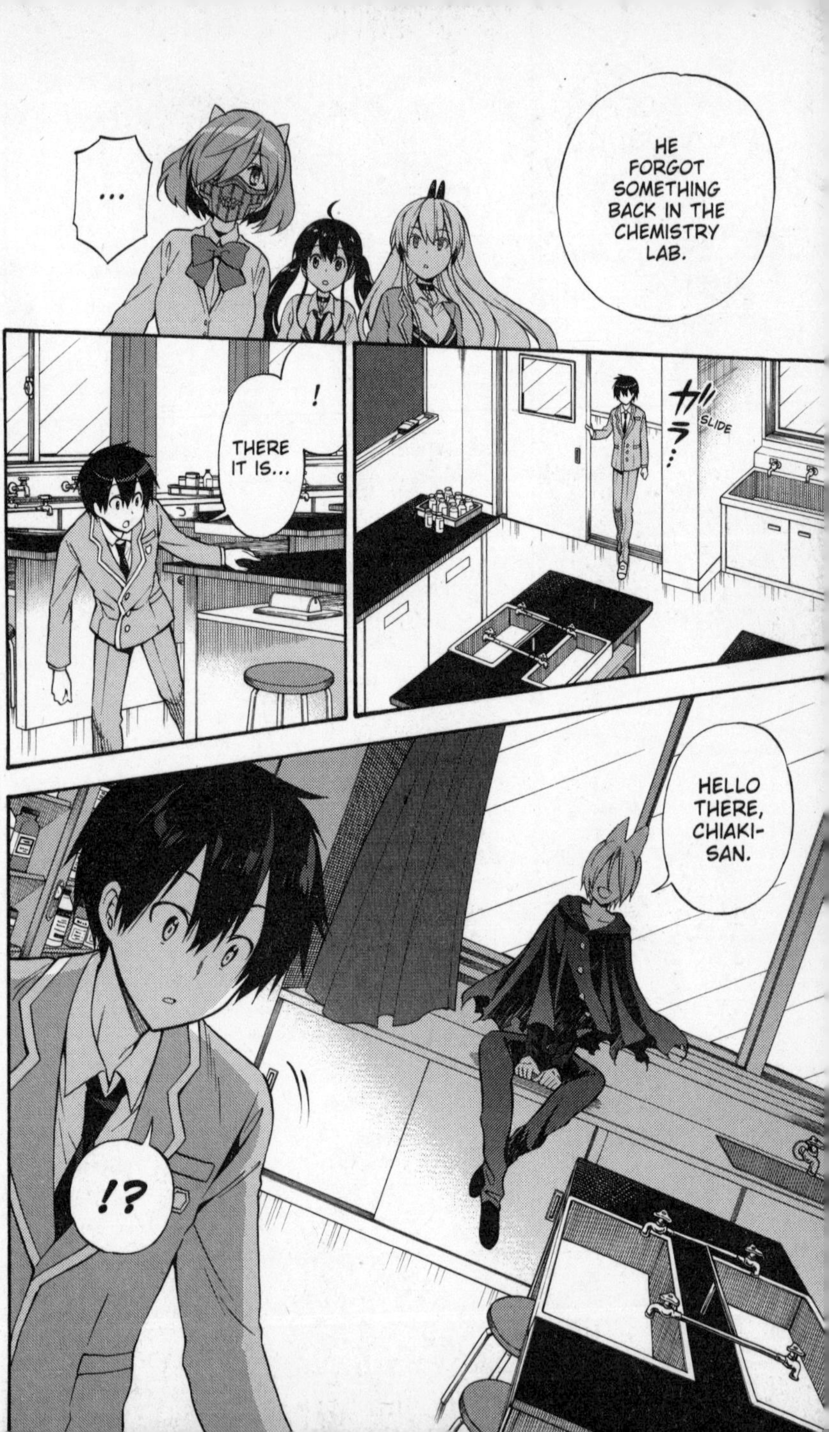
HE FORGOT SOMETHING BACK IN THE CHEMISTRY LAB.
...
ガラ
SLIDE
!
THERE IT IS...
HELLO THERE, CHIAKI-SAN.
!?

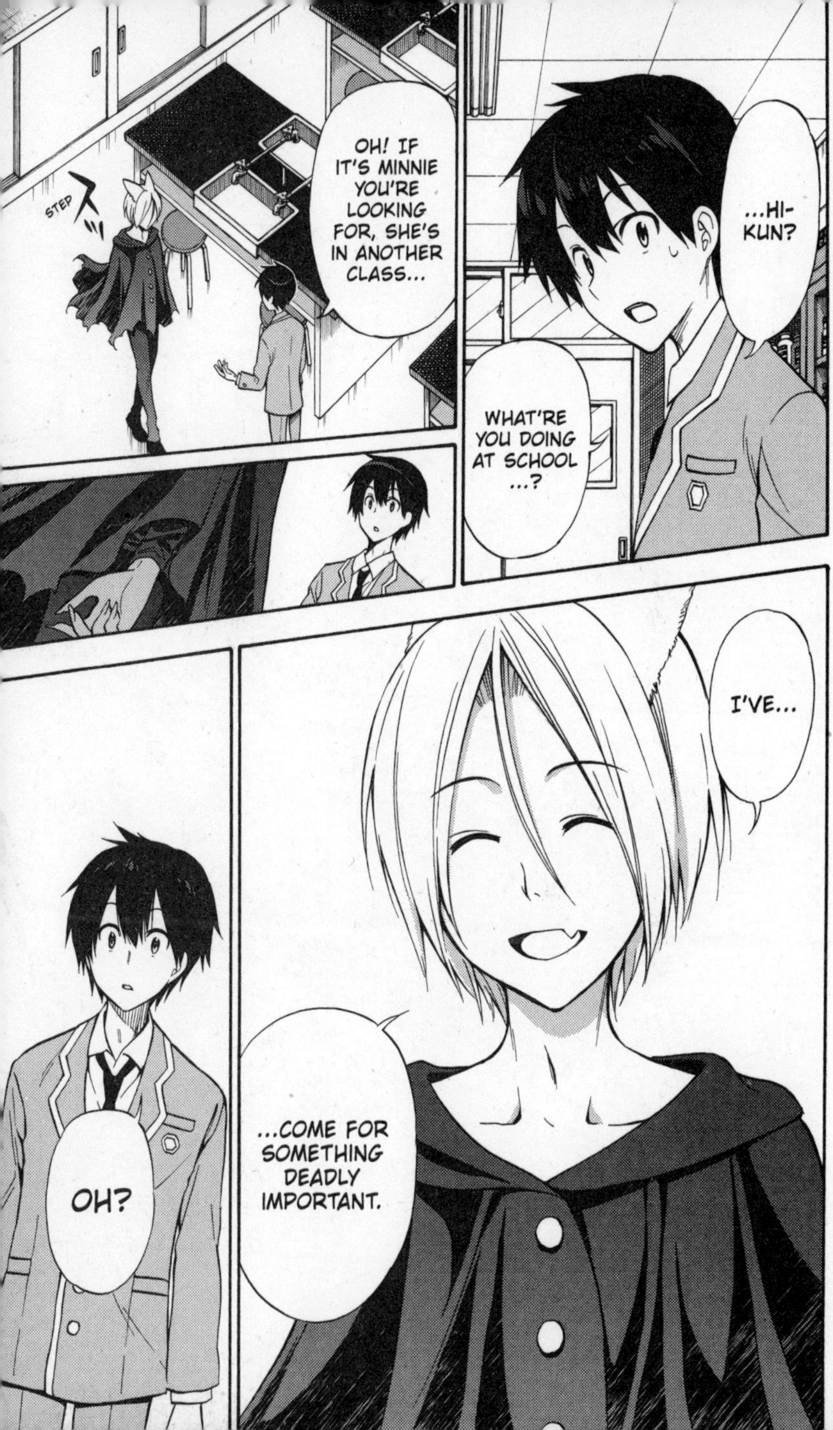
...HI-KUN?
WHAT'RE YOU DOING AT SCHOOL ...?
OH! IF IT'S MINNIE YOU'RE LOOKING FOR, SHE'S IN ANOTHER CLASS...
STEP
I'VE...
...COME FOR SOMETHING DEADLY IMPORTANT.
OH?

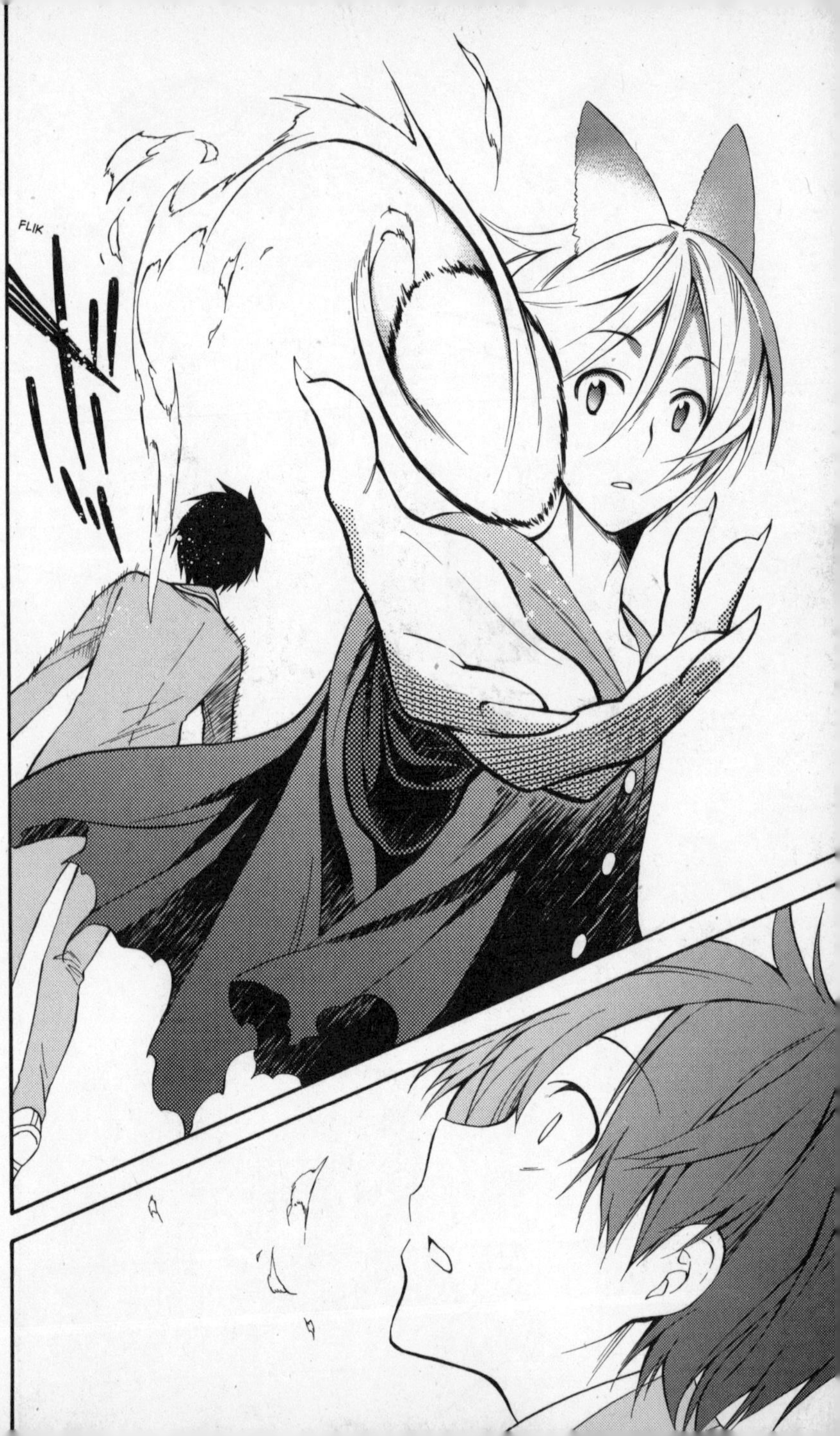
FLIK

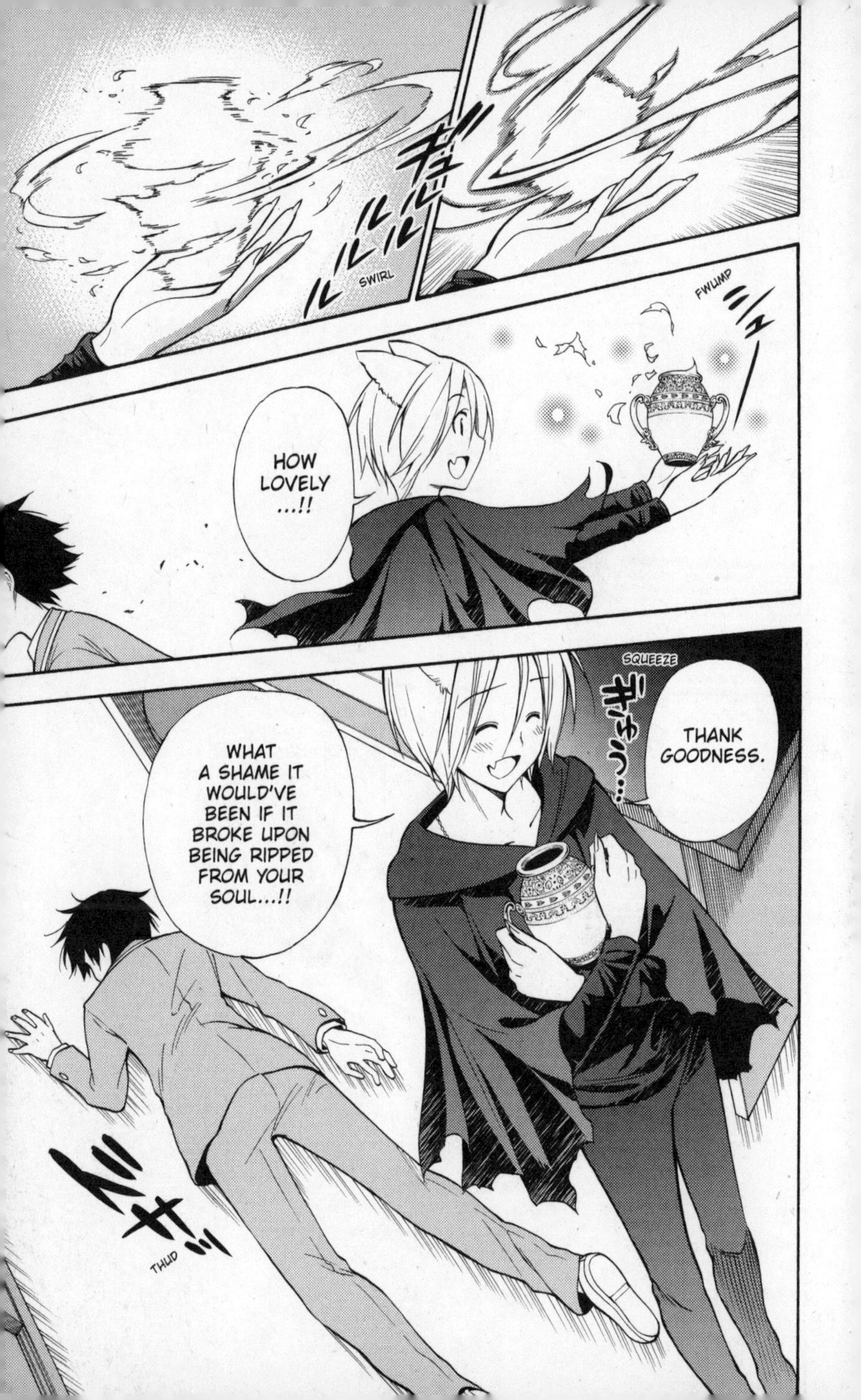
SWIRL
FWUMP
HOW LOVELY ...!!
SQUEEZE
THANK GOODNESS.
WHAT A SHAME IT WOULD'VE BEEN IF IT BROKE UPON BEING RIPPED FROM YOUR SOUL...!!
THUD

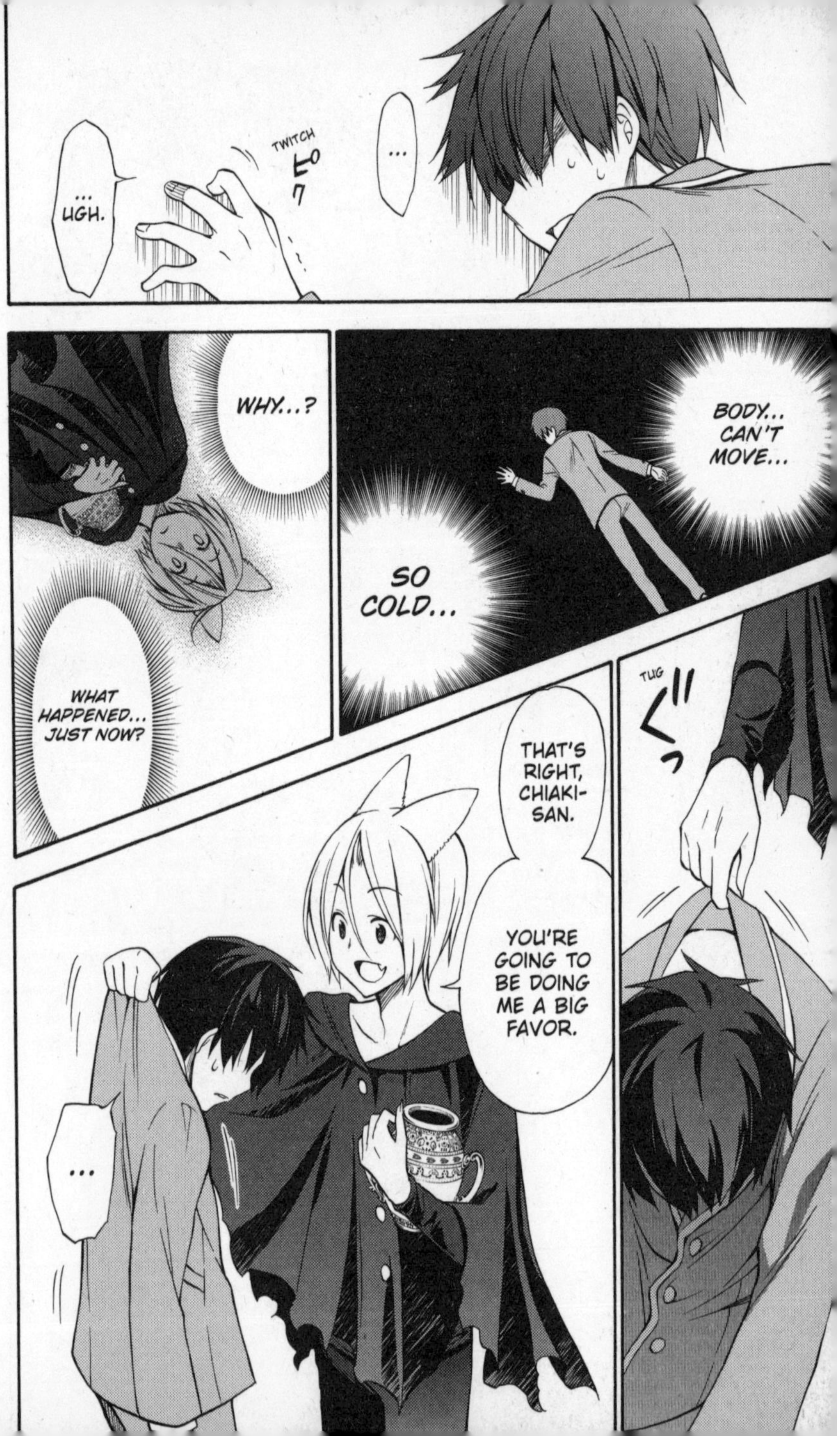
...
TWITCH
ピク
... UGH.
BODY... CAN'T MOVE...
SO COLD...
WHY...?
WHAT HAPPENED... JUST NOW?
TUG
ぐっ
THAT'S RIGHT, CHIAKI-SAN.
YOU'RE GOING TO BE DOING ME A BIG FAVOR.
...

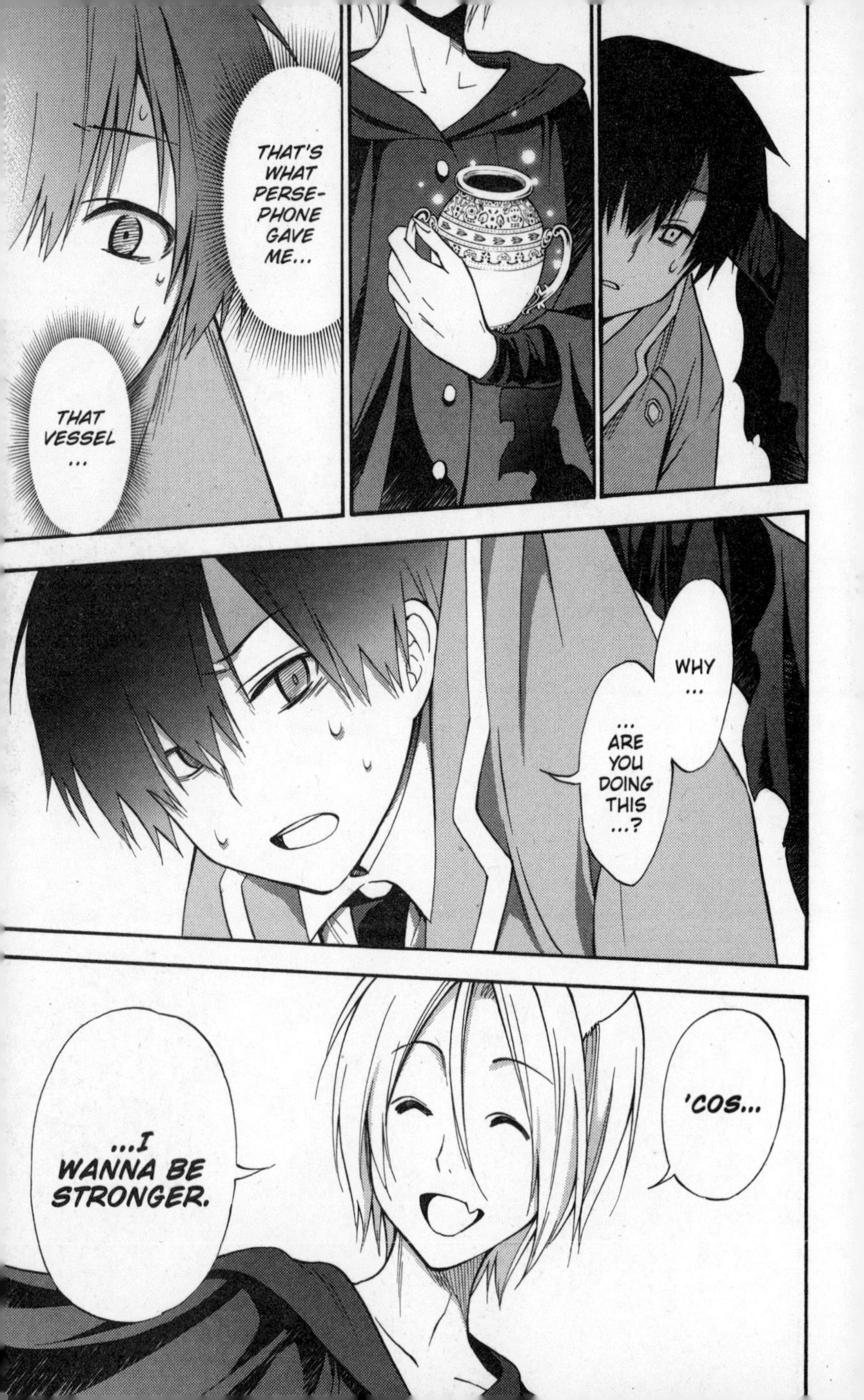
THAT'S WHAT PERSE-PHONE GAVE ME...
THAT VESSEL ...
WHY ...
... ARE YOU DOING THIS ...?
'COS...
...I WANNA BE STRONGER.

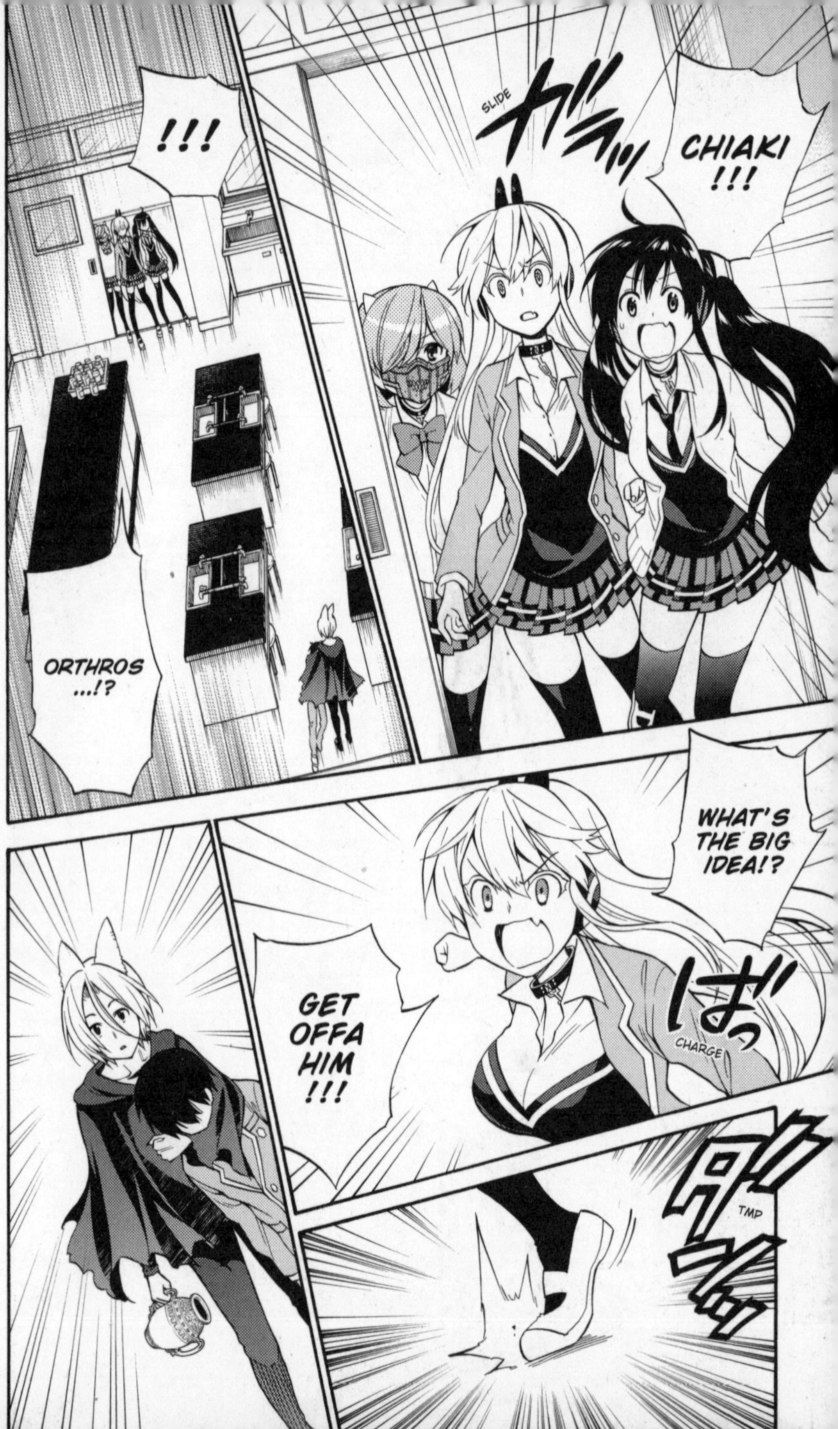
SLIDE
CHIAKI !!!
!!!
ORTHROS ...!?
WHAT'S THE BIG IDEA!?
CHARGE
GET OFFA HIM !!!
TMP

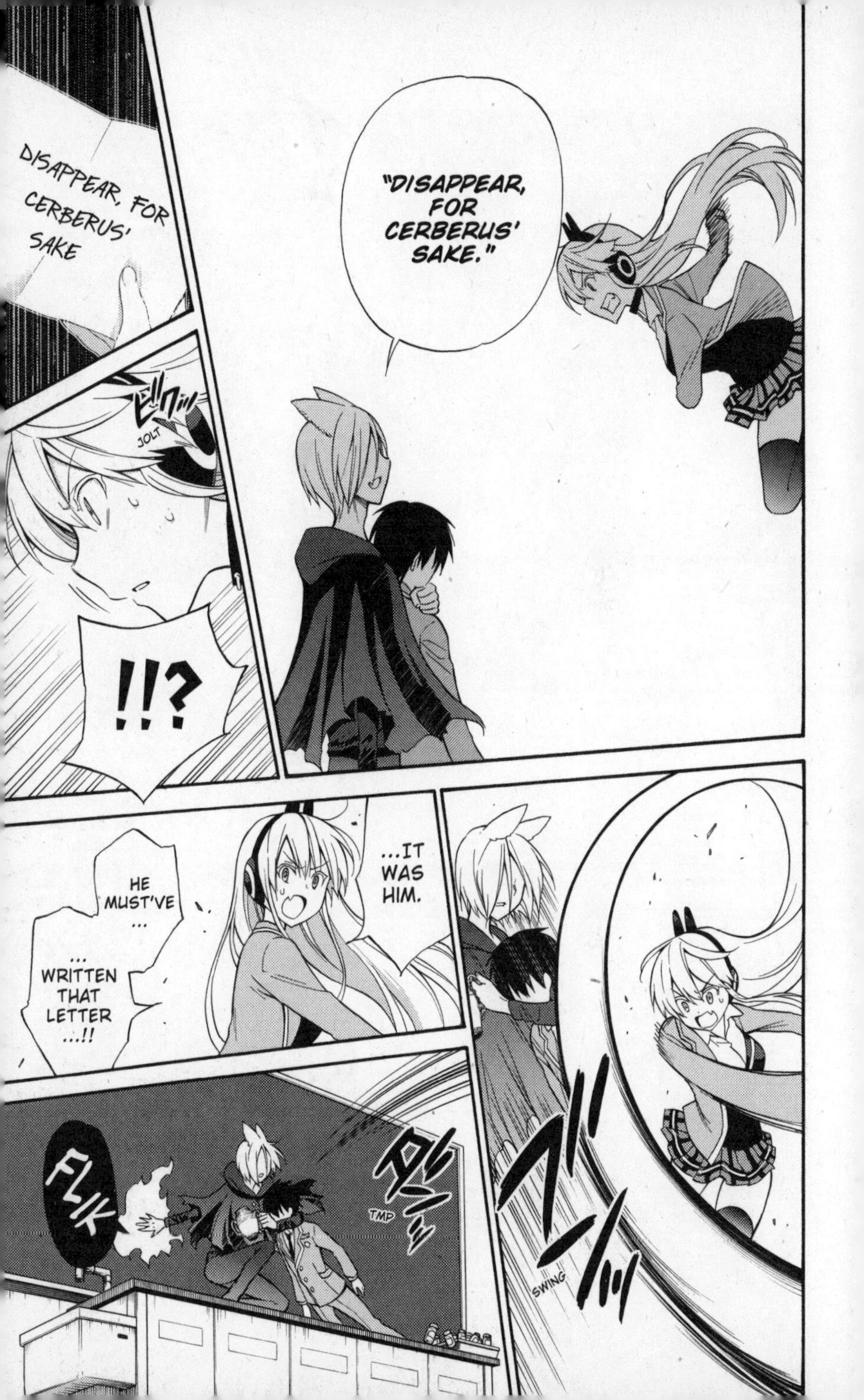
"DISAPPEAR, FOR CERBERUS' SAKE."
DISAPPEAR, FOR CERBERUS' SAKE
JOLT
!!?
SWING
...IT WAS HIM.
HE MUST'VE ... ... WRITTEN THAT LETTER ...!!
TMP
FLIK

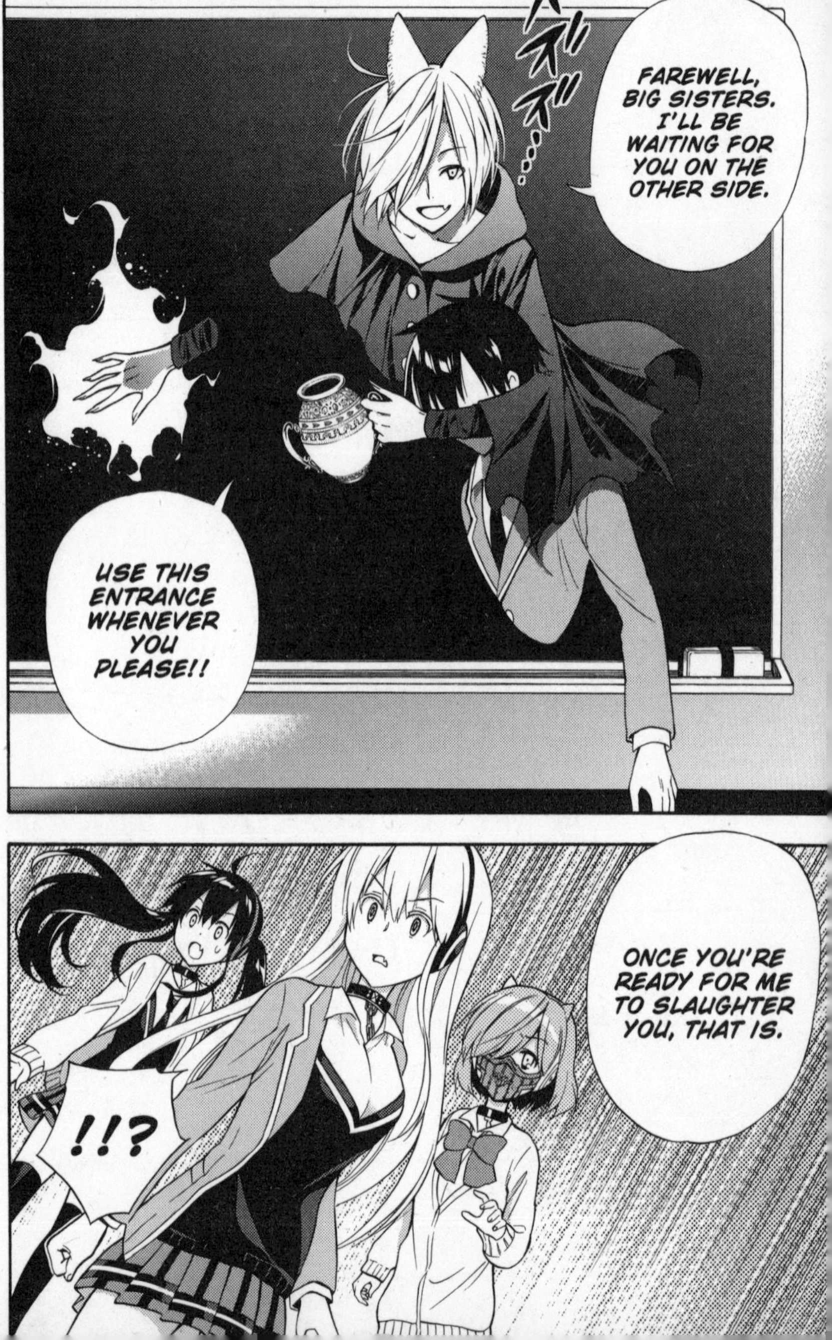
SINK
FAREWELL, BIG SISTERS. I'LL BE WAITING FOR YOU ON THE OTHER SIDE.
USE THIS ENTRANCE WHENEVER YOU PLEASE!!
ONCE YOU'RE READY FOR ME TO SLAUGHTER YOU, THAT IS.
!!?

❤ TODAY'S CERBERUS

I HAVE A BAD
FEELING, FOR
SOME REASON...

TODAY'S CERBERUS

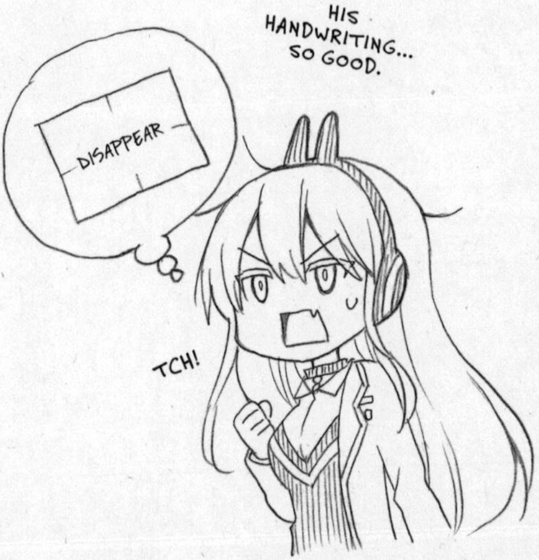
HIS HANDWRITING... SO GOOD.
DISAPPEAR
TCH!

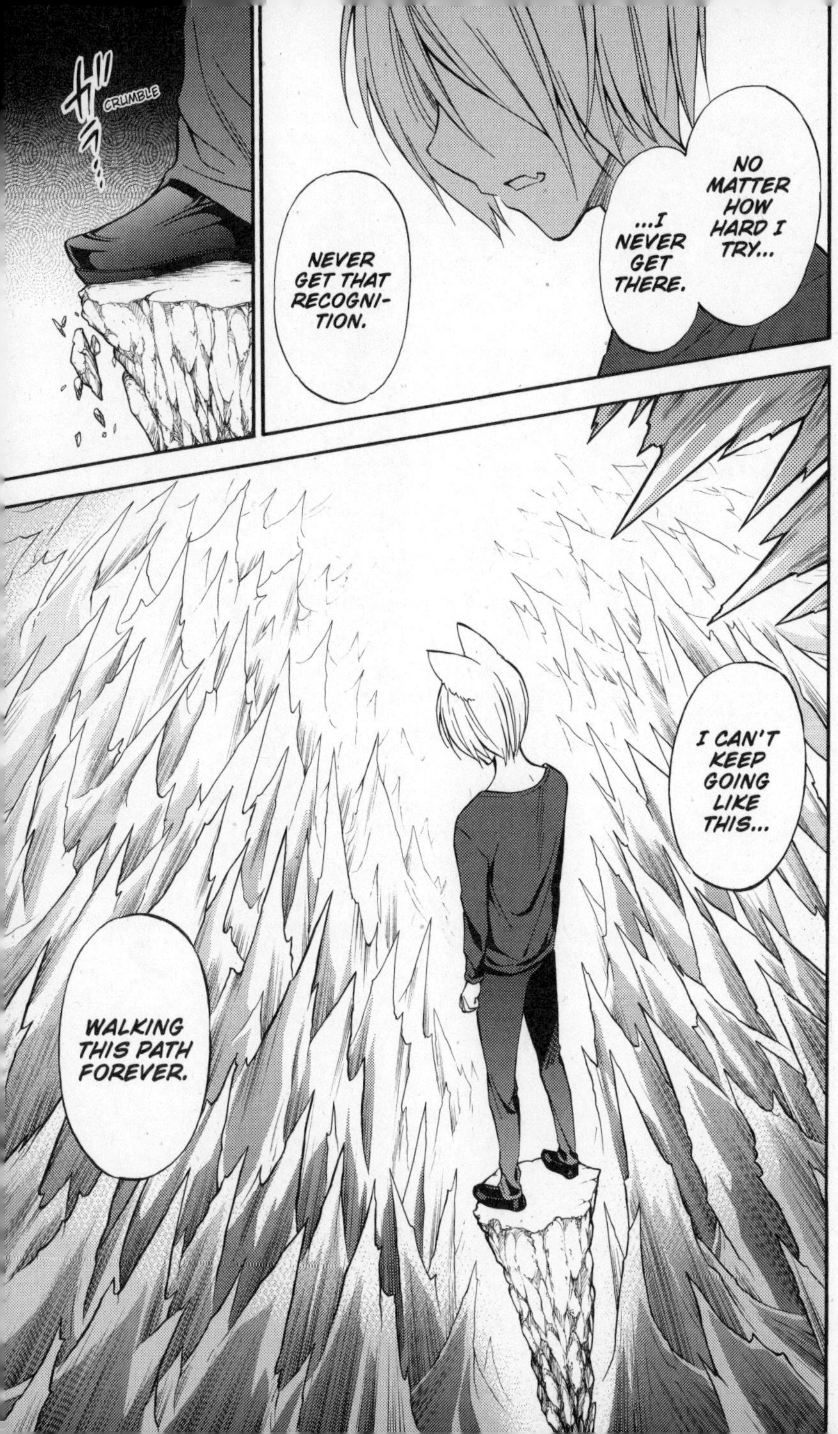
NO MATTER HOW HARD I TRY...
...I NEVER GET THERE.
NEVER GET THAT RECOGNITION.
CRUMBLE
I CAN'T KEEP GOING LIKE THIS...
WALKING THIS PATH FOREVER.

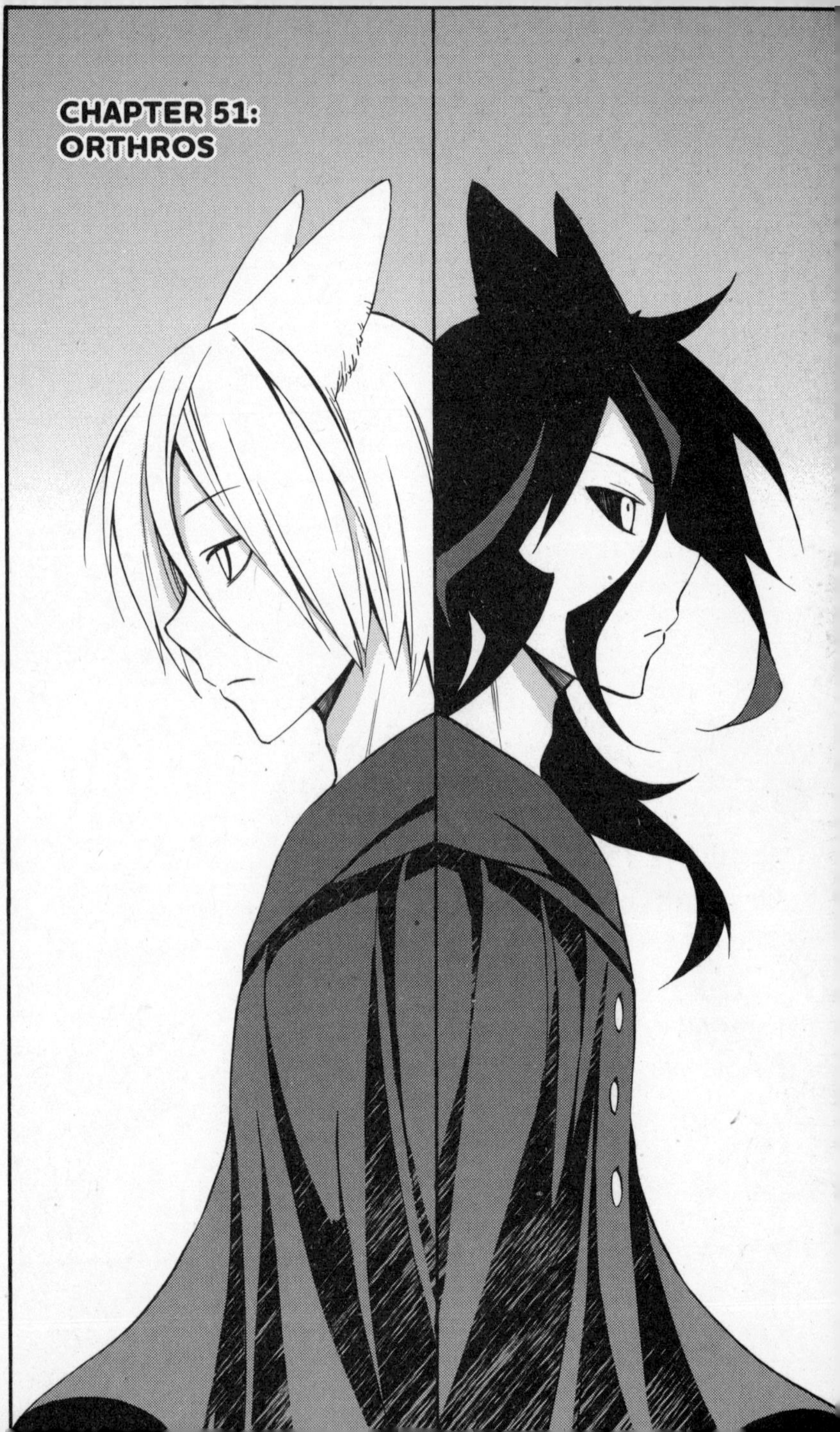
CHAPTER 51:
ORTHROS

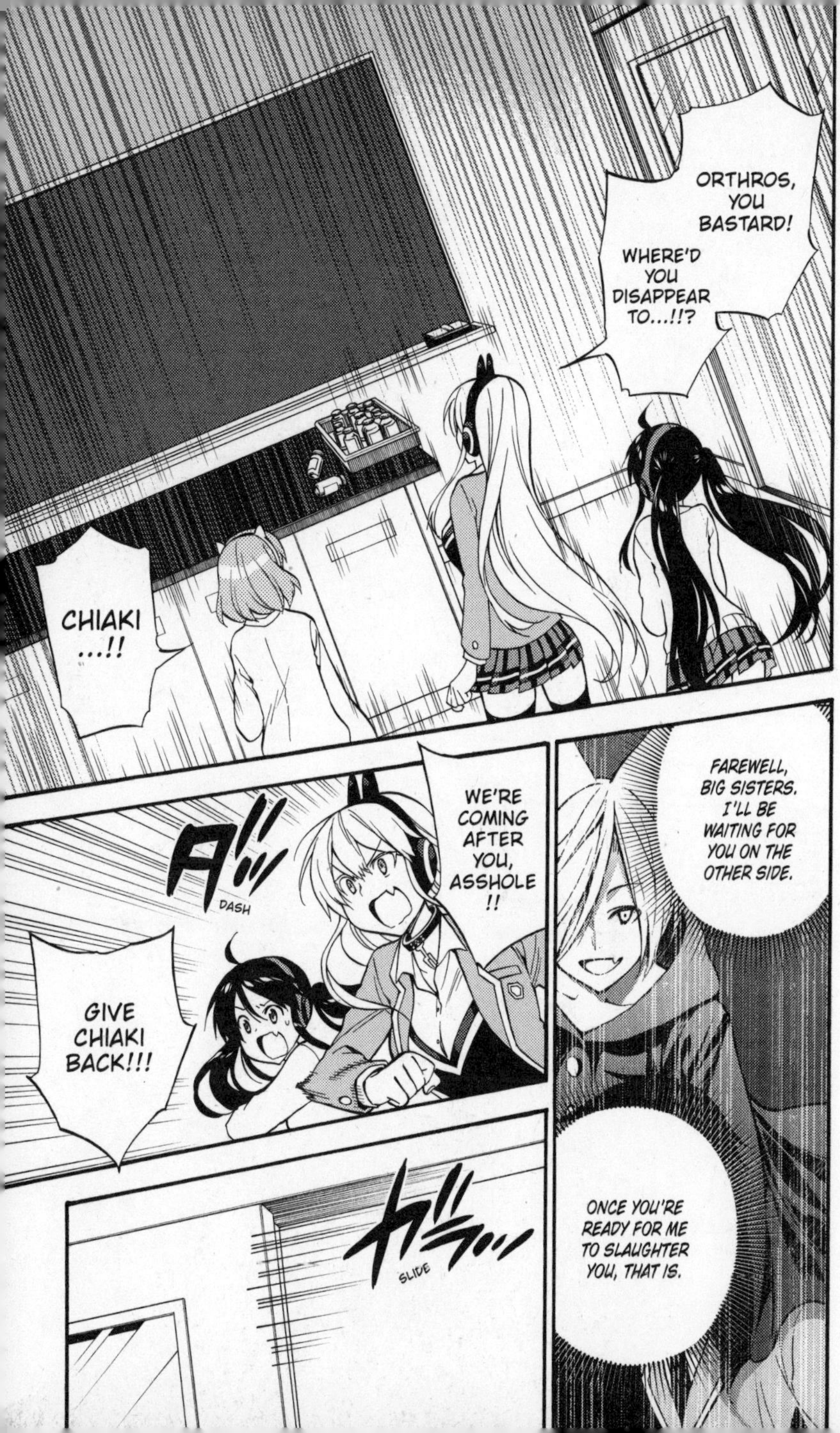
ORTHROS, YOU BASTARD!
WHERE'D YOU DISAPPEAR TO...!!?
CHIAKI ...!!
FAREWELL, BIG SISTERS. I'LL BE WAITING FOR YOU ON THE OTHER SIDE.
ONCE YOU'RE READY FOR ME TO SLAUGHTER YOU, THAT IS.
WE'RE COMING AFTER YOU, ASSHOLE !!
DASH
GIVE CHIAKI BACK!!!
SLIDE

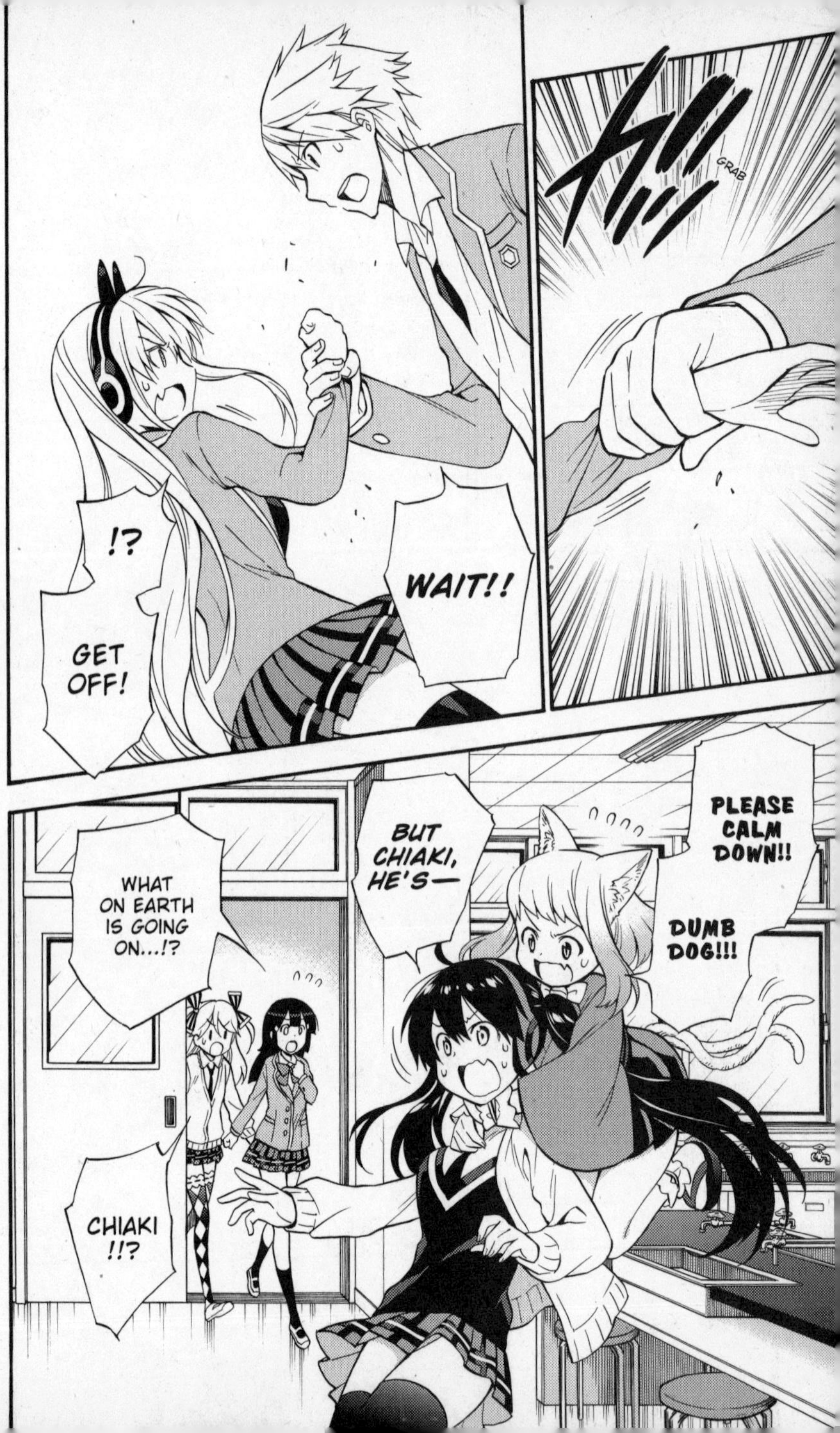
GRAB
WAIT!!
!?
GET OFF!
PLEASE CALM DOWN!!
DUMB DOG!!!
BUT CHIAKI, HE'S—
WHAT ON EARTH IS GOING ON...!?
CHIAKI!!?

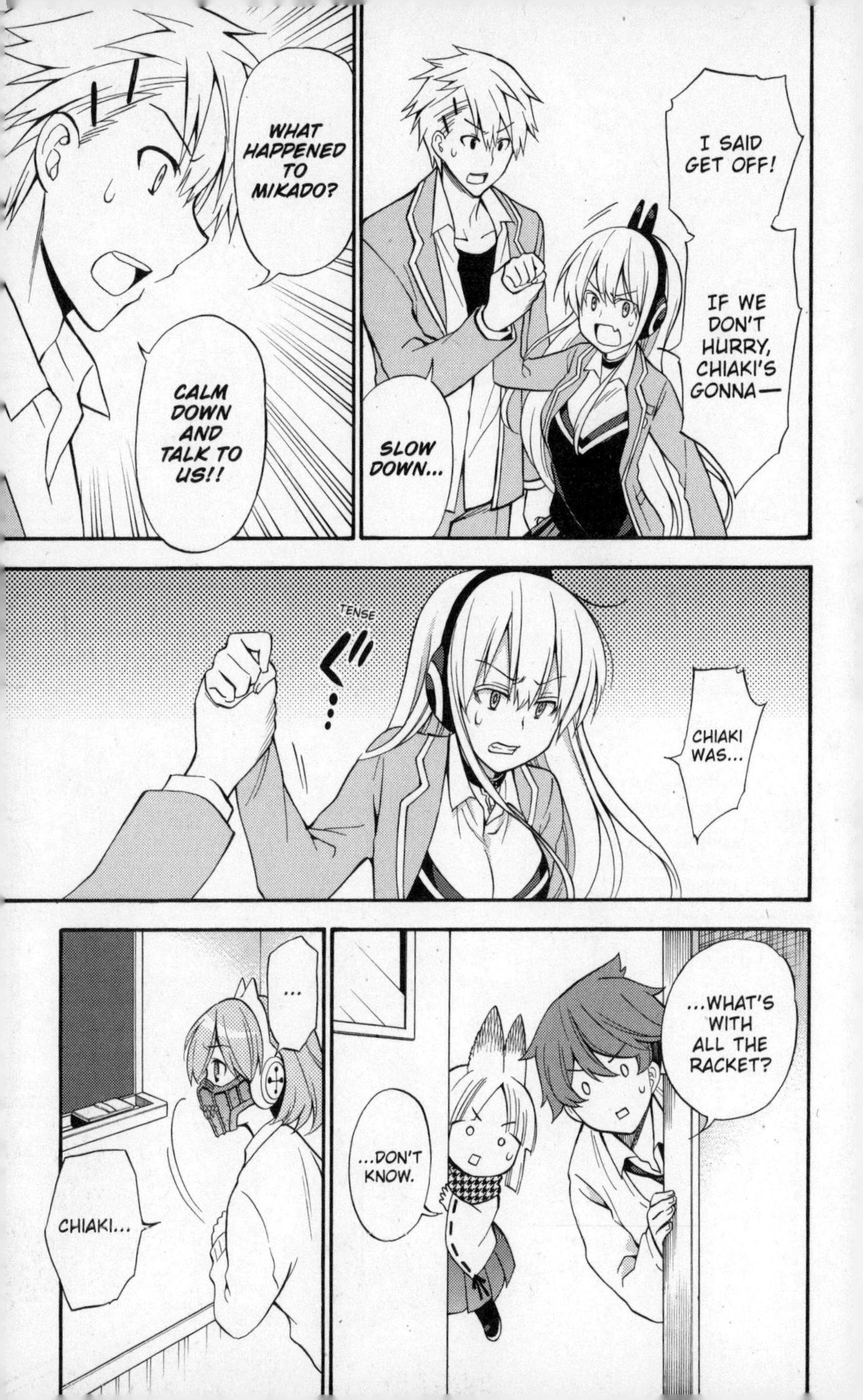
I SAID GET OFF!
IF WE DON'T HURRY, CHIAKI'S GONNA—
SLOW DOWN...
WHAT HAPPENED TO MIKADO?
CALM DOWN AND TALK TO US!!
TENSE
CHIAKI WAS...
...WHAT'S WITH ALL THE RACKET?
...DON'T KNOW.
...
CHIAKI...

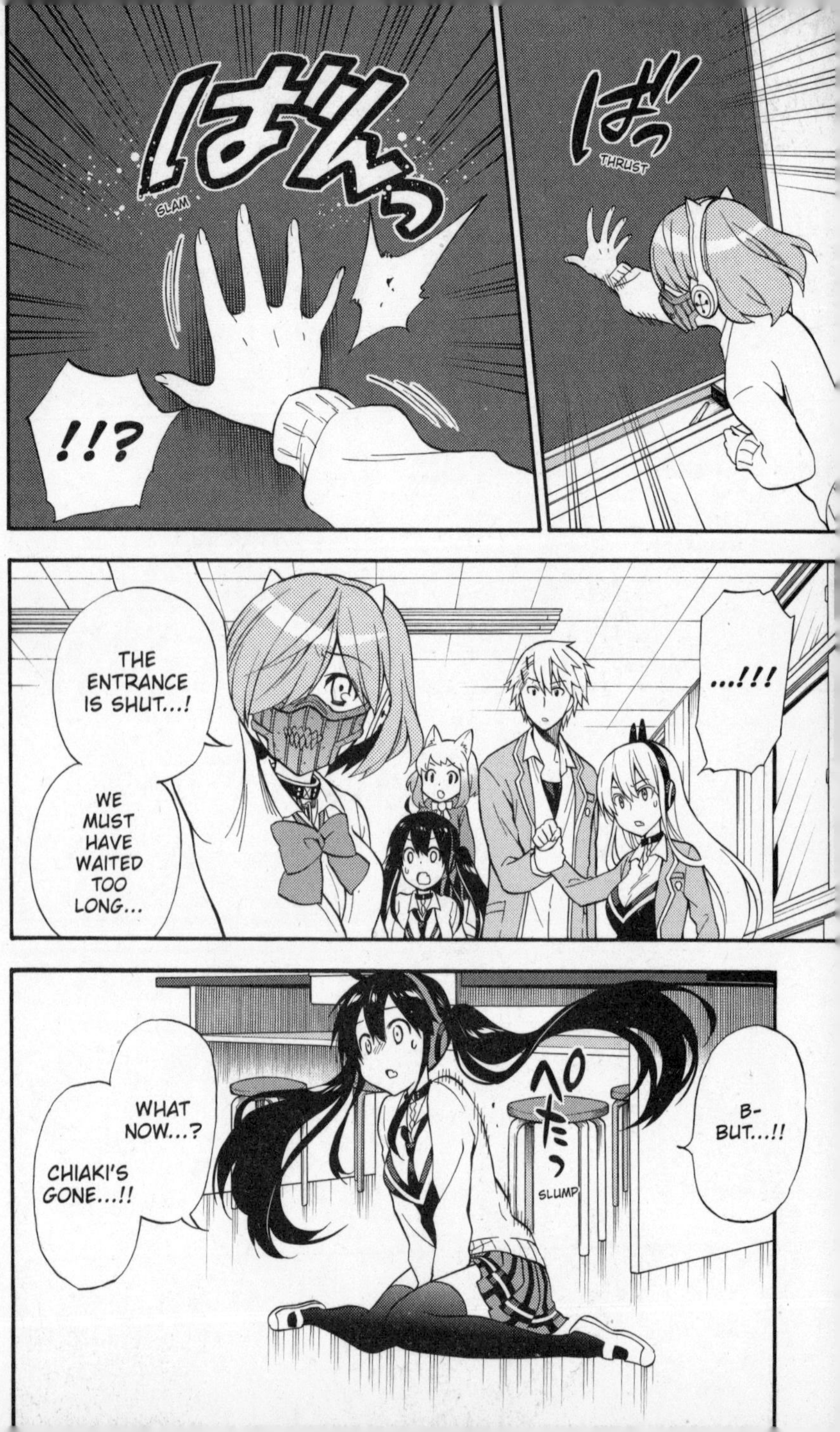
ばっ
THRUST
ばんっ
SLAM
!!?
...!!!
THE ENTRANCE IS SHUT...!
WE MUST HAVE WAITED TOO LONG...
B-BUT...!!
へたっ
SLUMP
WHAT NOW...?
CHIAKI'S GONE...!!

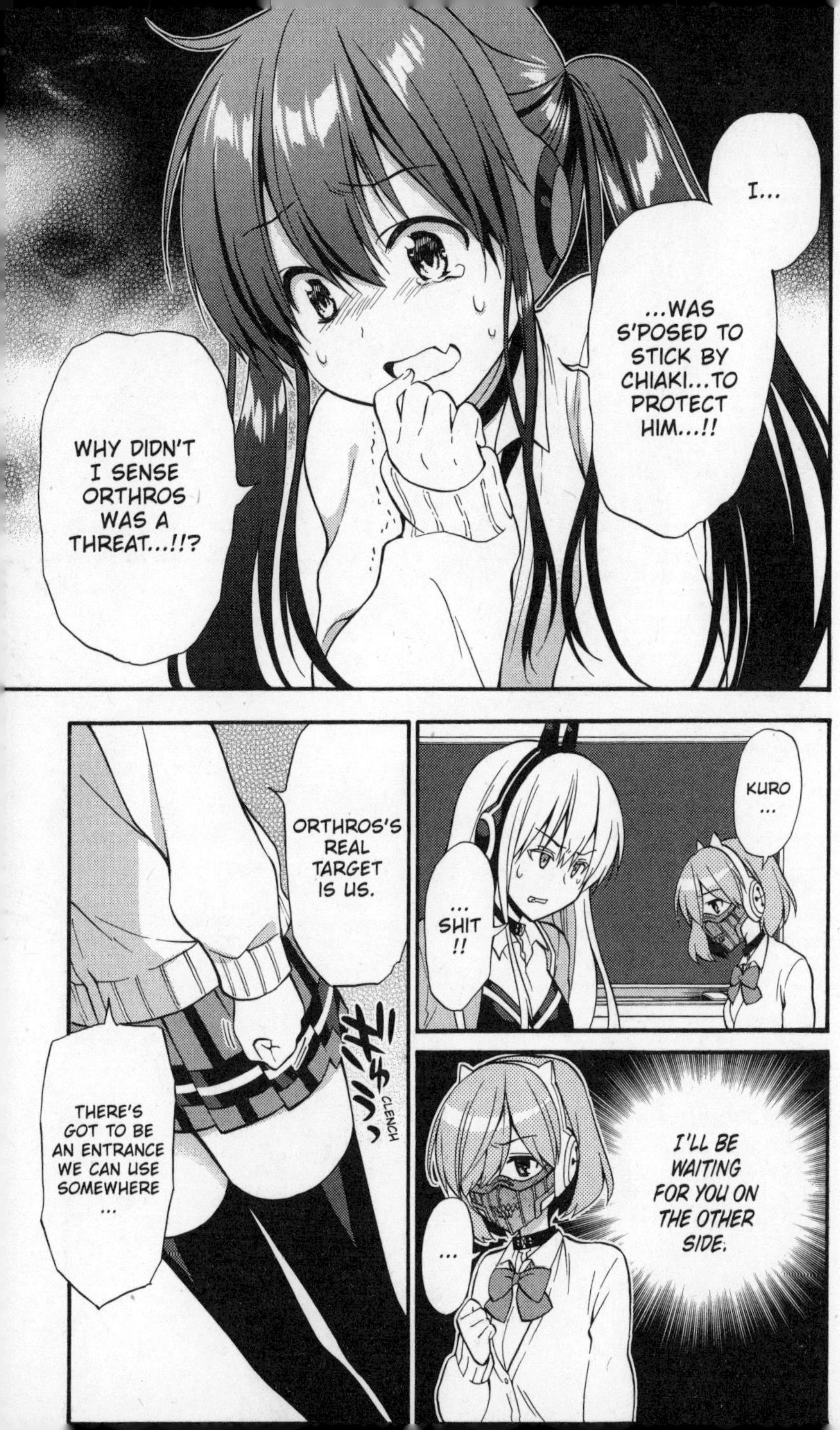
I...
...WAS S'POSED TO STICK BY CHIAKI...TO PROTECT HIM...!!
WHY DIDN'T I SENSE ORTHROS WAS A THREAT...!!?
KURO...
...SHIT!!
I'LL BE WAITING FOR YOU ON THE OTHER SIDE.
...
ORTHROS'S REAL TARGET IS US.
CLENCH
THERE'S GOT TO BE AN ENTRANCE WE CAN USE SOMEWHERE...

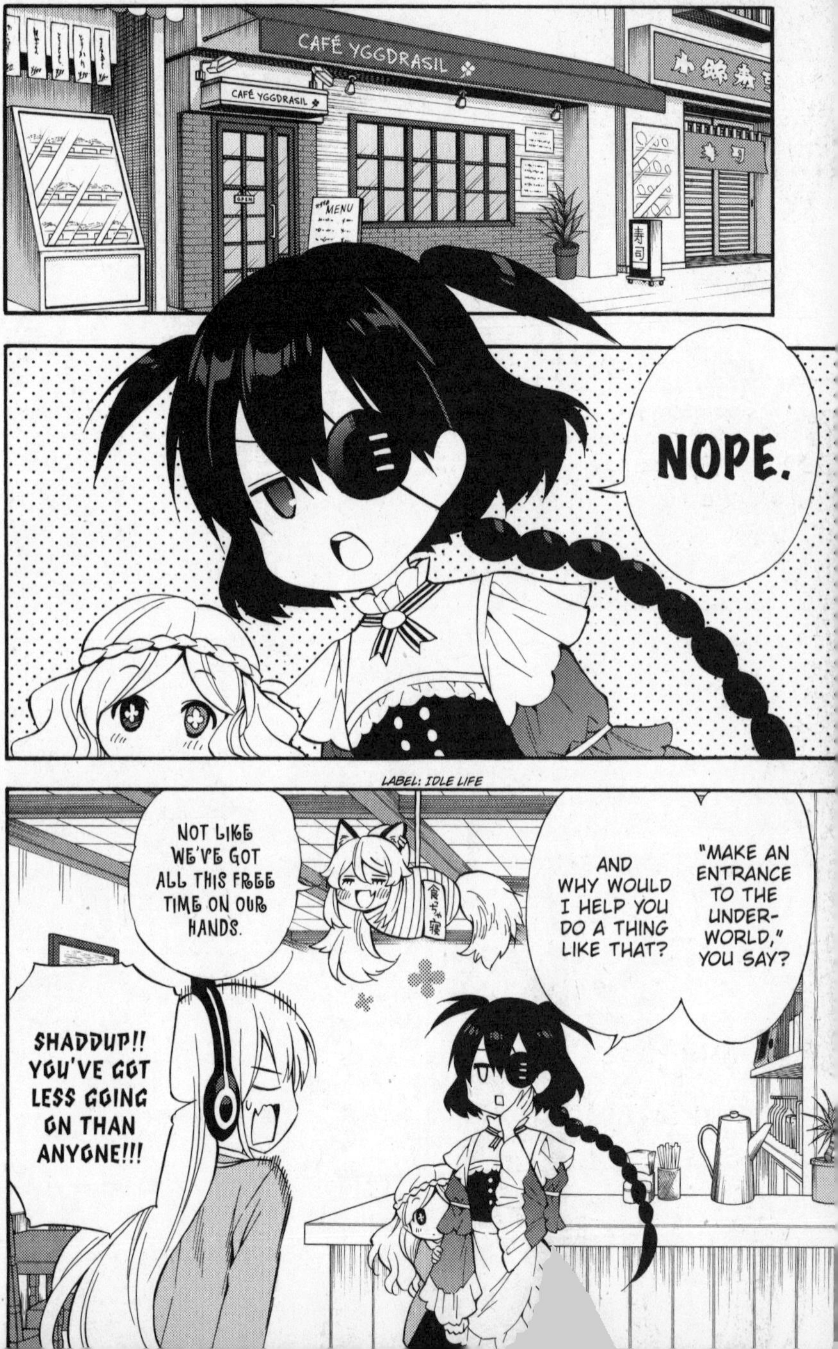
CAFÉ YGGDRASIL
CAFÉ YGGDRASIL
OPEN
MENU
寿司
NOPE.
LABEL: IDLE LIFE
"MAKE AN ENTRANCE TO THE UNDER-WORLD," YOU SAY?
AND WHY WOULD I HELP YOU DO A THING LIKE THAT?
NOT LIKE WE'VE GOT ALL THIS FREE TIME ON OUR HANDS.
SHADDUP!! YOU'VE GOT LESS GOING ON THAN ANYONE!!!

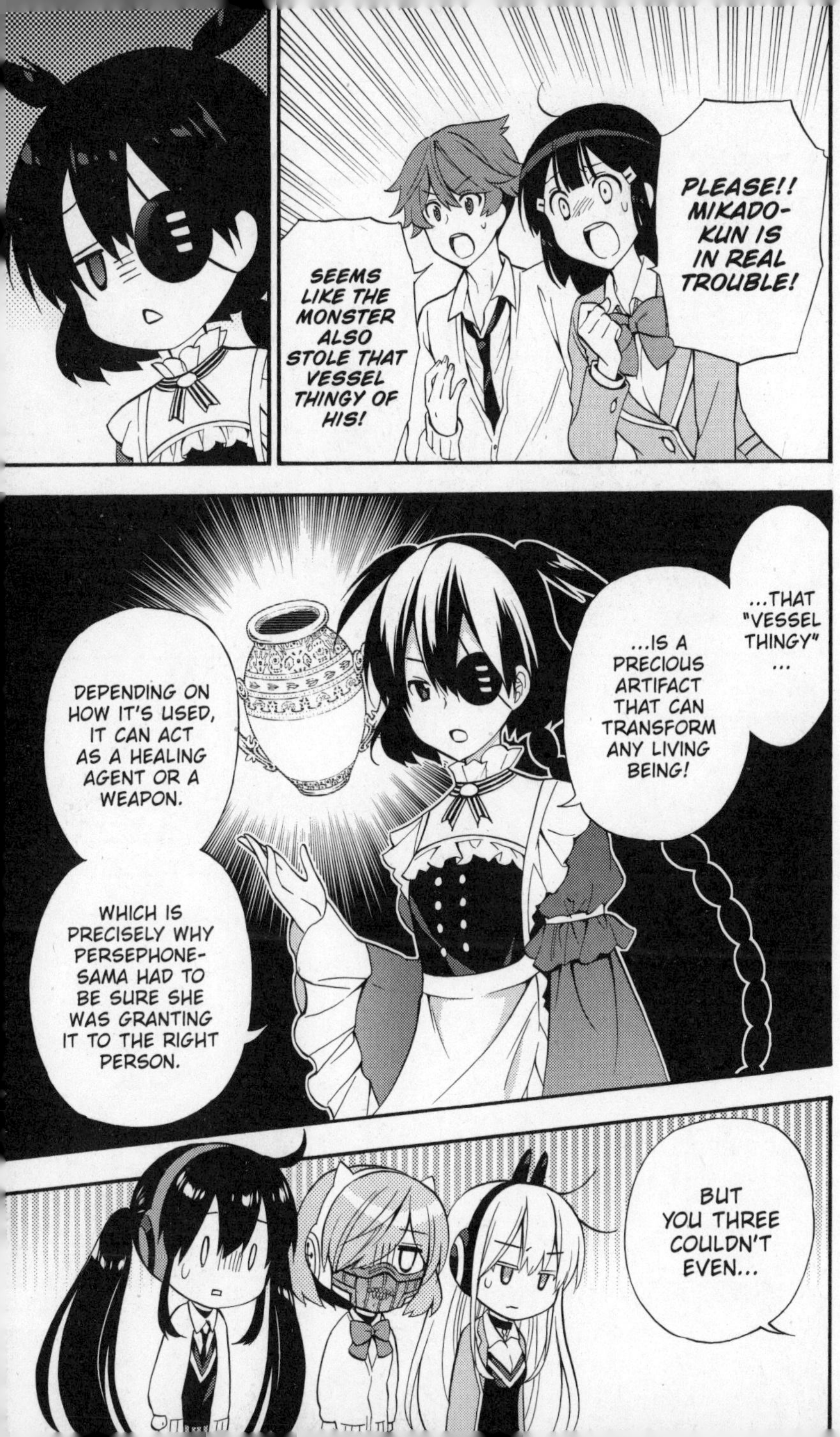
PLEASE!! MIKADO-KUN IS IN REAL TROUBLE!
SEEMS LIKE THE MONSTER ALSO STOLE THAT VESSEL THINGY OF HIS!
...THAT "VESSEL THINGY" ...
...IS A PRECIOUS ARTIFACT THAT CAN TRANSFORM ANY LIVING BEING!
DEPENDING ON HOW IT'S USED, IT CAN ACT AS A HEALING AGENT OR A WEAPON.
WHICH IS PRECISELY WHY PERSEPHONE-SAMA HAD TO BE SURE SHE WAS GRANTING IT TO THE RIGHT PERSON.
BUT YOU THREE COULDN'T EVEN...

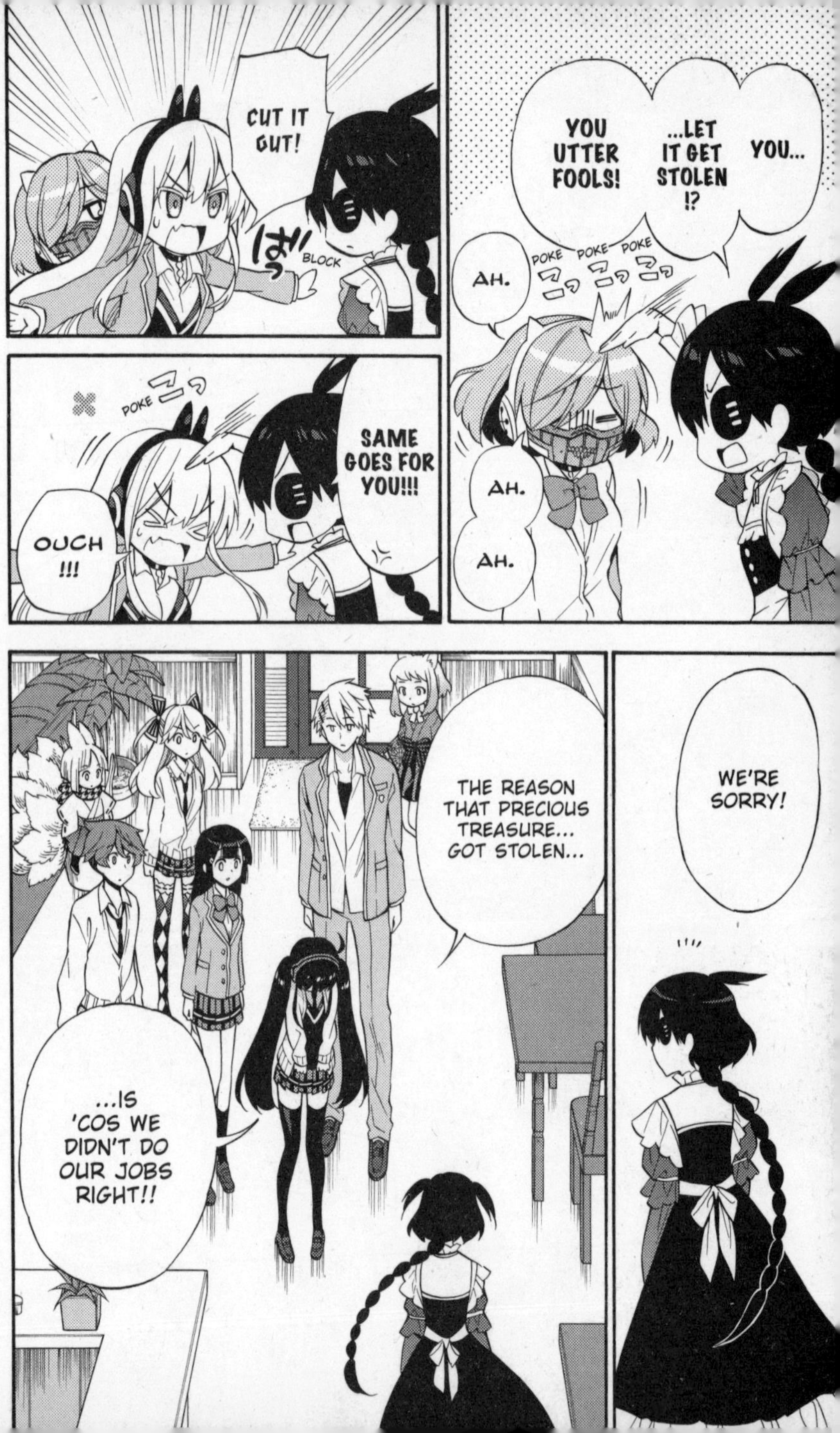
YOU... ...LET IT GET STOLEN !? YOU UTTER FOOLS!
POKE POKE POKE
AH.
AH.
AH.
CUT IT OUT!
BLOCK
POKE
SAME GOES FOR YOU!!!
OUCH !!!
WE'RE SORRY!
!!!
THE REASON THAT PRECIOUS TREASURE... GOT STOLEN...
...IS 'COS WE DIDN'T DO OUR JOBS RIGHT!!

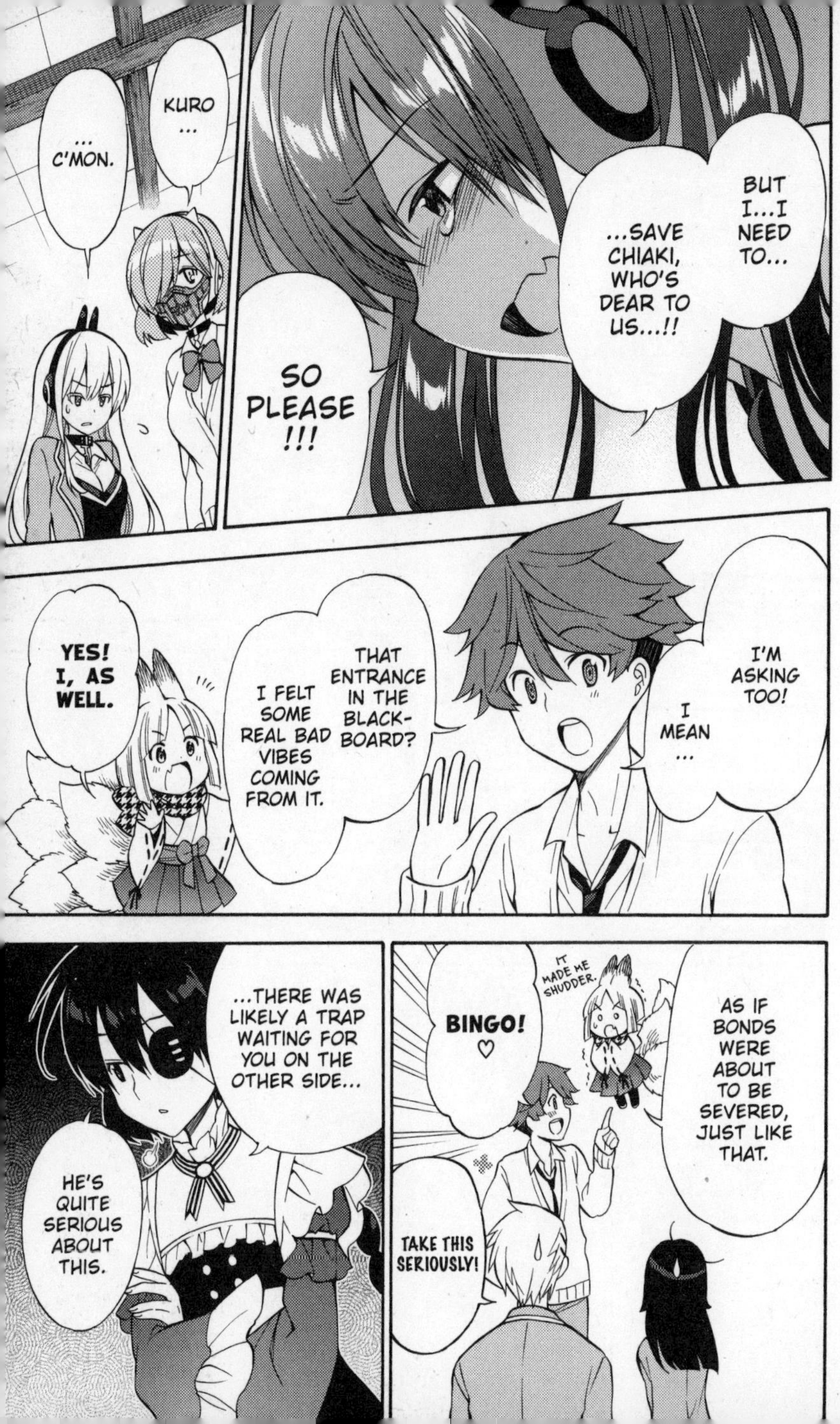
BUT I...I NEED TO...
...SAVE CHIAKI, WHO'S DEAR TO US...!!
SO PLEASE !!!
KURO ...
... C'MON.
I'M ASKING TOO!
I MEAN ...
THAT ENTRANCE IN THE BLACK-BOARD?
I FELT SOME REAL BAD VIBES COMING FROM IT.
YES! I, AS WELL.
AS IF BONDS WERE ABOUT TO BE SEVERED, JUST LIKE THAT.
IT MADE ME SHUDDER.
BINGO! ♡
TAKE THIS SERIOUSLY!
...THERE WAS LIKELY A TRAP WAITING FOR YOU ON THE OTHER SIDE...
HE'S QUITE SERIOUS ABOUT THIS.

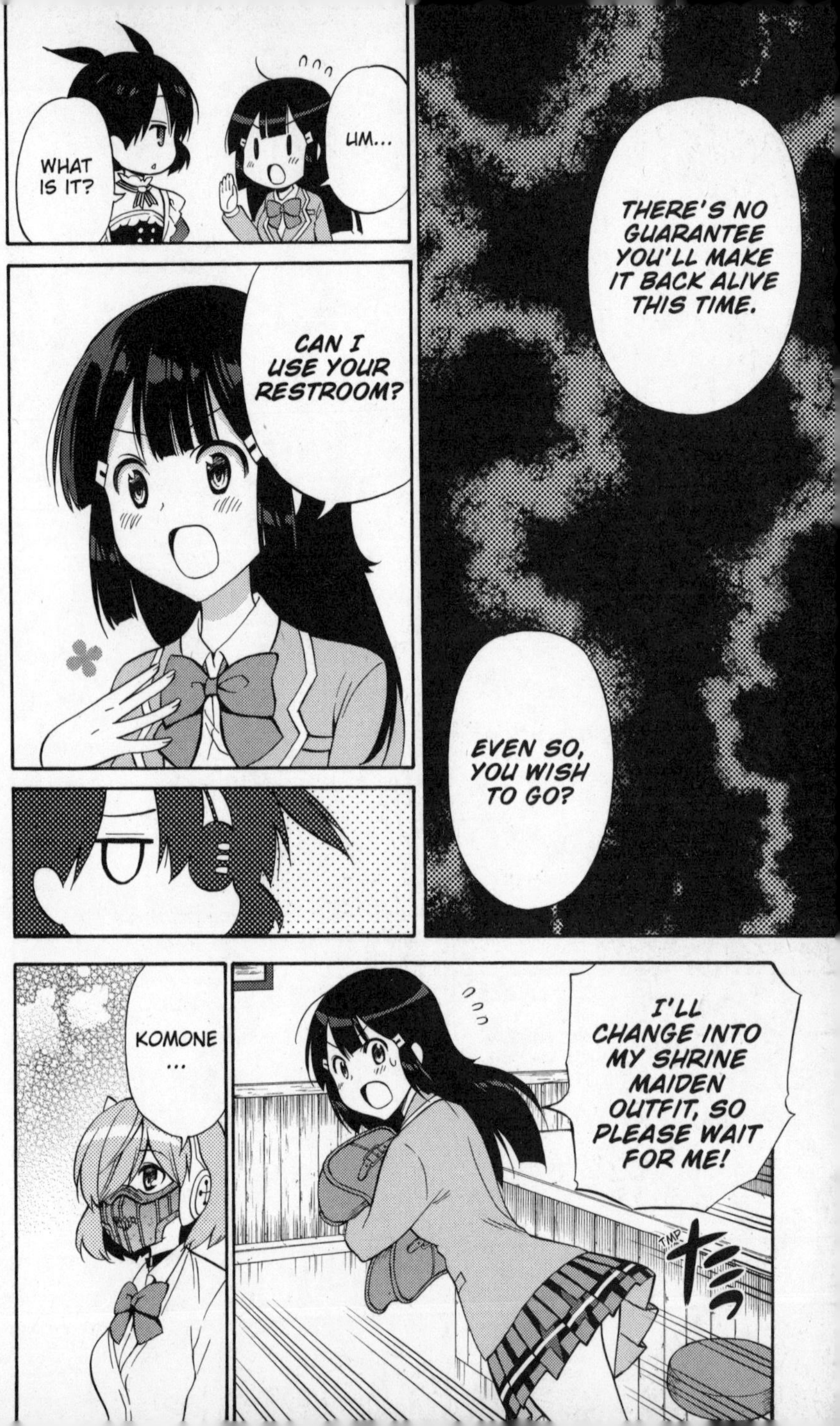
THERE'S NO GUARANTEE YOU'LL MAKE IT BACK ALIVE THIS TIME.
EVEN SO, YOU WISH TO GO?
UM...
WHAT IS IT?
CAN I USE YOUR RESTROOM?
I'LL CHANGE INTO MY SHRINE MAIDEN OUTFIT, SO PLEASE WAIT FOR ME!
TMP
KOMONE...

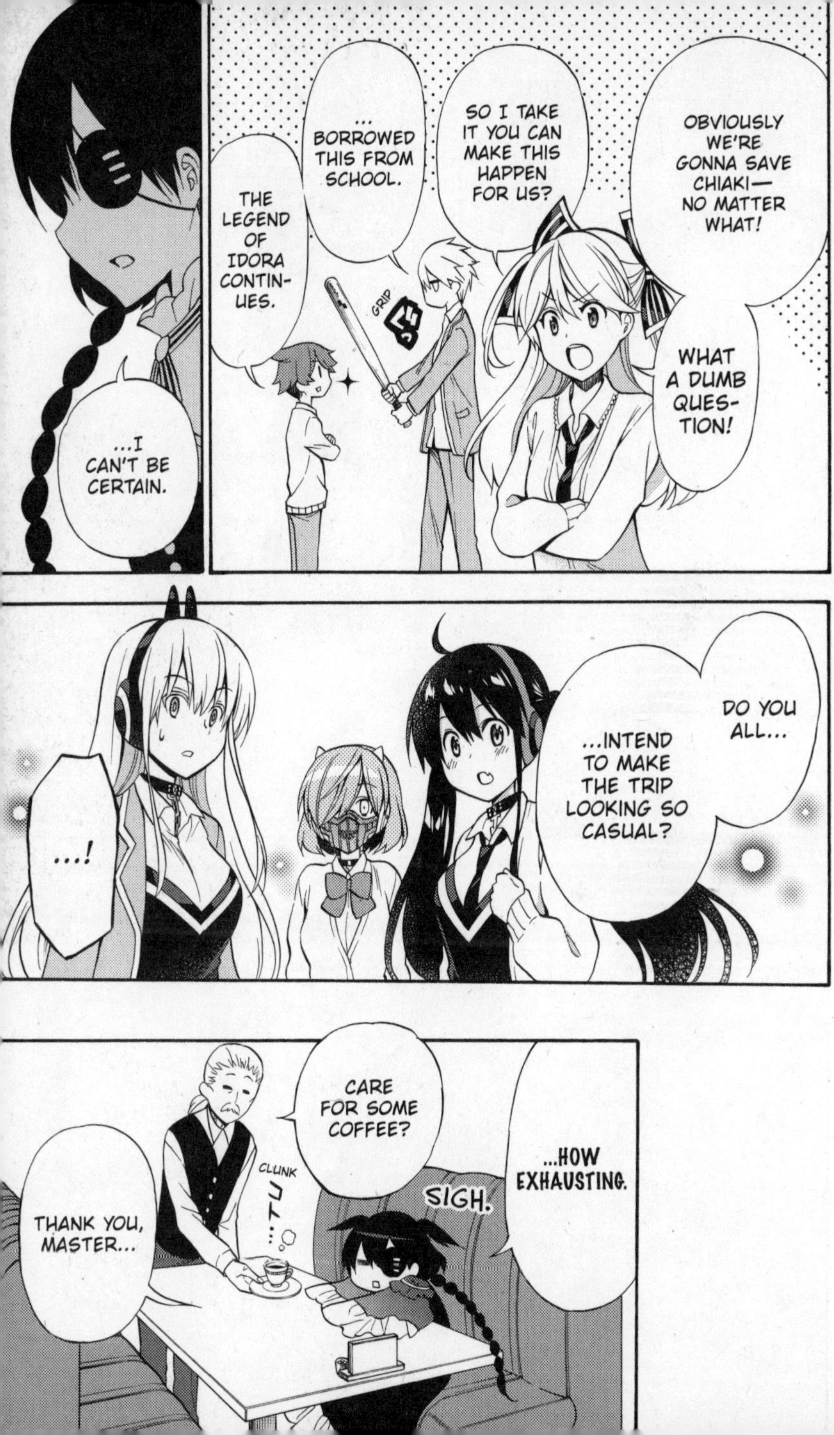
OBVIOUSLY WE'RE GONNA SAVE CHIAKI— NO MATTER WHAT!
WHAT A DUMB QUESTION!
SO I TAKE IT YOU CAN MAKE THIS HAPPEN FOR US?
...BORROWED THIS FROM SCHOOL.
GRIP
THE LEGEND OF IDORA CONTINUES.
...I CAN'T BE CERTAIN.
DO YOU ALL...
...INTEND TO MAKE THE TRIP LOOKING SO CASUAL?
...!
...HOW EXHAUSTING.
SIGH.
CARE FOR SOME COFFEE?
CLUNK
THANK YOU, MASTER...

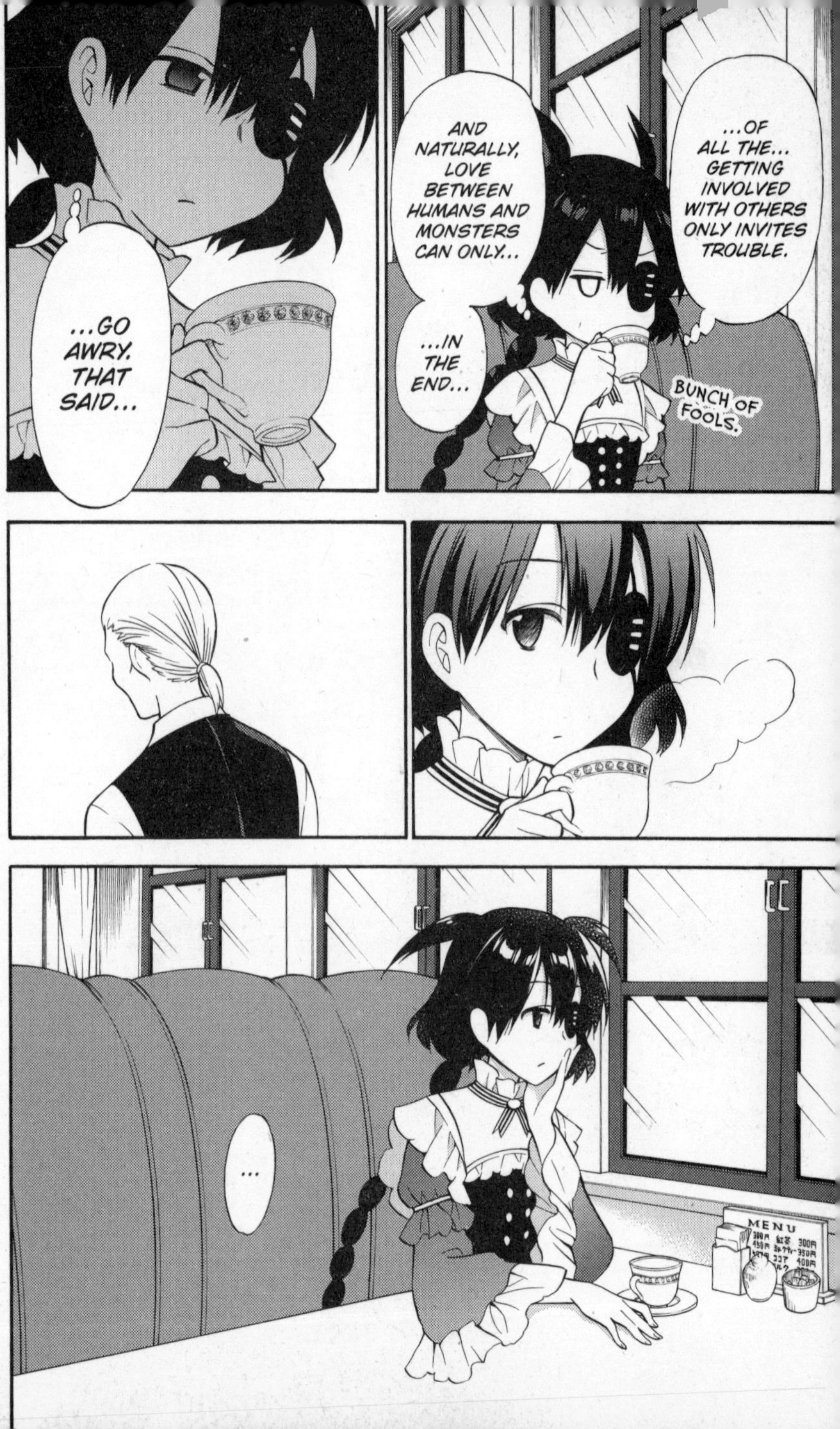
...OF ALL THE... GETTING INVOLVED WITH OTHERS ONLY INVITES TROUBLE.
AND NATURALLY, LOVE BETWEEN HUMANS AND MONSTERS CAN ONLY...
BUNCH OF FOOLS.
...IN THE END...
...GO AWRY. THAT SAID...
...
MENU

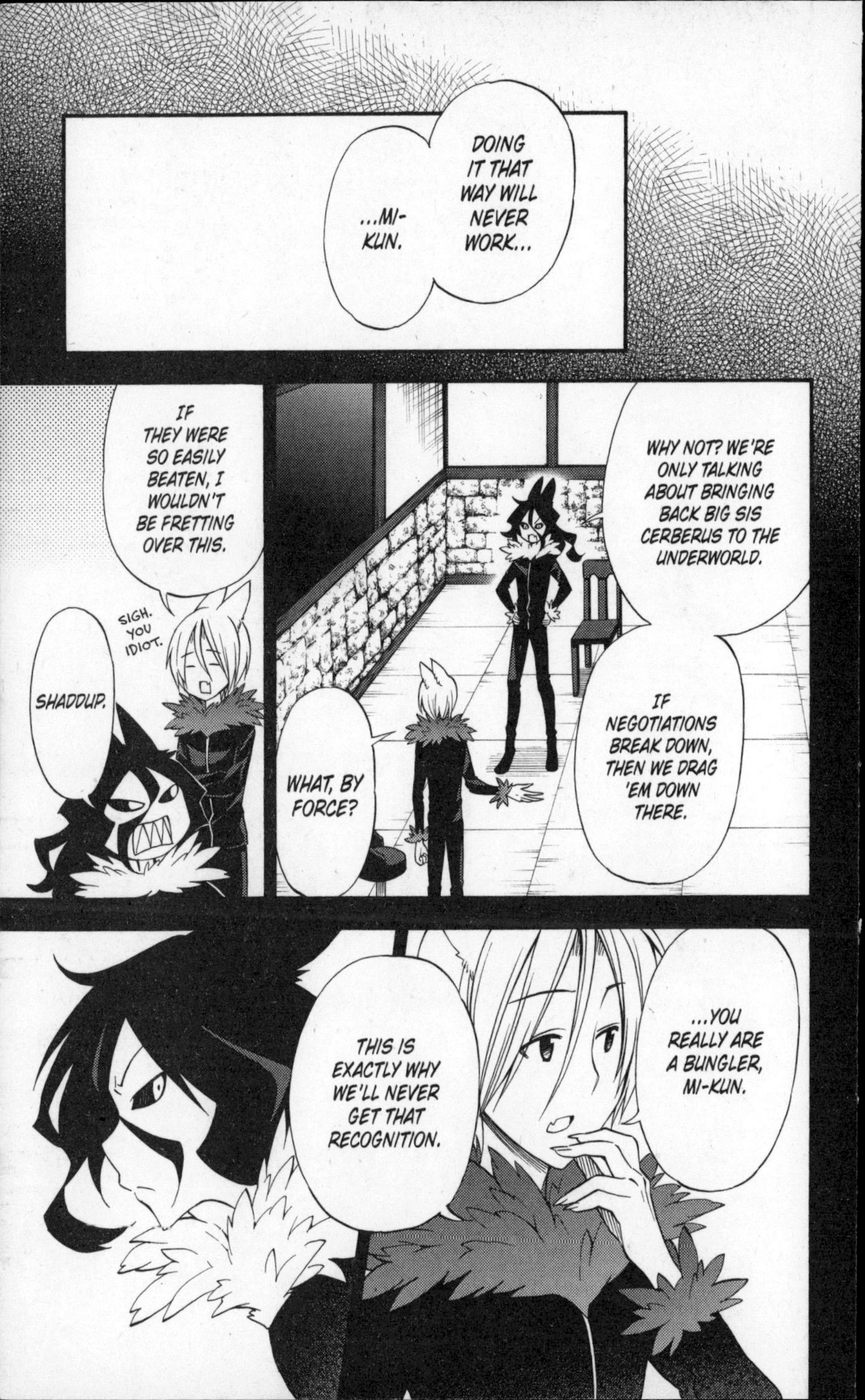

DOING IT THAT WAY WILL NEVER WORK...
...MI-KUN.
WHY NOT? WE'RE ONLY TALKING ABOUT BRINGING BACK BIG SIS CERBERUS TO THE UNDERWORLD.
IF NEGOTIATIONS BREAK DOWN, THEN WE DRAG 'EM DOWN THERE.
WHAT, BY FORCE?
IF THEY WERE SO EASILY BEATEN, I WOULDN'T BE FRETTING OVER THIS.
SIGH. YOU IDIOT.
SHADDUP.
...YOU REALLY ARE A BUNGLER, MI-KUN.
THIS IS EXACTLY WHY WE'LL NEVER GET THAT RECOGNITION.

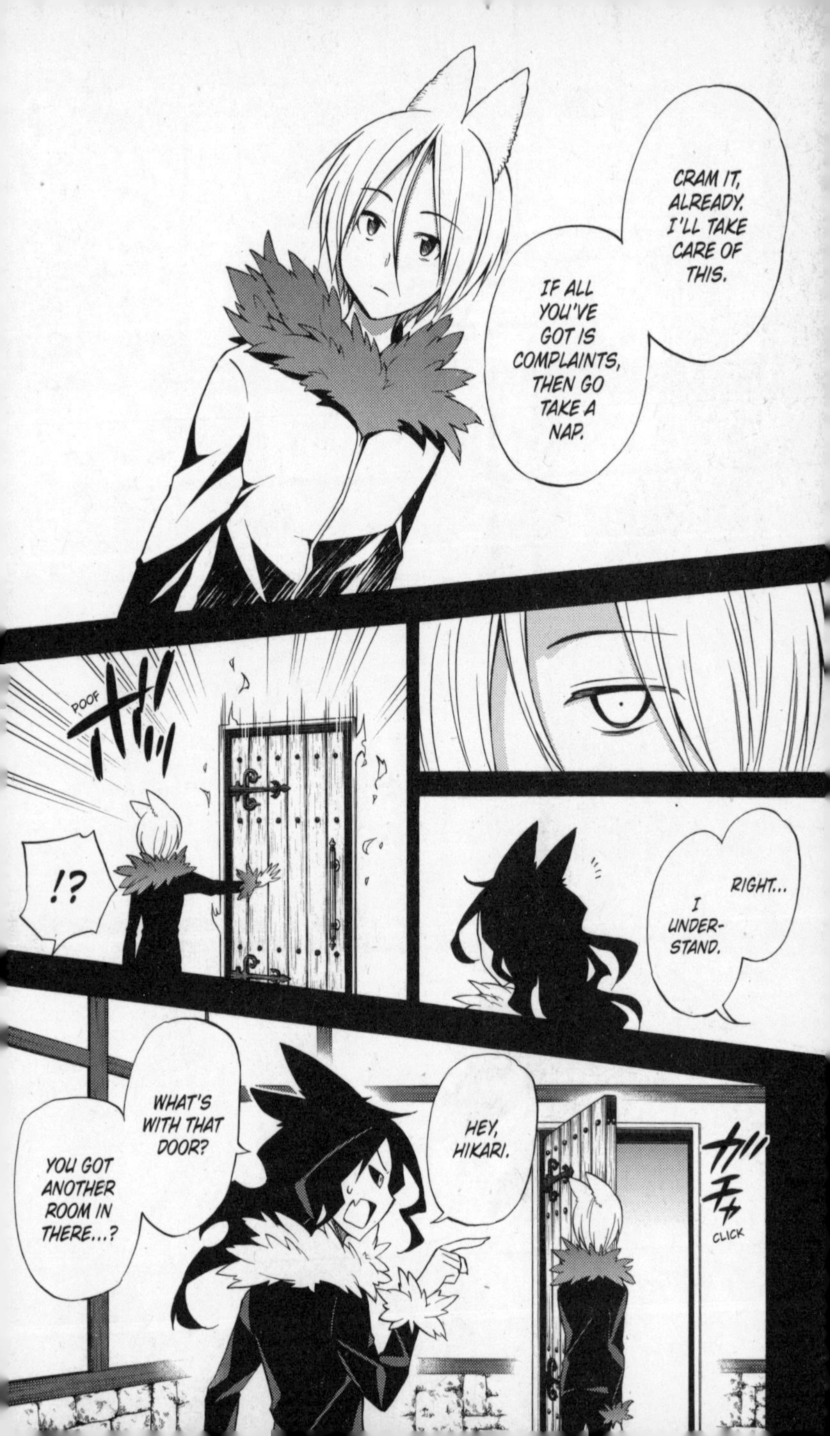
CRAM IT, ALREADY. I'LL TAKE CARE OF THIS.
IF ALL YOU'VE GOT IS COMPLAINTS, THEN GO TAKE A NAP.
RIGHT... I UNDER-STAND.
POOF
!?
CLICK
HEY, HIKARI.
WHAT'S WITH THAT DOOR?
YOU GOT ANOTHER ROOM IN THERE...?

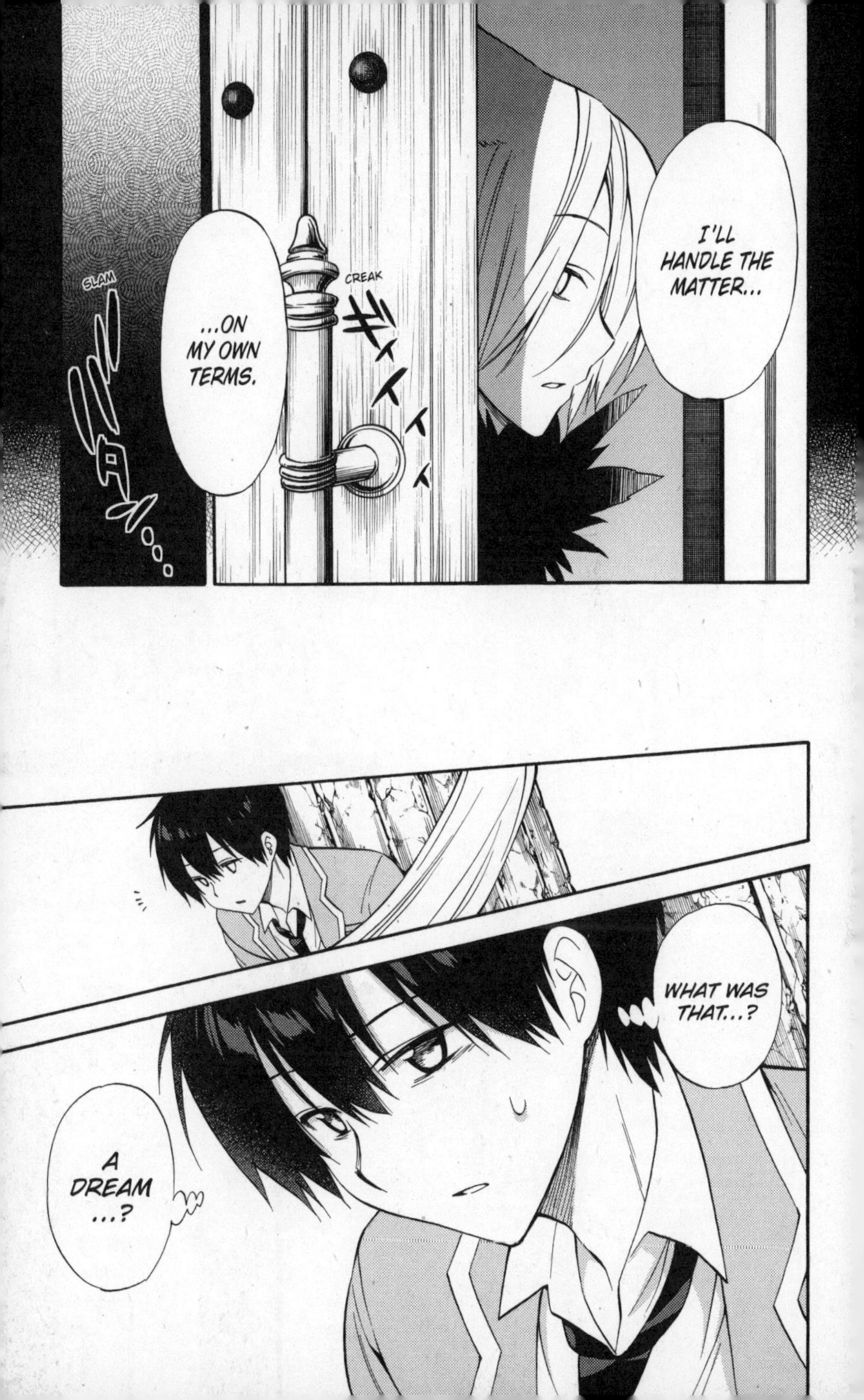
I'LL HANDLE THE MATTER...
CREAK
...ON MY OWN TERMS.
SLAM
WHAT WAS THAT...?
A DREAM ...?

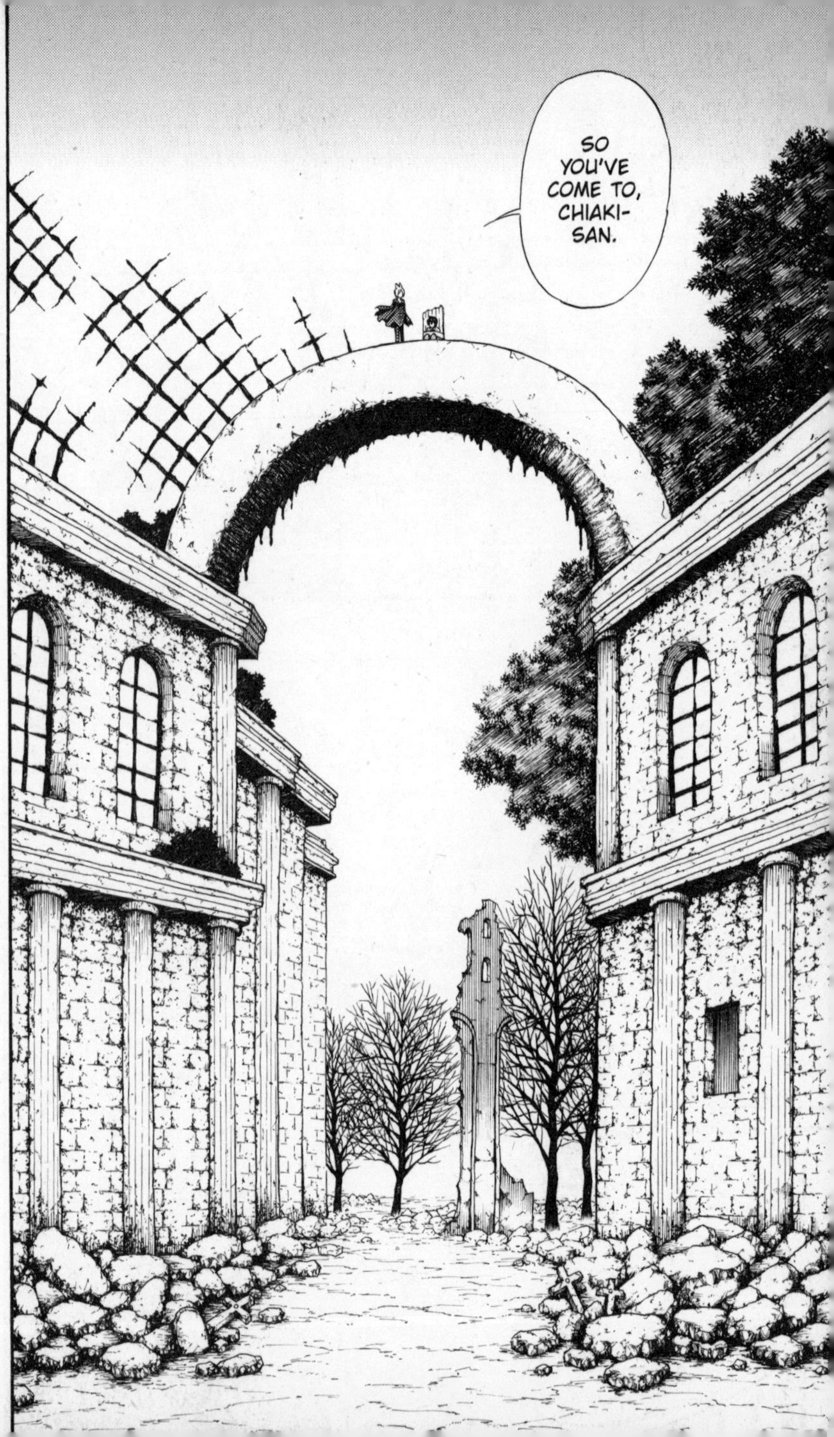
SO YOU'VE COME TO, CHIAKI-SAN.

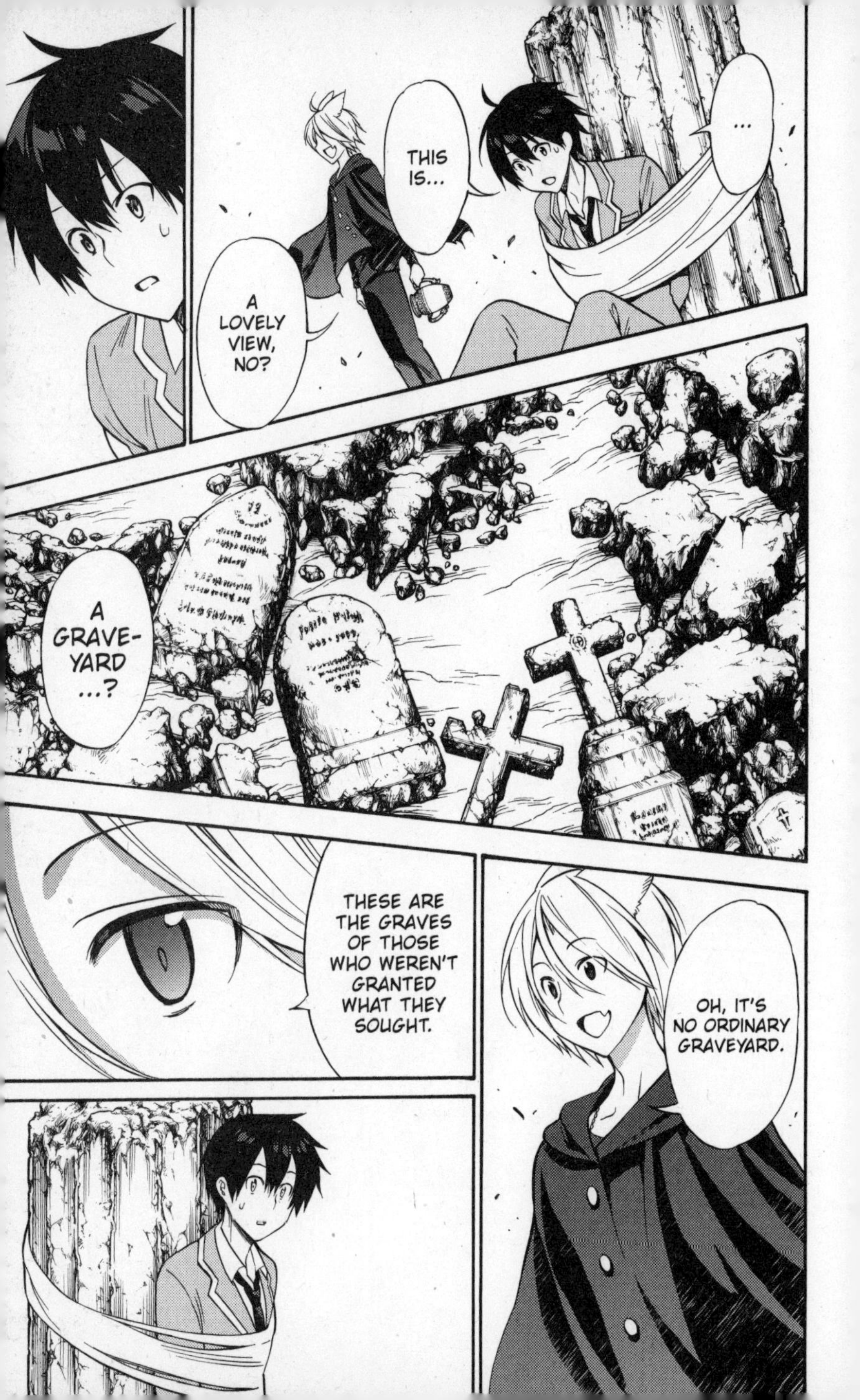
...
THIS IS...
A LOVELY VIEW, NO?
A GRAVEYARD...?
OH, IT'S NO ORDINARY GRAVEYARD.
THESE ARE THE GRAVES OF THOSE WHO WEREN'T GRANTED WHAT THEY SOUGHT.

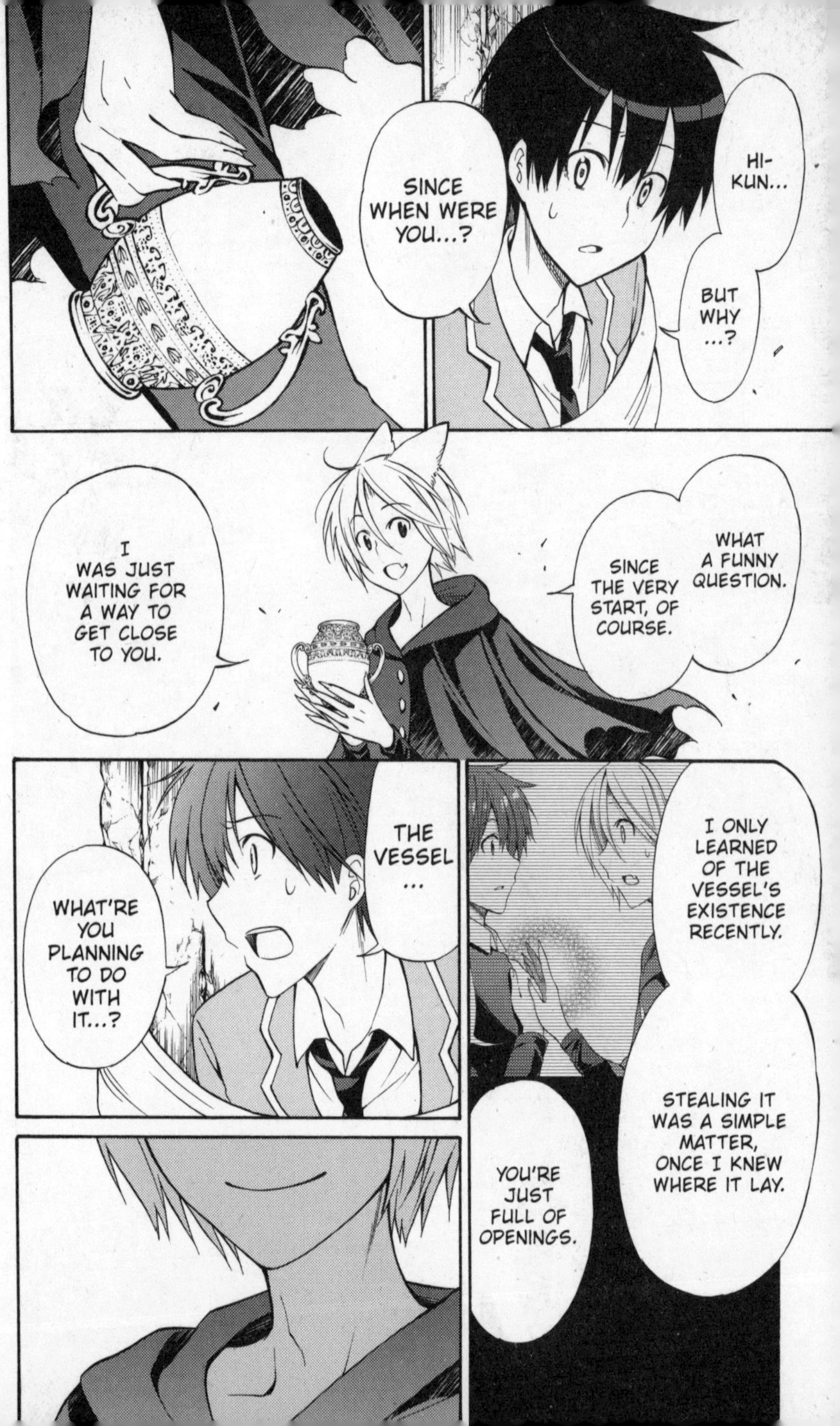
HI-KUN...
BUT WHY...?
SINCE WHEN WERE YOU...?
WHAT A FUNNY QUESTION.
SINCE THE VERY START, OF COURSE.
I WAS JUST WAITING FOR A WAY TO GET CLOSE TO YOU.
I ONLY LEARNED OF THE VESSEL'S EXISTENCE RECENTLY.
STEALING IT WAS A SIMPLE MATTER, ONCE I KNEW WHERE IT LAY.
YOU'RE JUST FULL OF OPENINGS.
THE VESSEL...
WHAT'RE YOU PLANNING TO DO WITH IT...?

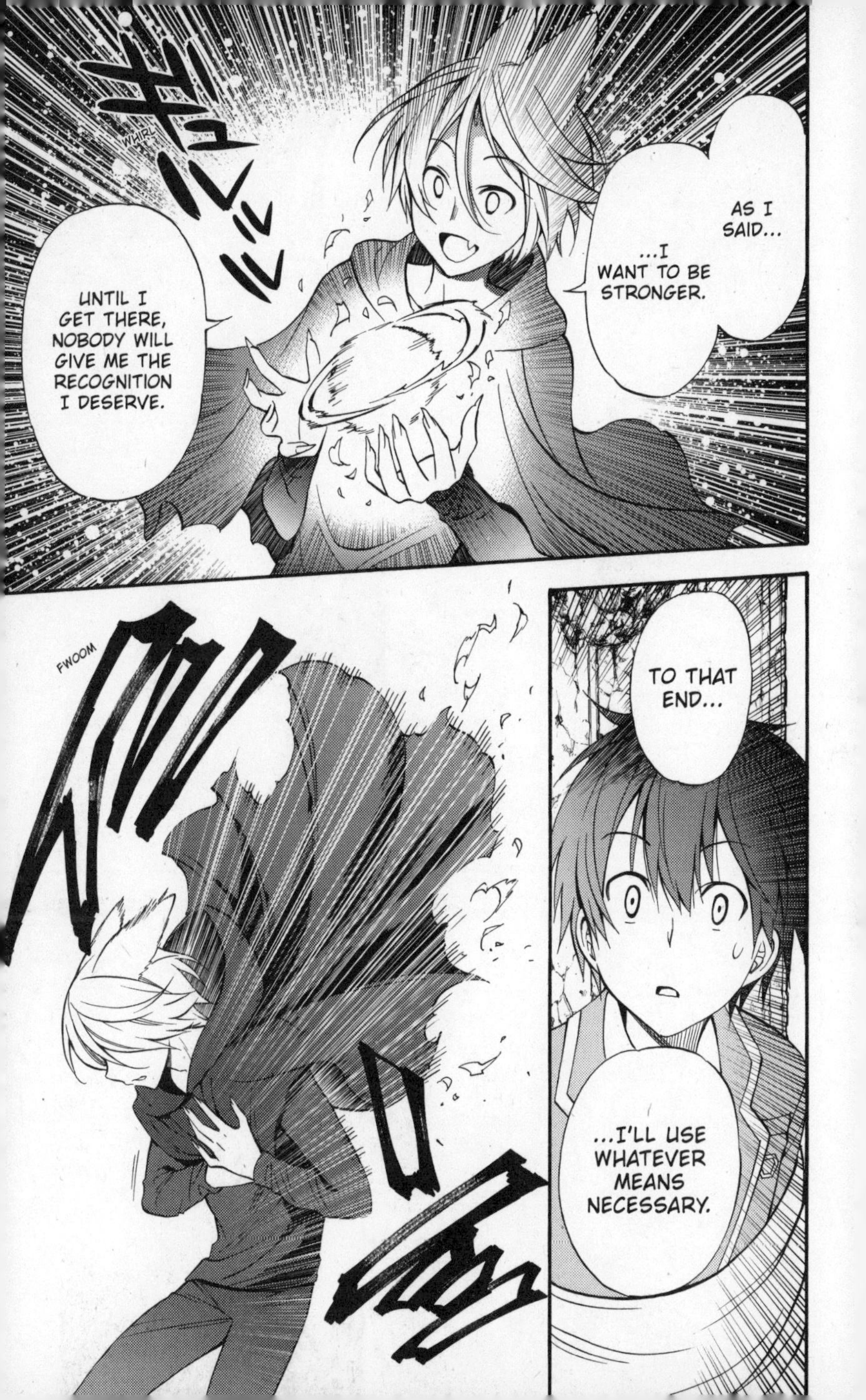
AS I SAID...
...I WANT TO BE STRONGER.
WHIRL
UNTIL I GET THERE, NOBODY WILL GIVE ME THE RECOGNITION I DESERVE.
TO THAT END...
...I'LL USE WHATEVER MEANS NECESSARY.
FWOOM

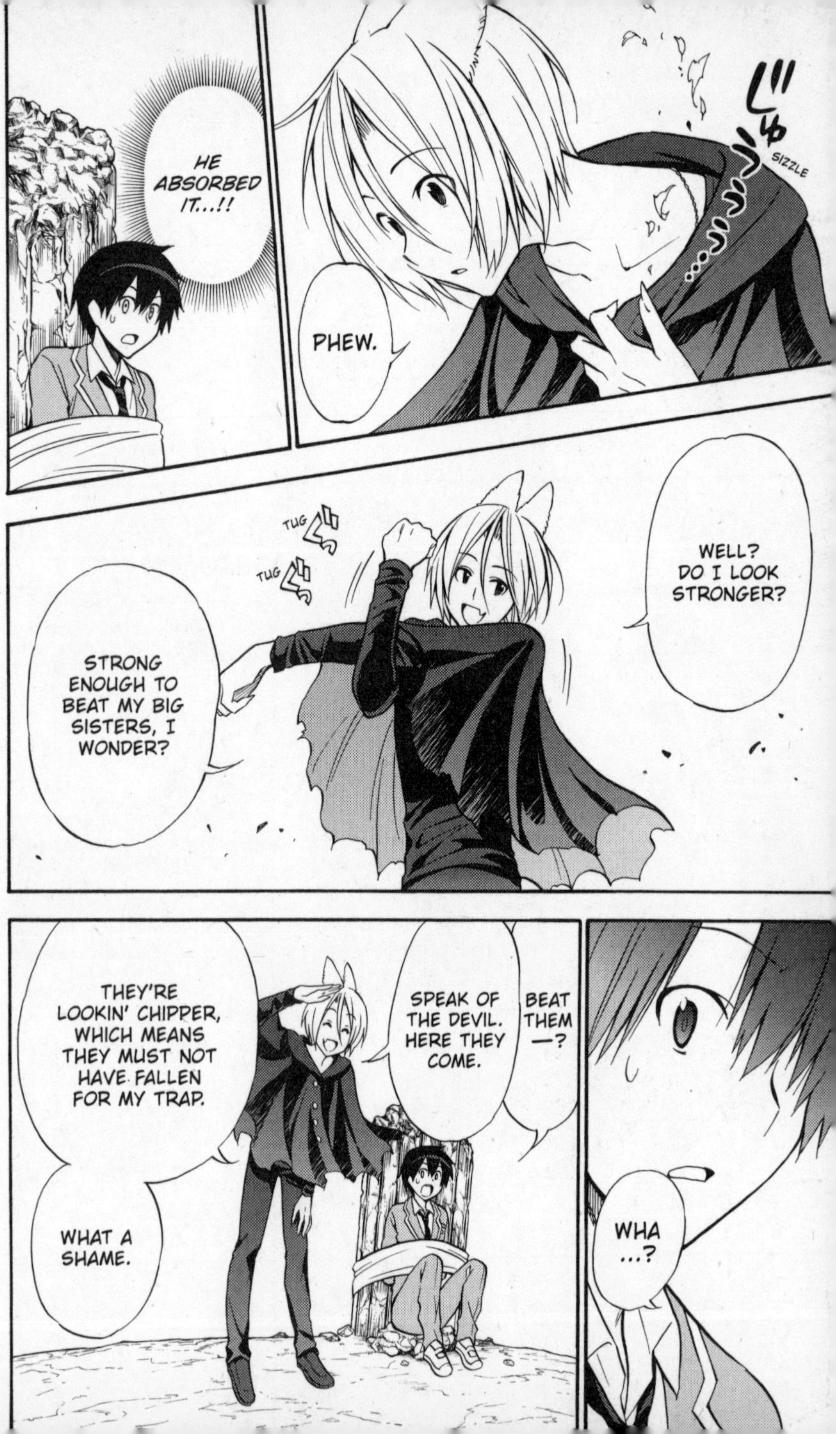
SIZZLE
PHEW.
HE ABSORBED IT...!!
WELL? DO I LOOK STRONGER?
TUG
TUG
STRONG ENOUGH TO BEAT MY BIG SISTERS, I WONDER?
WHA ...?
BEAT THEM —?
SPEAK OF THE DEVIL. HERE THEY COME.
THEY'RE LOOKIN' CHIPPER, WHICH MEANS THEY MUST NOT HAVE FALLEN FOR MY TRAP.
WHAT A SHAME.

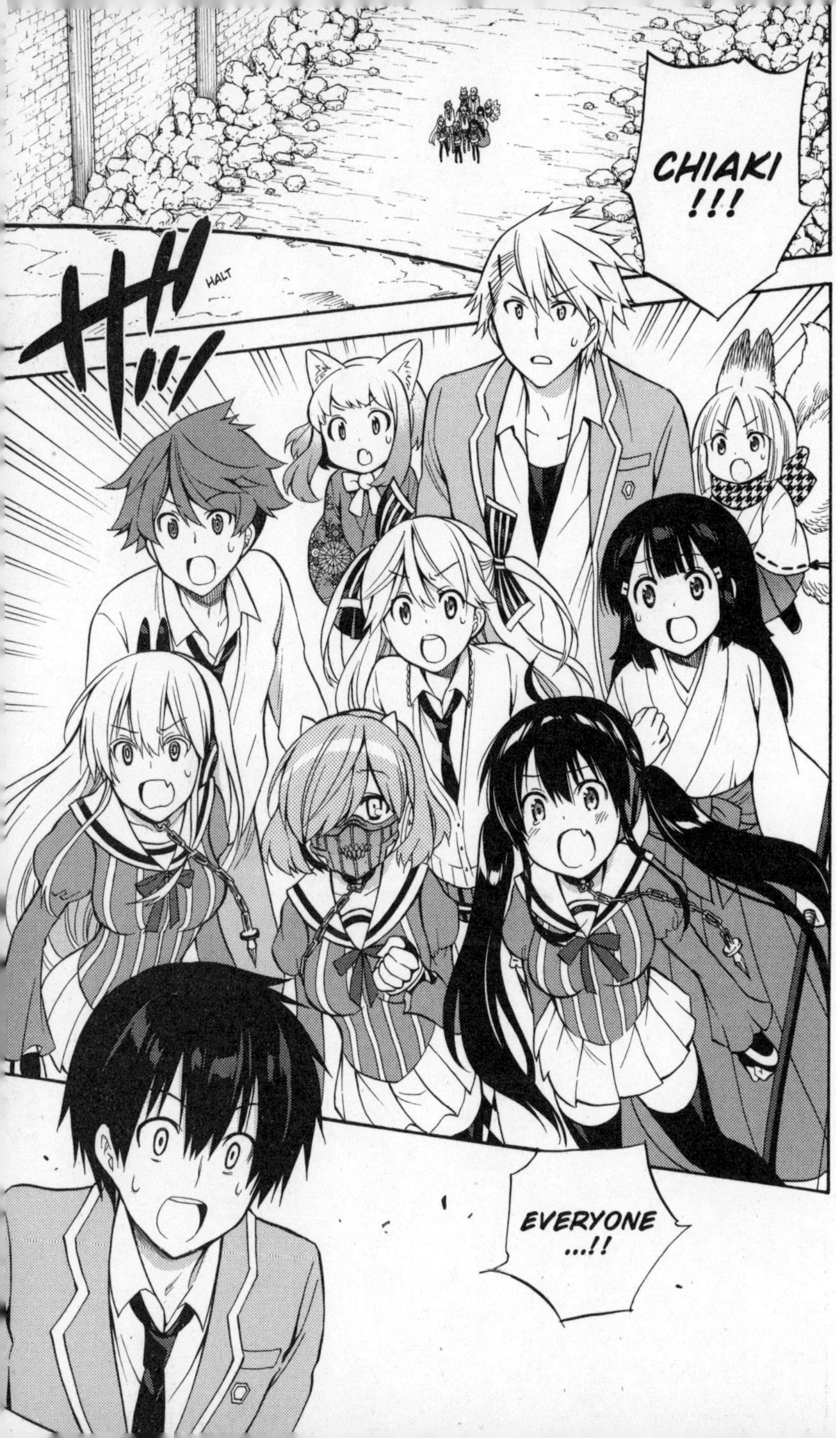
CHIAKI
!!!
HALT
EVERYONE
...!!

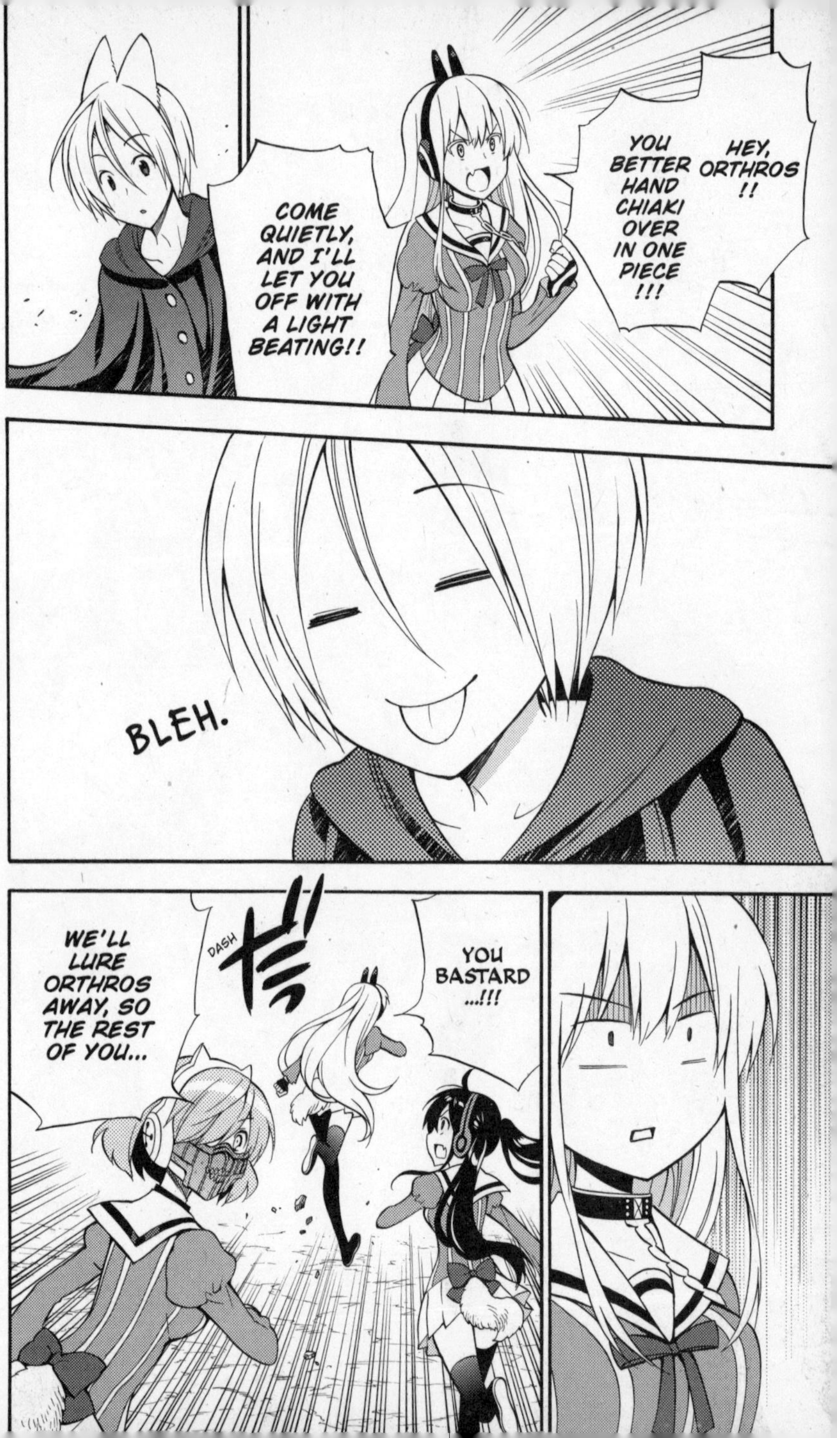
HEY, ORTHROS!!
YOU BETTER HAND CHIAKI OVER IN ONE PIECE!!!
COME QUIETLY, AND I'LL LET YOU OFF WITH A LIGHT BEATING!!
BLEH.
YOU BASTARD...!!!
DASH
WE'LL LURE ORTHROS AWAY, SO THE REST OF YOU...

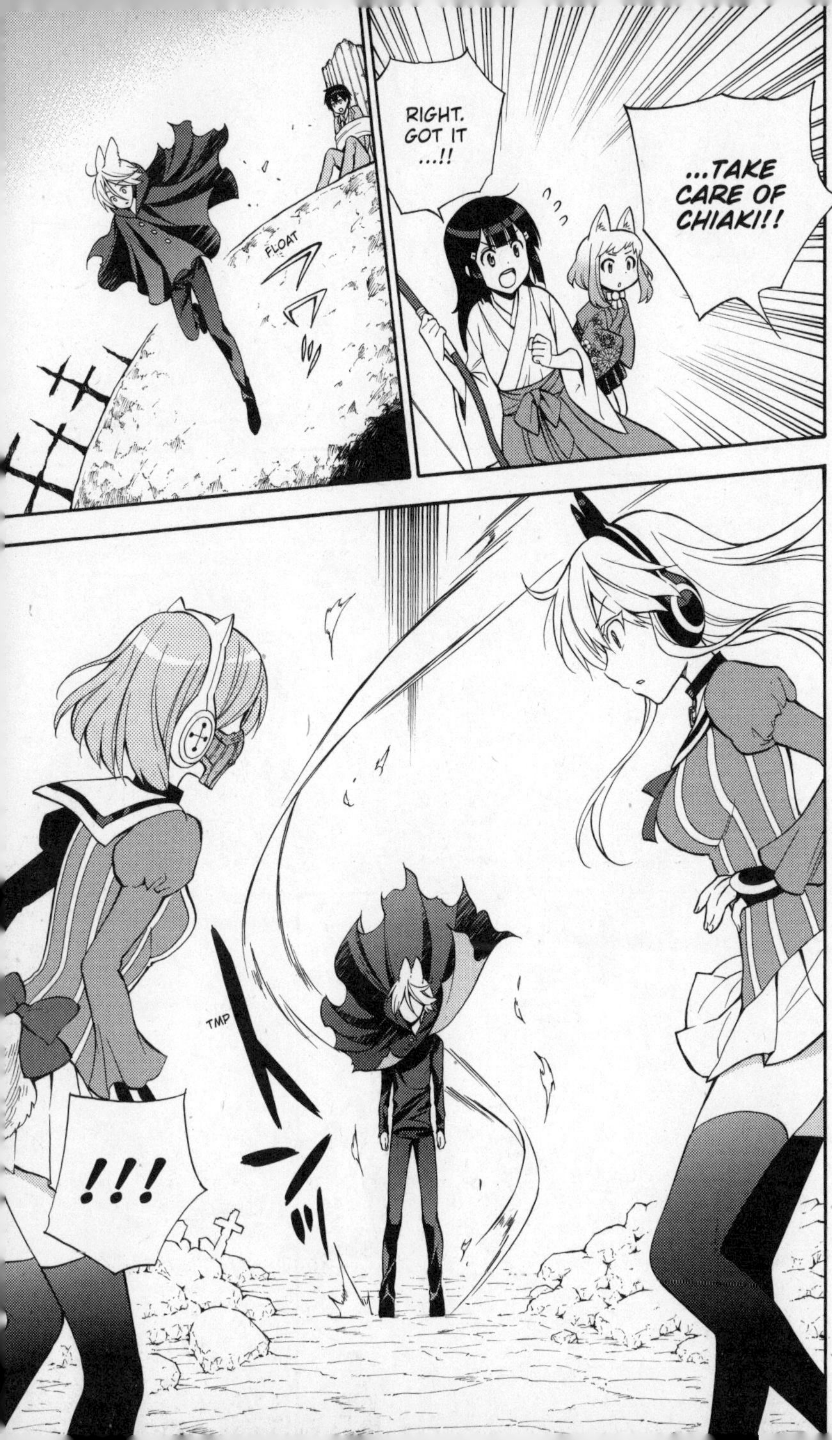
...TAKE CARE OF CHIAKI!!
RIGHT. GOT IT ...!!
FLOAT
TMP
!!!

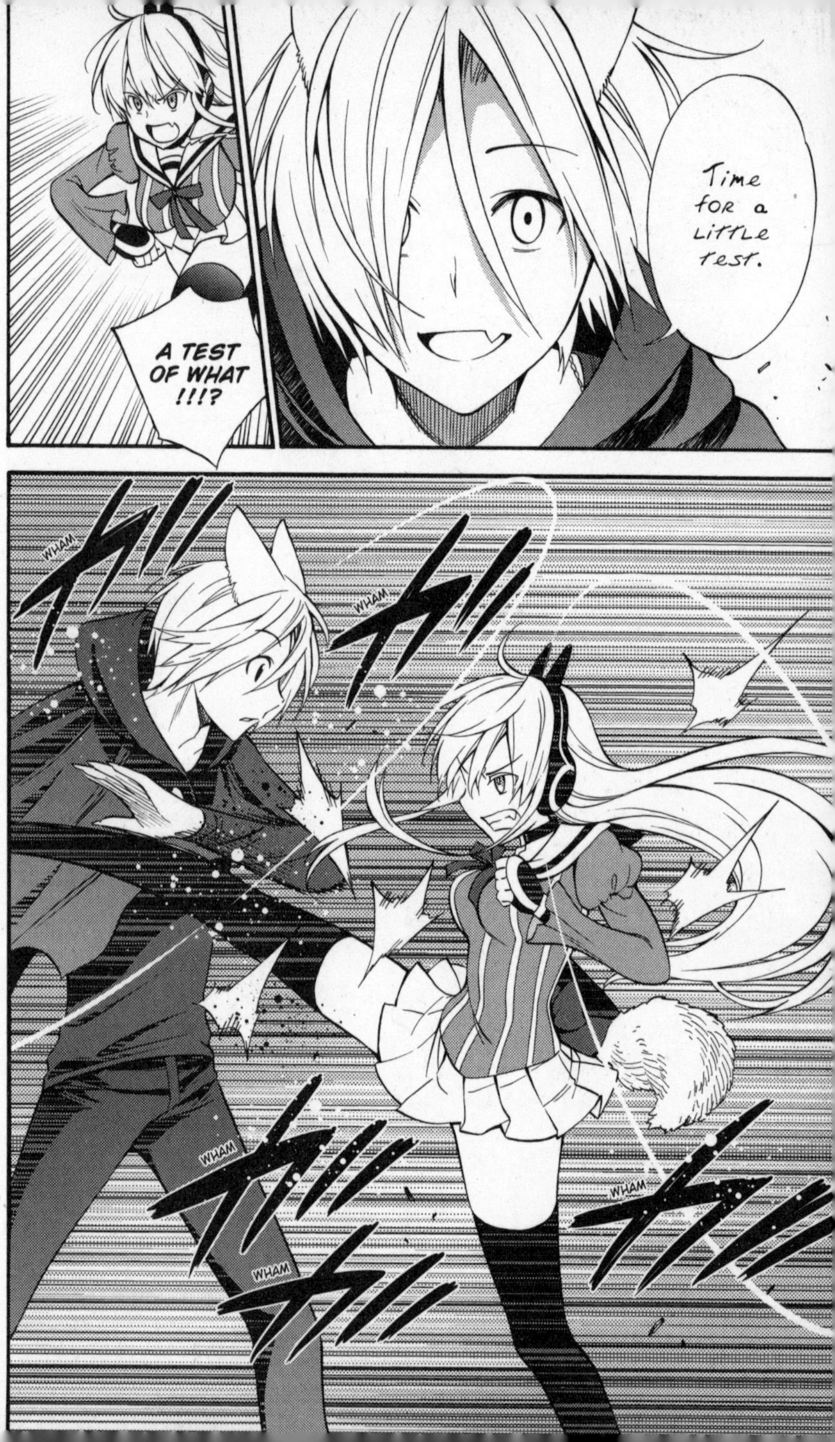

Time for a little test.
A TEST OF WHAT !!!?
WHAM
WHAM
WHAM
WHAM
WHAM

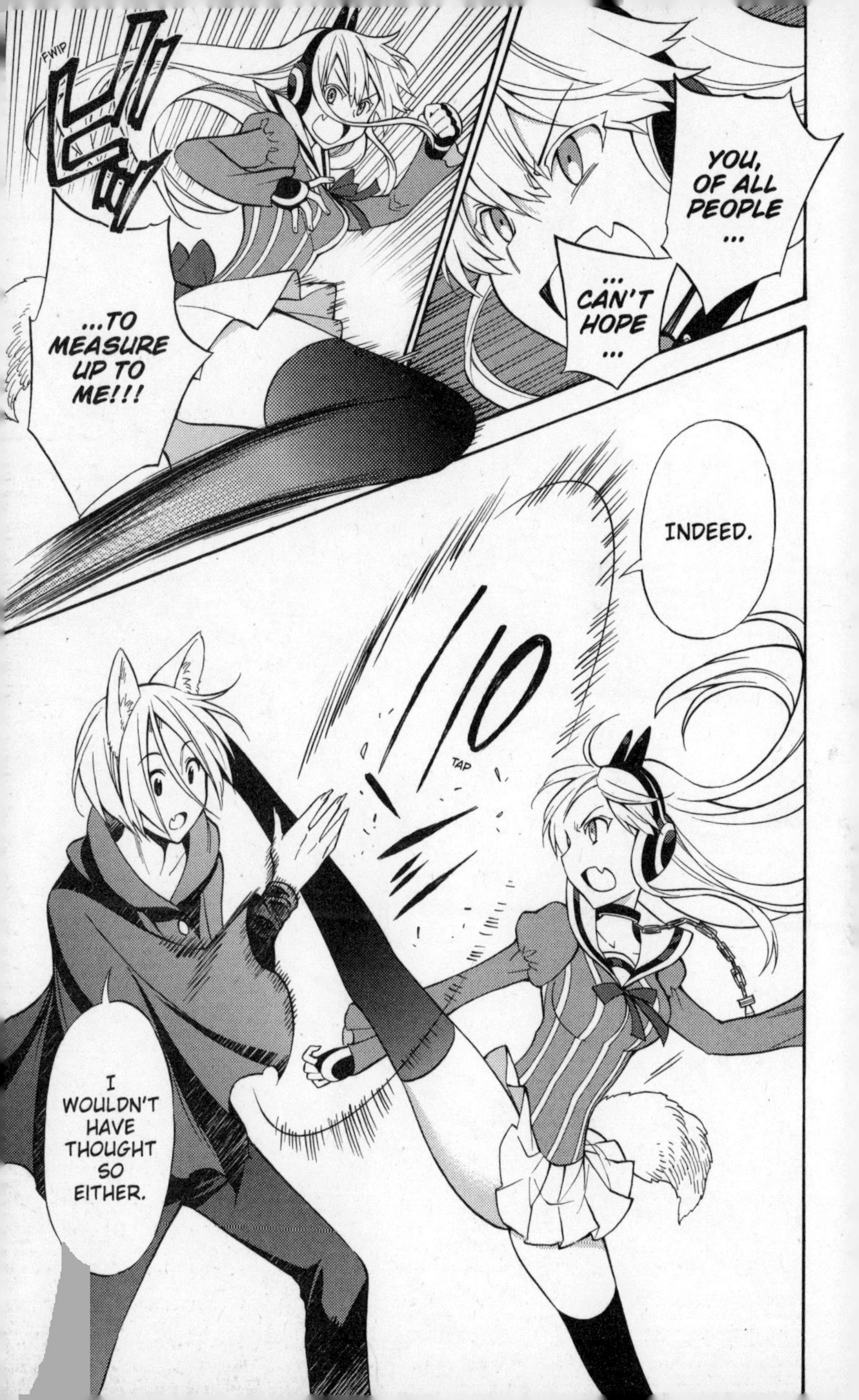
YOU, OF ALL PEOPLE ...
... CAN'T HOPE ...
FWIP
...TO MEASURE UP TO ME!!!
INDEED.
TAP
I WOULDN'T HAVE THOUGHT SO EITHER.

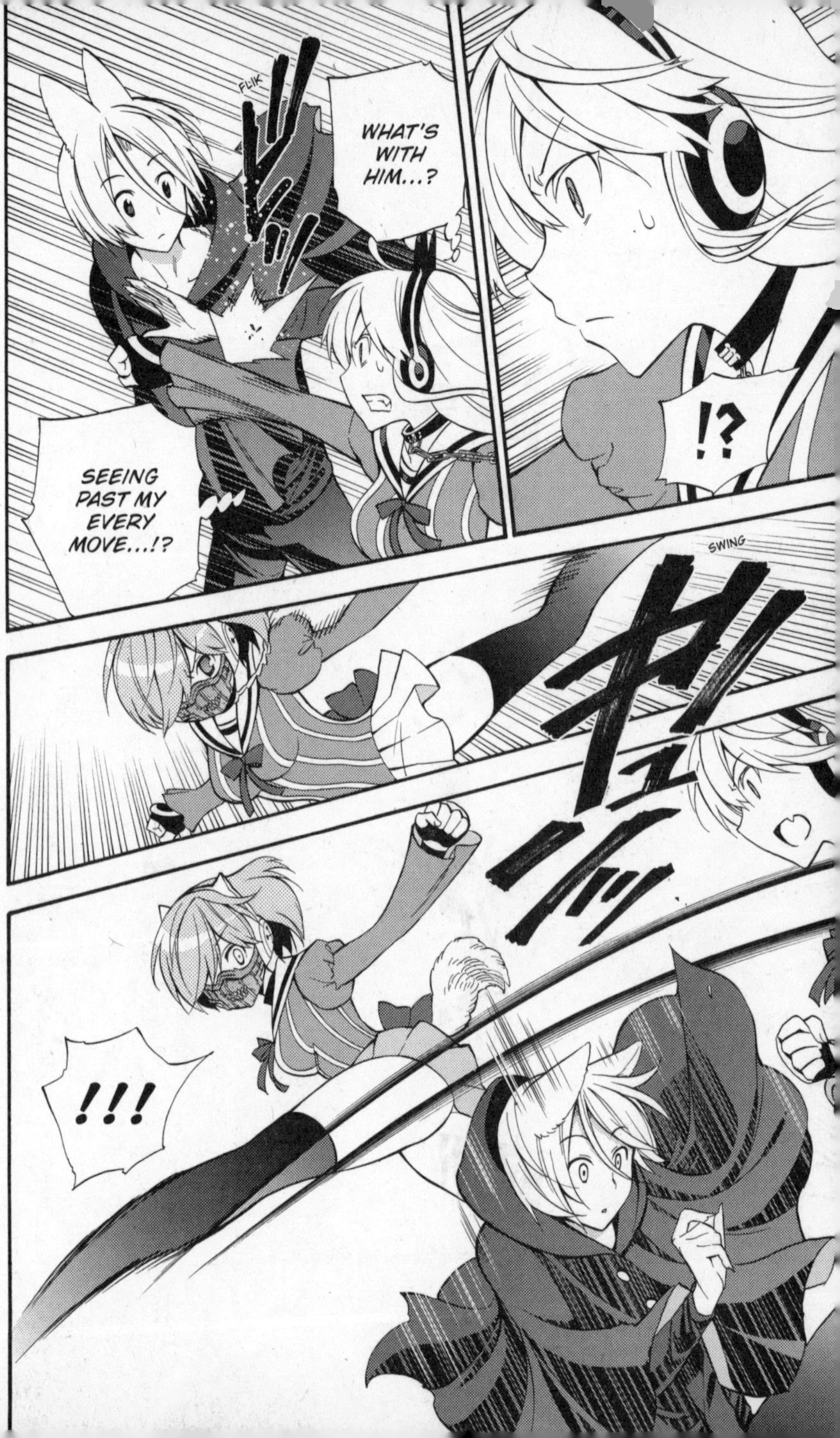
!?
WHAT'S WITH HIM...?
FLIK
SEEING PAST MY EVERY MOVE...!?
SWING
!!!

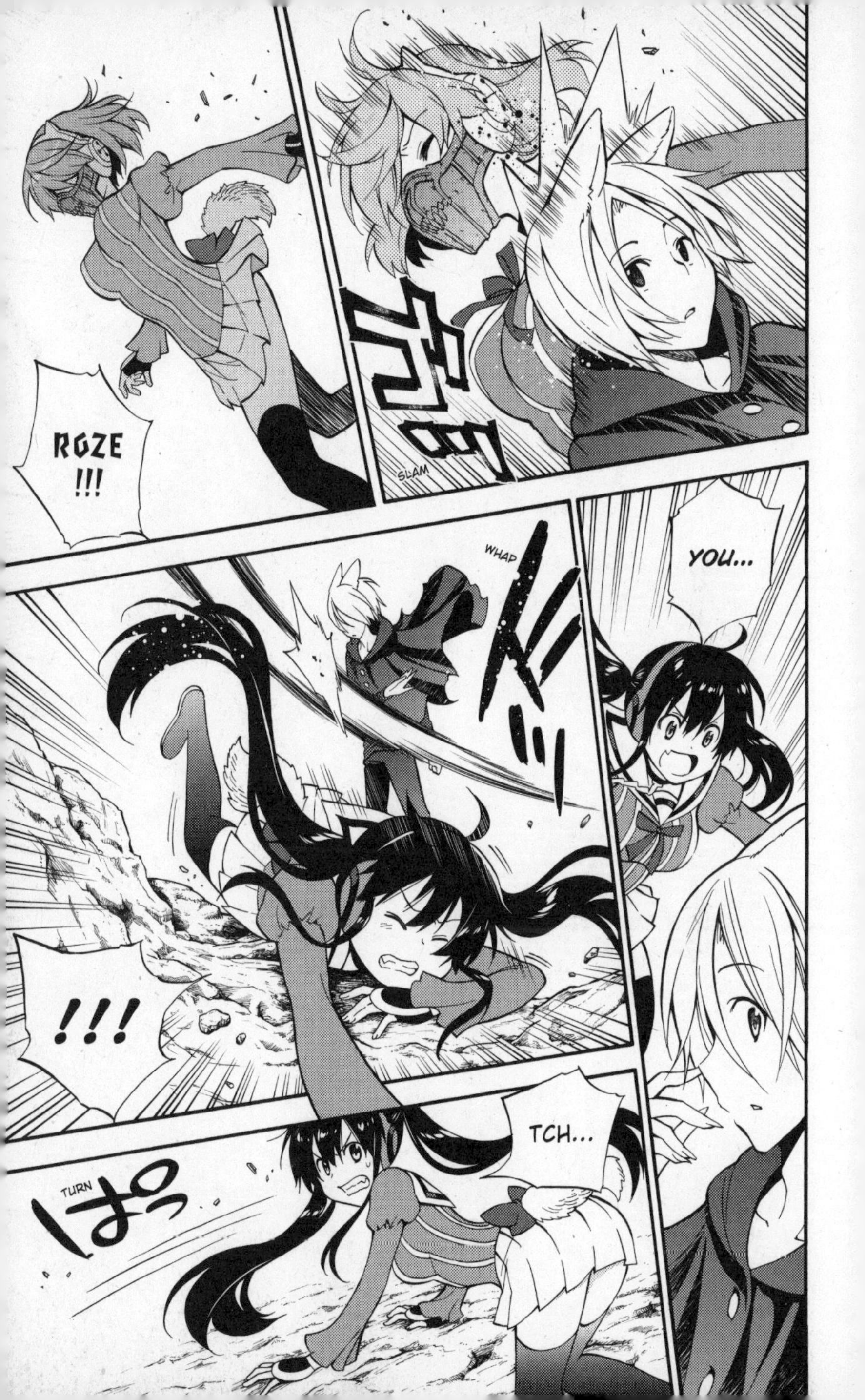

SLAM
ROZE !!!
YOU...
WHAP
!!!
TCH...
TURN

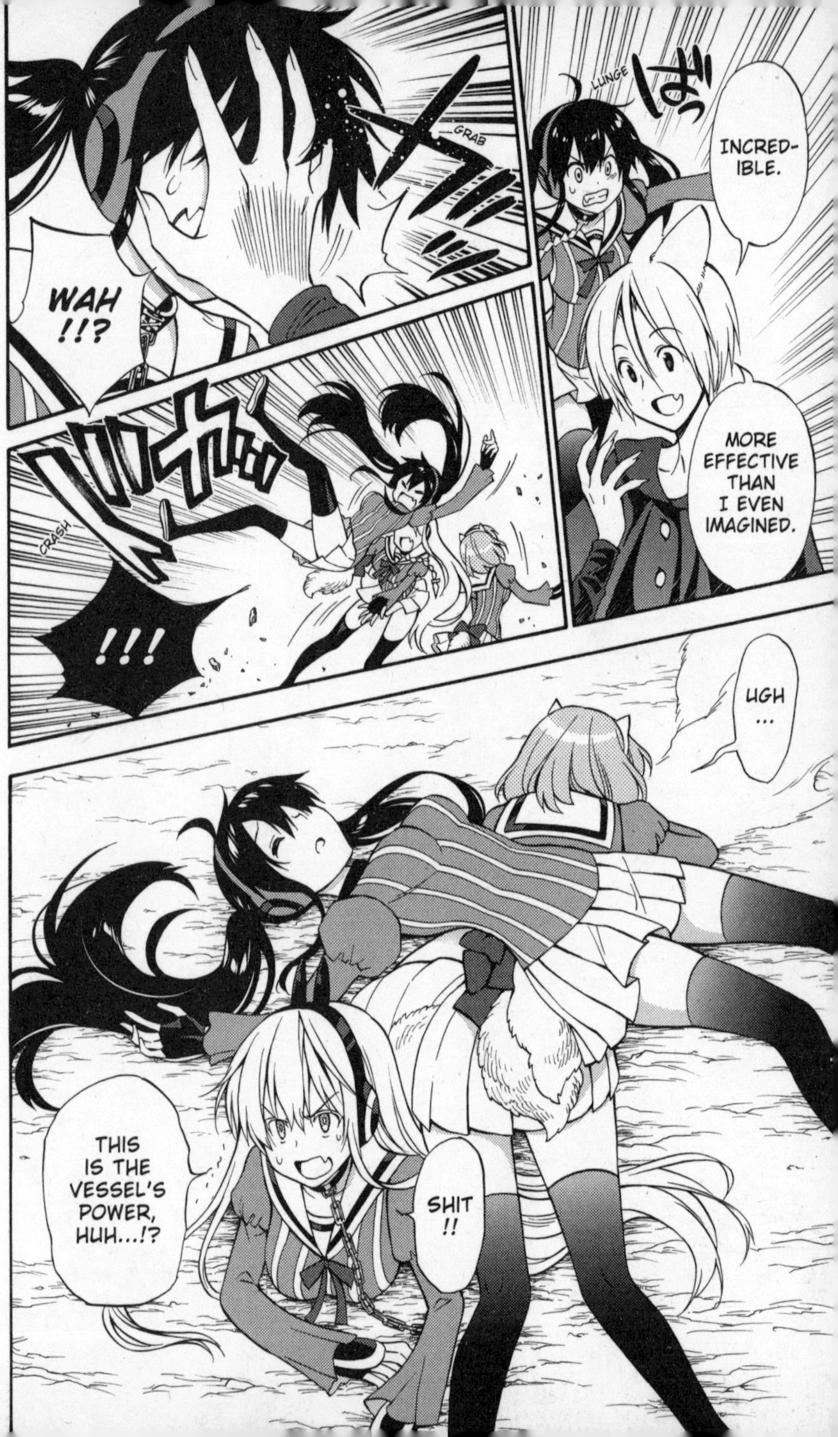
LUNGE
ばっ
INCREDIBLE.
MORE EFFECTIVE THAN I EVEN IMAGINED.
GRAB
WAH!!?
CRASH
!!!
UGH...
SHIT!!
THIS IS THE VESSEL'S POWER, HUH...!?

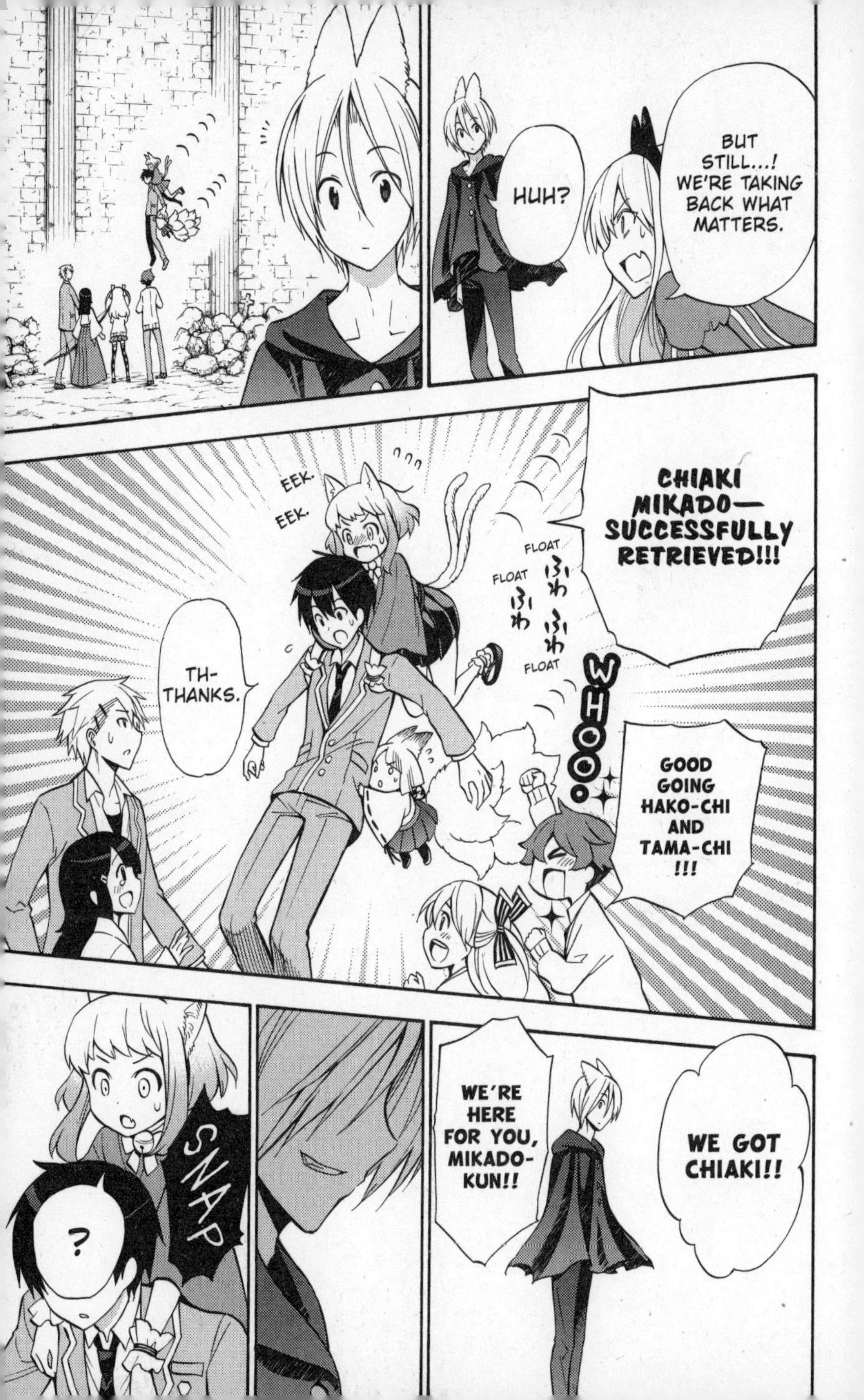
BUT STILL...! WE'RE TAKING BACK WHAT MATTERS.
HUH?
CHIAKI MIKADO— SUCCESSFULLY RETRIEVED!!!
EEK.
EEK.
FLOAT
ふわ
FLOAT
ふわ
ふわ
FLOAT
WHOOO.
GOOD GOING HAKO-CHI AND TAMA-CHI !!!
TH-THANKS.
WE GOT CHIAKI!!
WE'RE HERE FOR YOU, MIKADO-KUN!!
SNAP
?

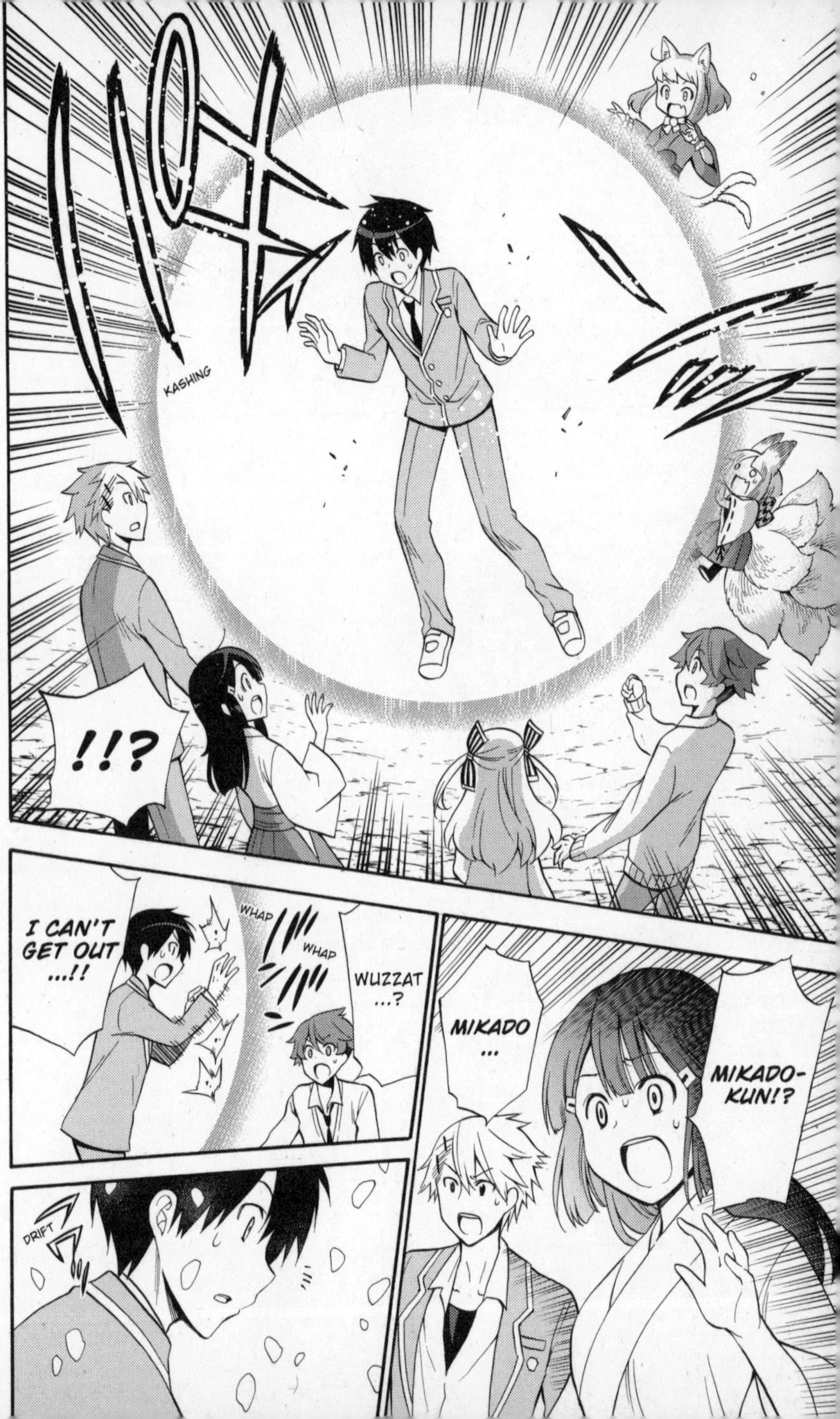
KASHING
!!?
MIKADO-KUN!?
MIKADO ...
WUZZAT ...?
WHAP
WHAP
I CAN'T GET OUT ...!!
DRIFT

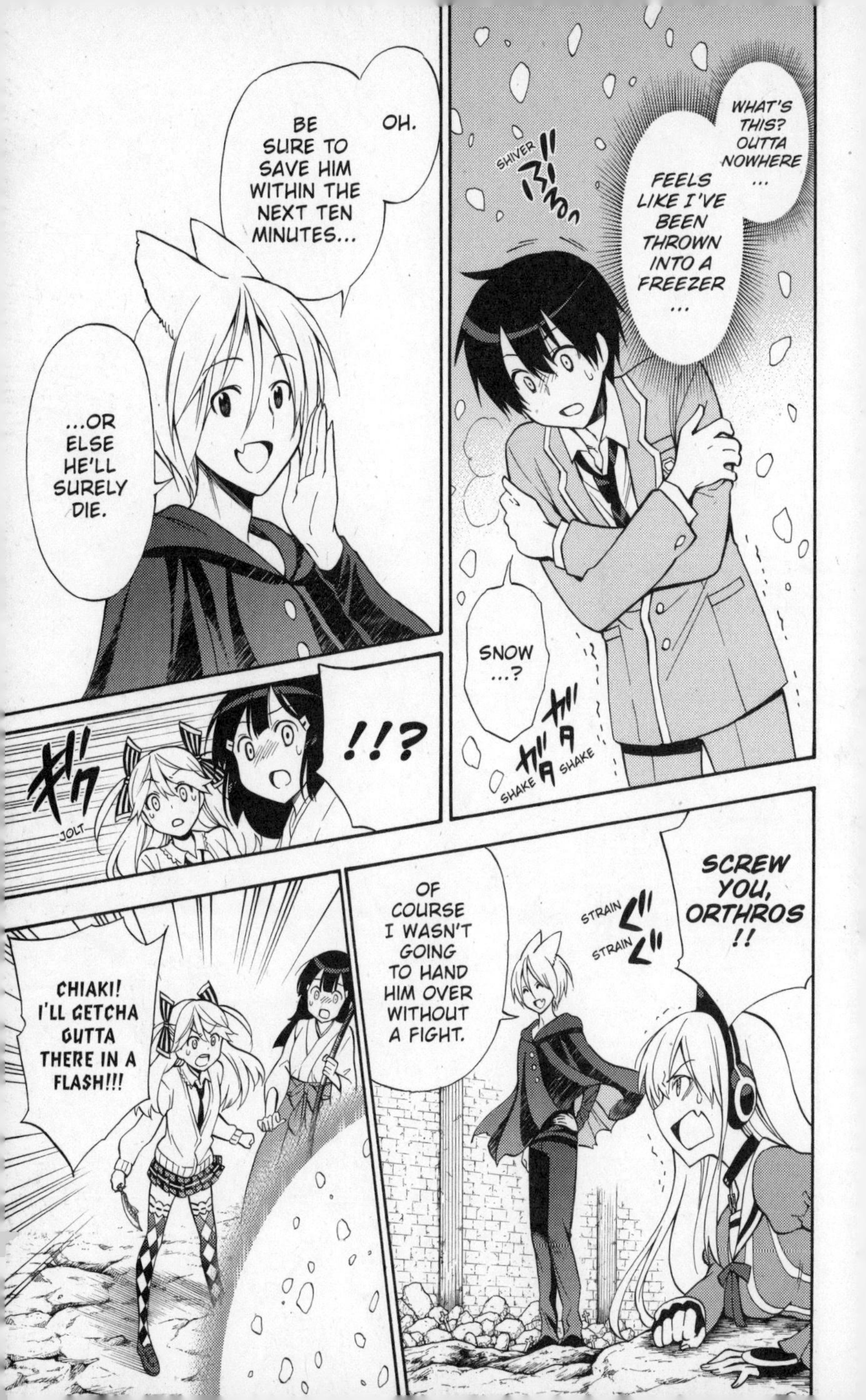
WHAT'S THIS? OUTTA NOWHERE...
FEELS LIKE I'VE BEEN THROWN INTO A FREEZER...
SHIVER
SNOW...?
SHAKE SHAKE
OH.
BE SURE TO SAVE HIM WITHIN THE NEXT TEN MINUTES...
...OR ELSE HE'LL SURELY DIE.
!!?
JOLT
SCREW YOU, ORTHROS!!
STRAIN STRAIN
OF COURSE I WASN'T GOING TO HAND HIM OVER WITHOUT A FIGHT.
CHIAKI! I'LL GETCHA OUTTA THERE IN A FLASH!!!

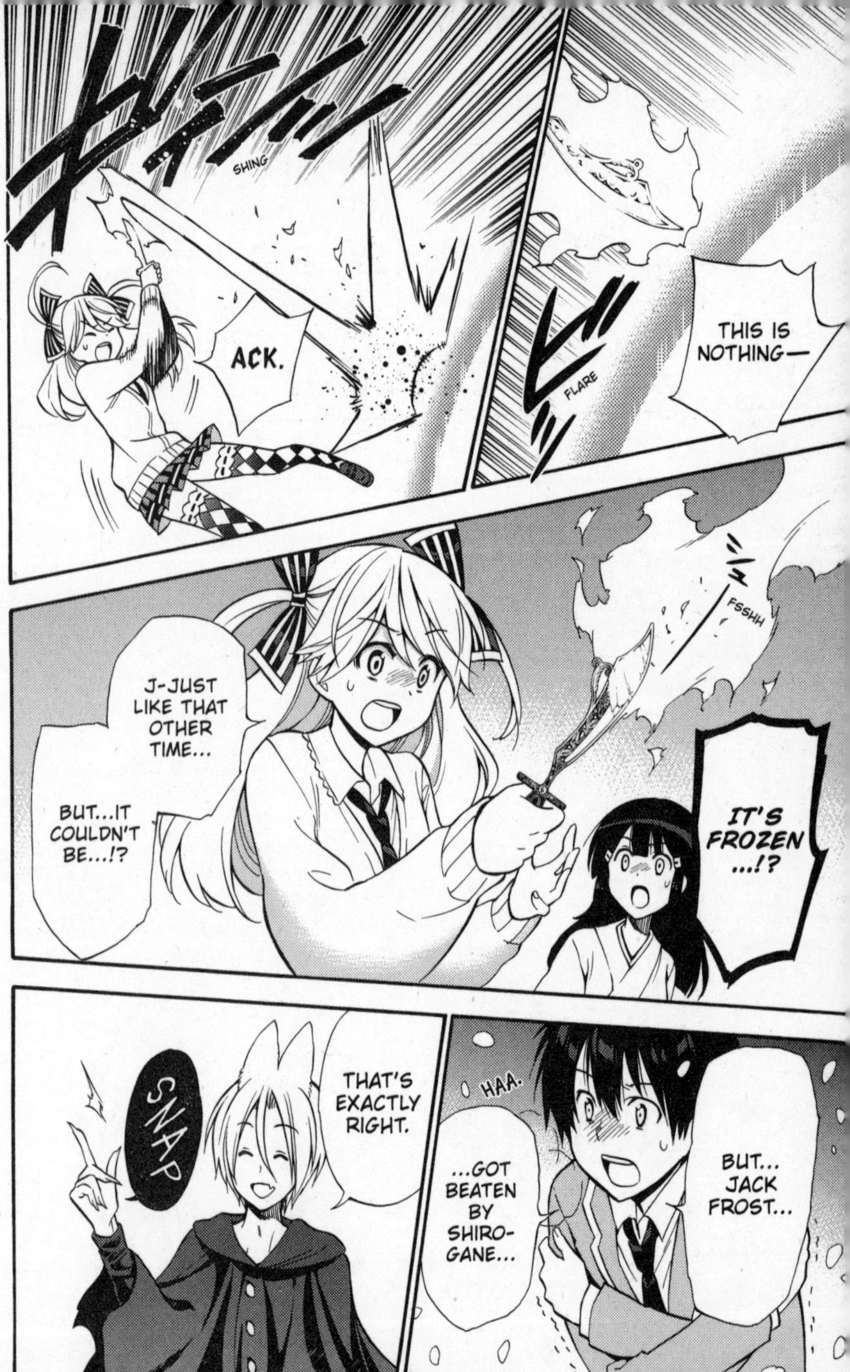
THIS IS NOTHING—
FLARE
SHING
ACK.
FSSHH
IT'S FROZEN ...!?
J-JUST LIKE THAT OTHER TIME...
BUT...IT COULDN'T BE...!?
HAA.
BUT... JACK FROST...
...GOT BEATEN BY SHIRO-GANE...
THAT'S EXACTLY RIGHT.
SNAP

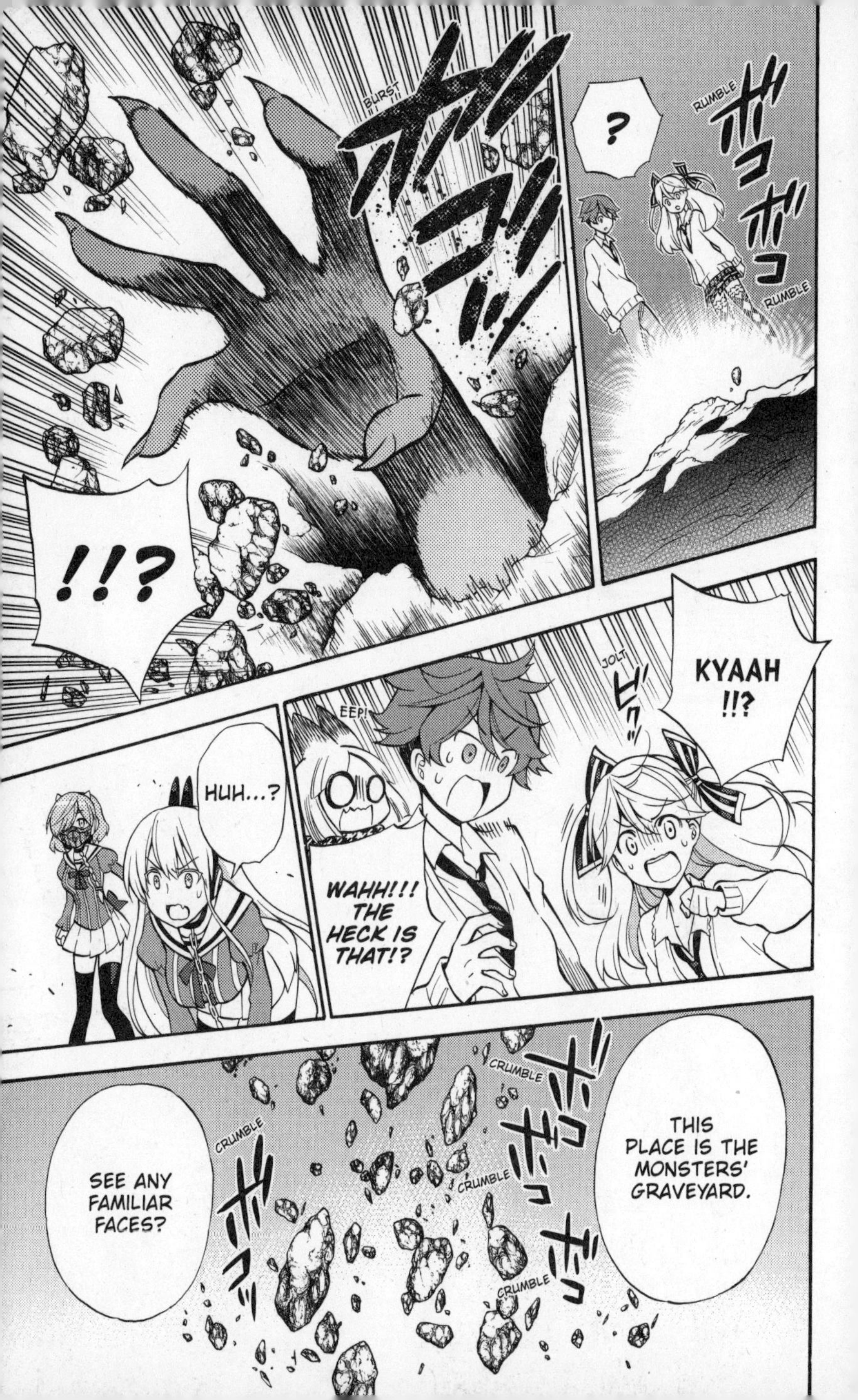
?
RUMBLE
ボコボコ
RUMBLE
BURST
!!?
KYAAH !!?
JOLT
EEP!
WAHH!!! THE HECK IS THAT!?
HUH...?
THIS PLACE IS THE MONSTERS' GRAVEYARD.
CRUMBLE
CRUMBLE
CRUMBLE
CRUMBLE
SEE ANY FAMILIAR FACES?

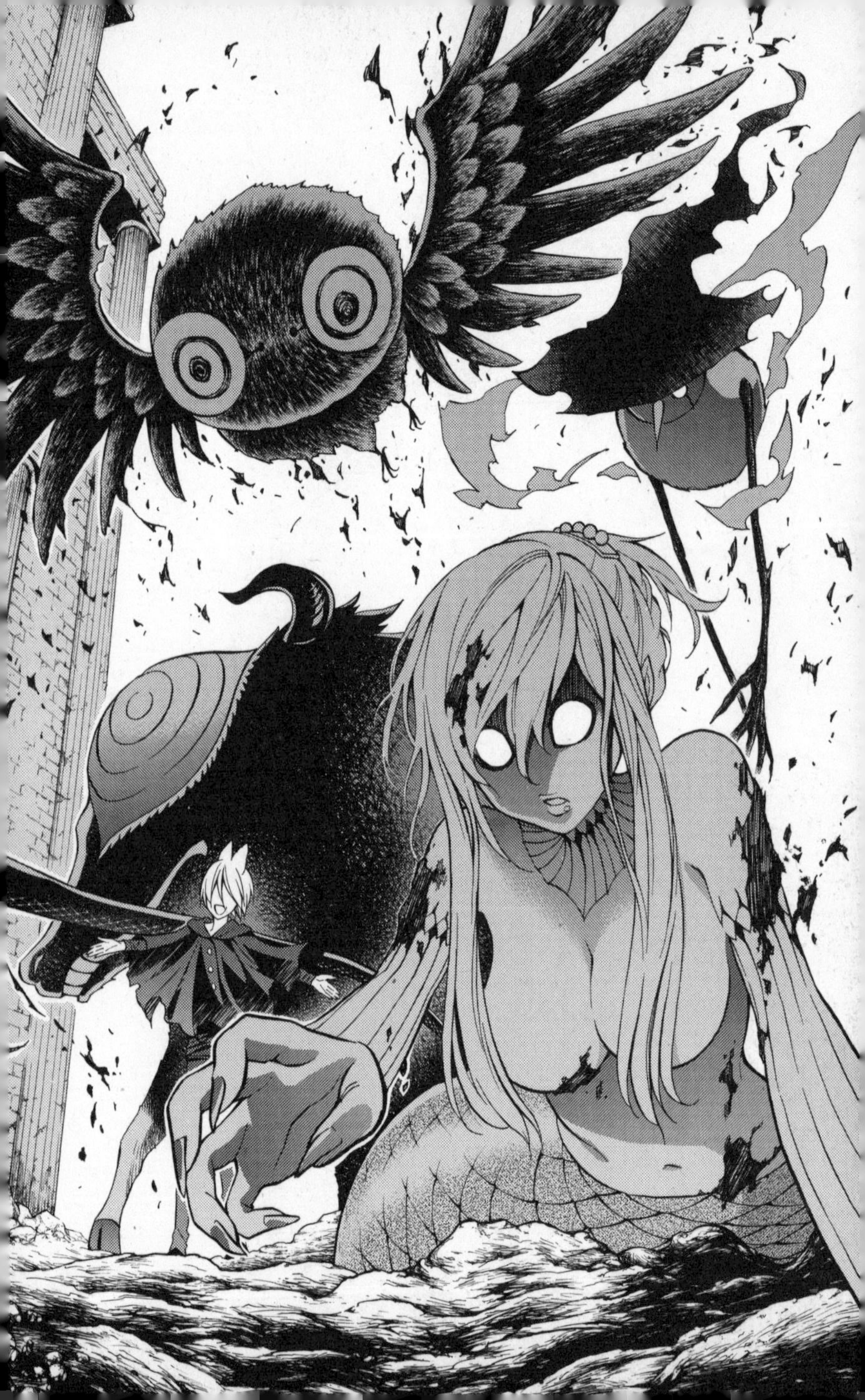

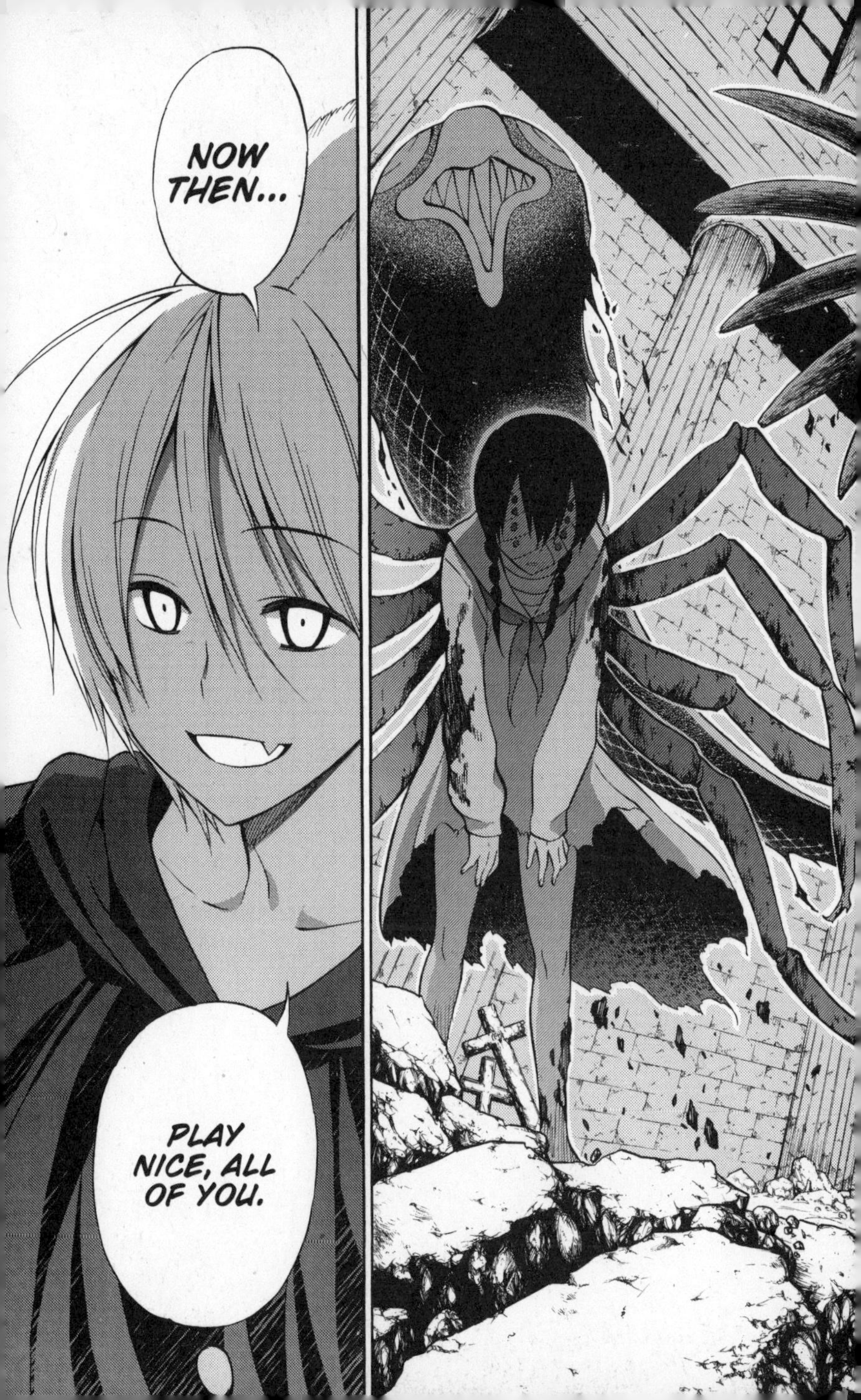
NOW THEN...
PLAY NICE, ALL OF YOU.

TODAY'S CERBERUS

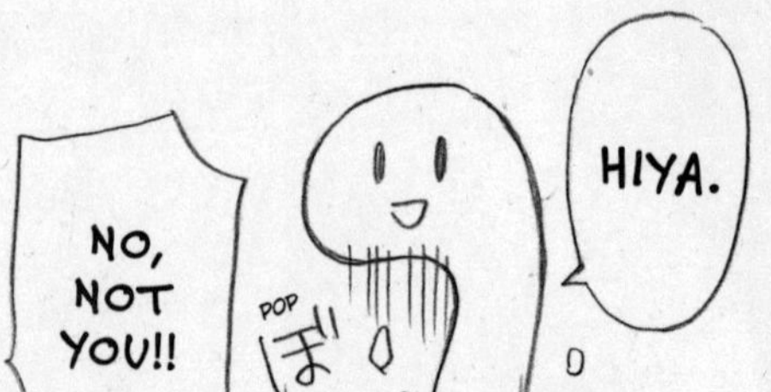
HIYA.
POP
ぼこっ
NO, NOT YOU!!

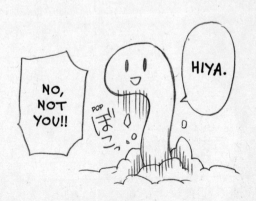

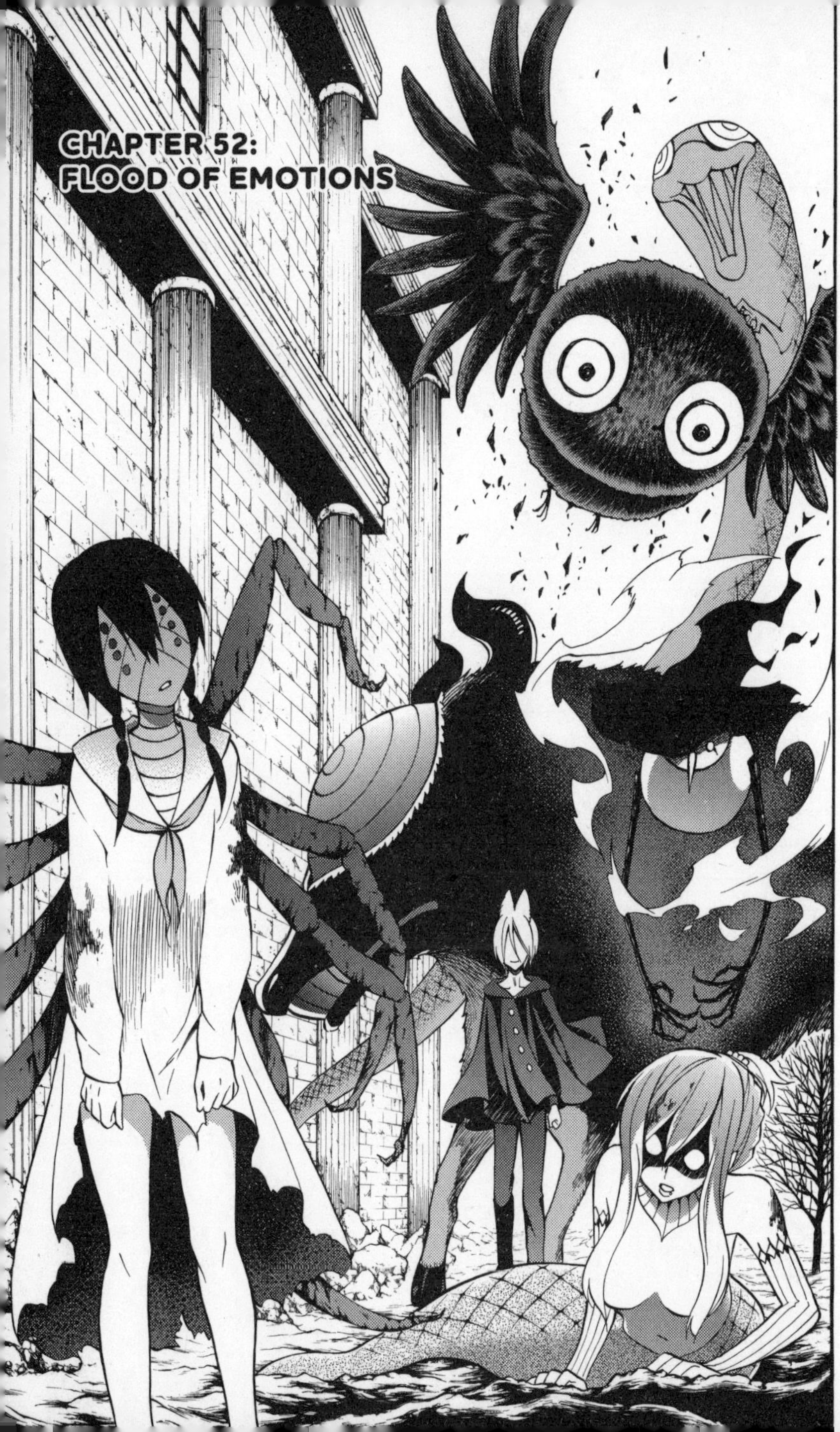
CHAPTER 52:
FLOOD OF EMOTIONS

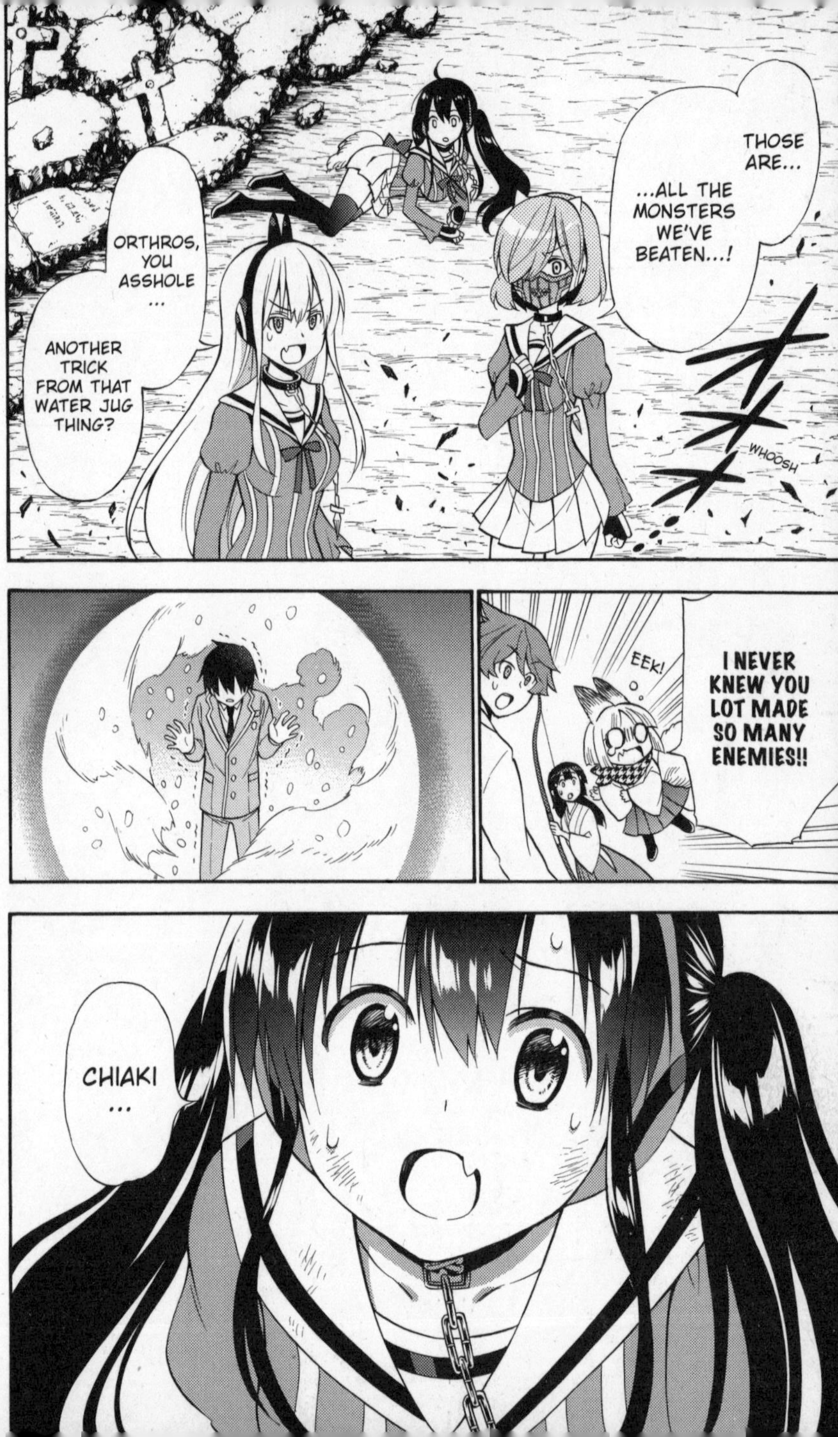
THOSE ARE... ...ALL THE MONSTERS WE'VE BEATEN...!
WHOOSH
ORTHROS, YOU ASSHOLE ... ANOTHER TRICK FROM THAT WATER JUG THING?
I NEVER KNEW YOU LOT MADE SO MANY ENEMIES!!
EEK!
CHIAKI ...

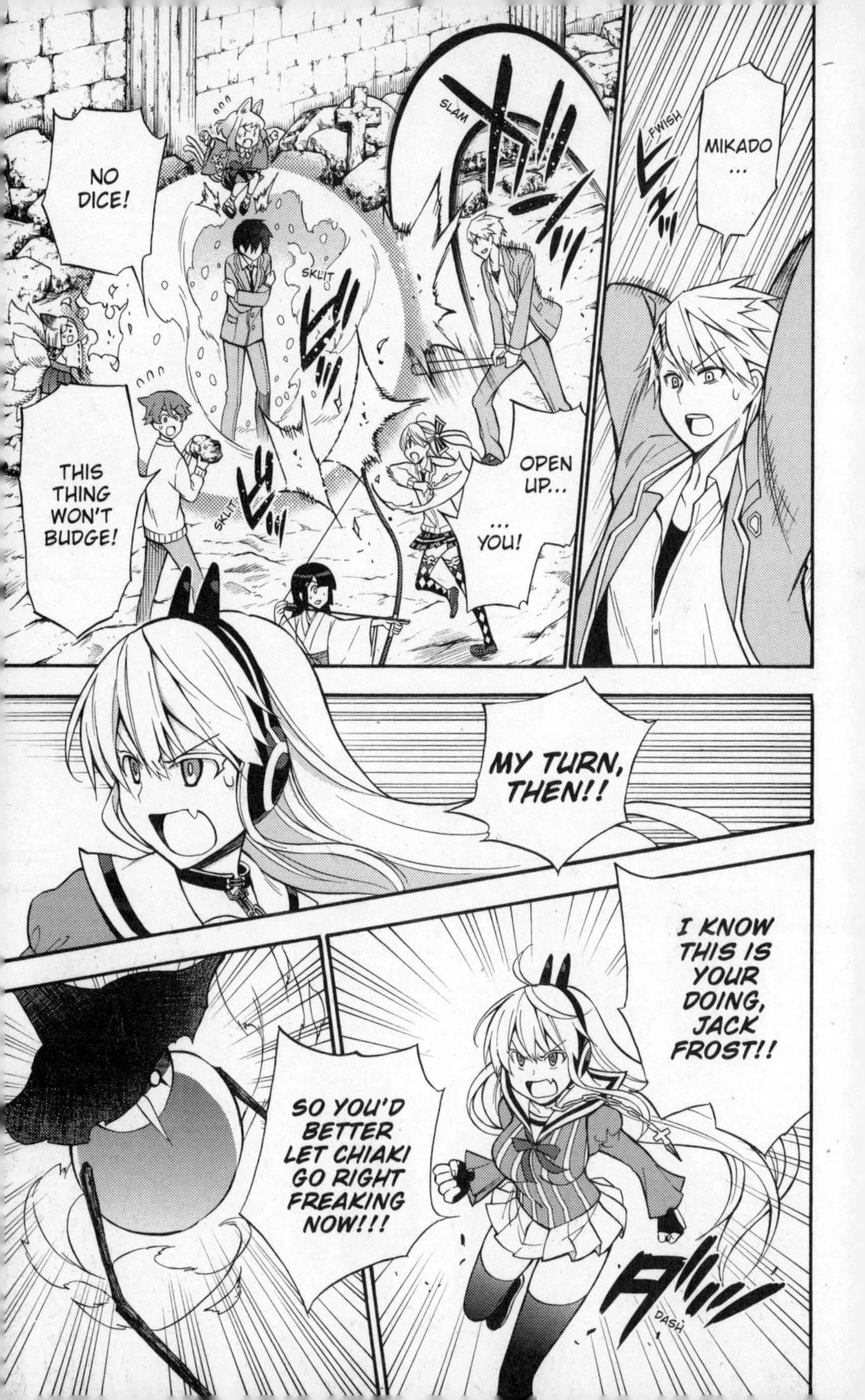
FWISH
MIKADO ...
SLAM
NO DICE!
SKLIT
OPEN UP...
... YOU!
THIS THING WON'T BUDGE!
SKLIT
MY TURN, THEN!!
I KNOW THIS IS YOUR DOING, JACK FROST!!
SO YOU'D BETTER LET CHIAKI GO RIGHT FREAKING NOW!!!
DASH

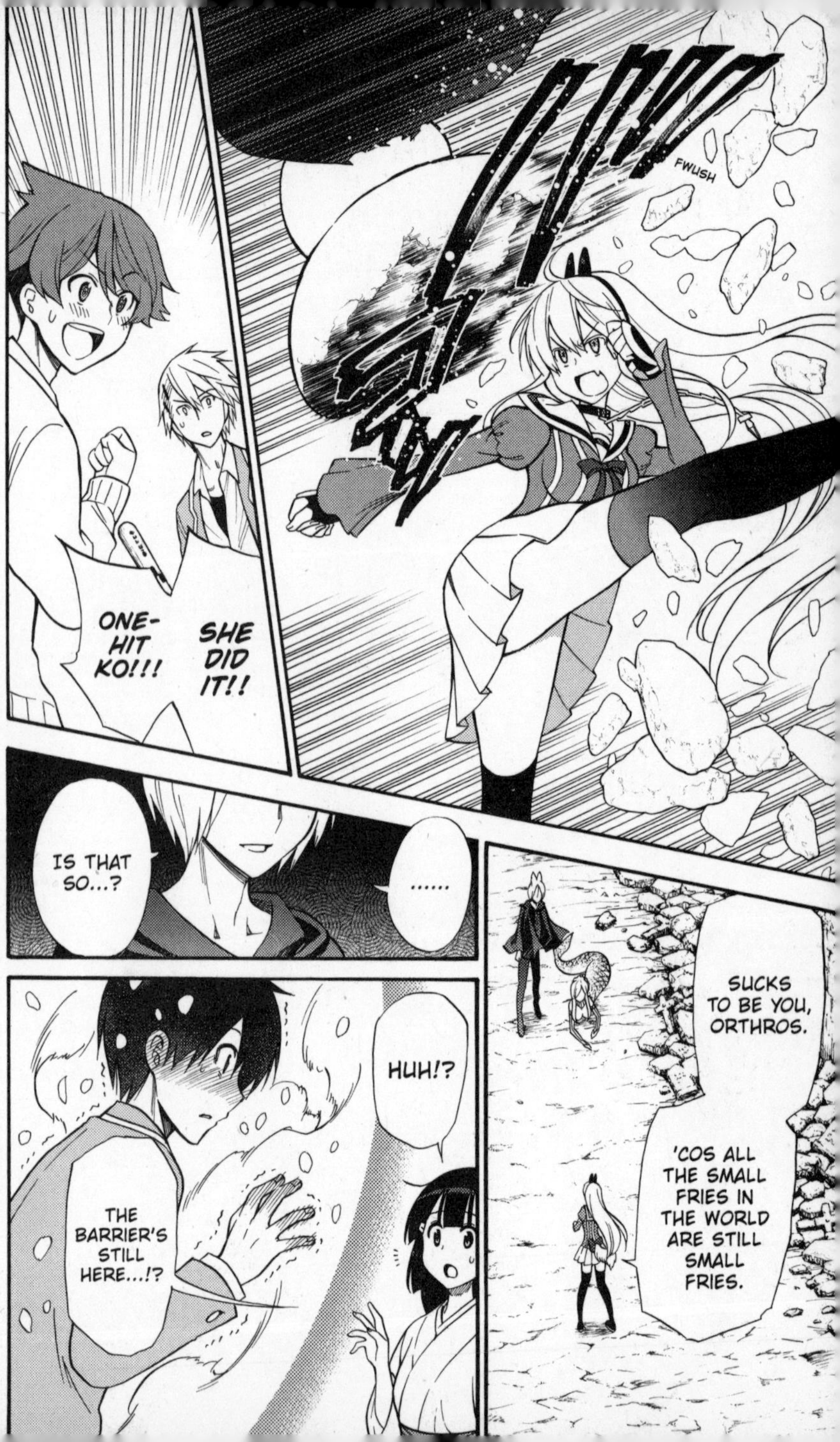
FWUSH
SHE DID IT!!
ONE-HIT KO!!!
SUCKS TO BE YOU, ORTHROS.
'COS ALL THE SMALL FRIES IN THE WORLD ARE STILL SMALL FRIES.
......
IS THAT SO...?
HUH!?
THE BARRIER'S STILL HERE...!?

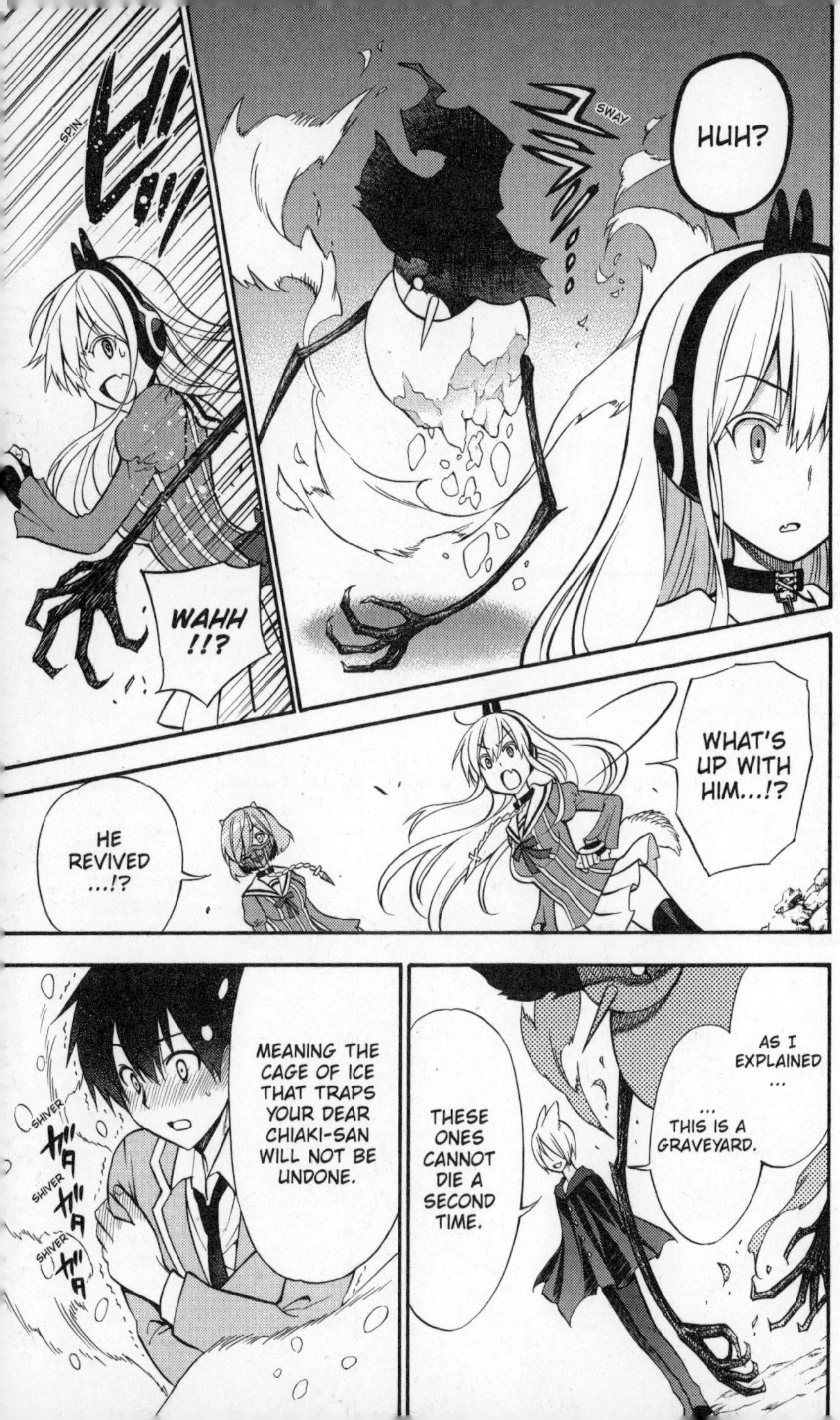
HUH?
SWAY
SPIN
WAHH!!?
WHAT'S UP WITH HIM...!?
HE REVIVED...!?
AS I EXPLAINED...
... THIS IS A GRAVEYARD.
THESE ONES CANNOT DIE A SECOND TIME.
MEANING THE CAGE OF ICE THAT TRAPS YOUR DEAR CHIAKI-SAN WILL NOT BE UNDONE.
SHIVER
SHIVER
SHIVER

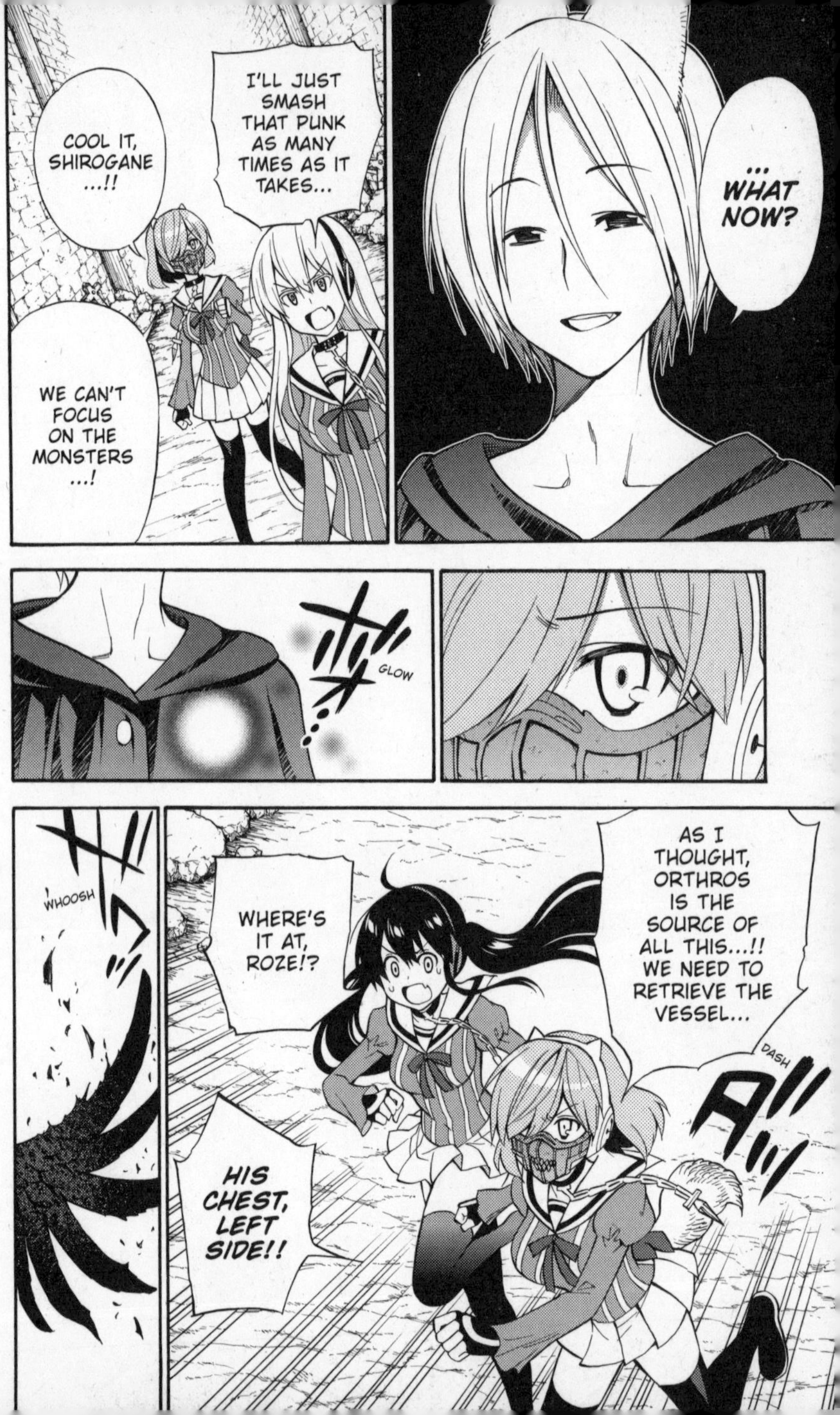
... WHAT NOW?
I'LL JUST SMASH THAT PUNK AS MANY TIMES AS IT TAKES...
COOL IT, SHIROGANE ...!!
WE CAN'T FOCUS ON THE MONSTERS ...!
GLOW
AS I THOUGHT, ORTHROS IS THE SOURCE OF ALL THIS...!! WE NEED TO RETRIEVE THE VESSEL...
DASH
WHERE'S IT AT, ROZE!?
HIS CHEST, LEFT SIDE!!
WHOOSH

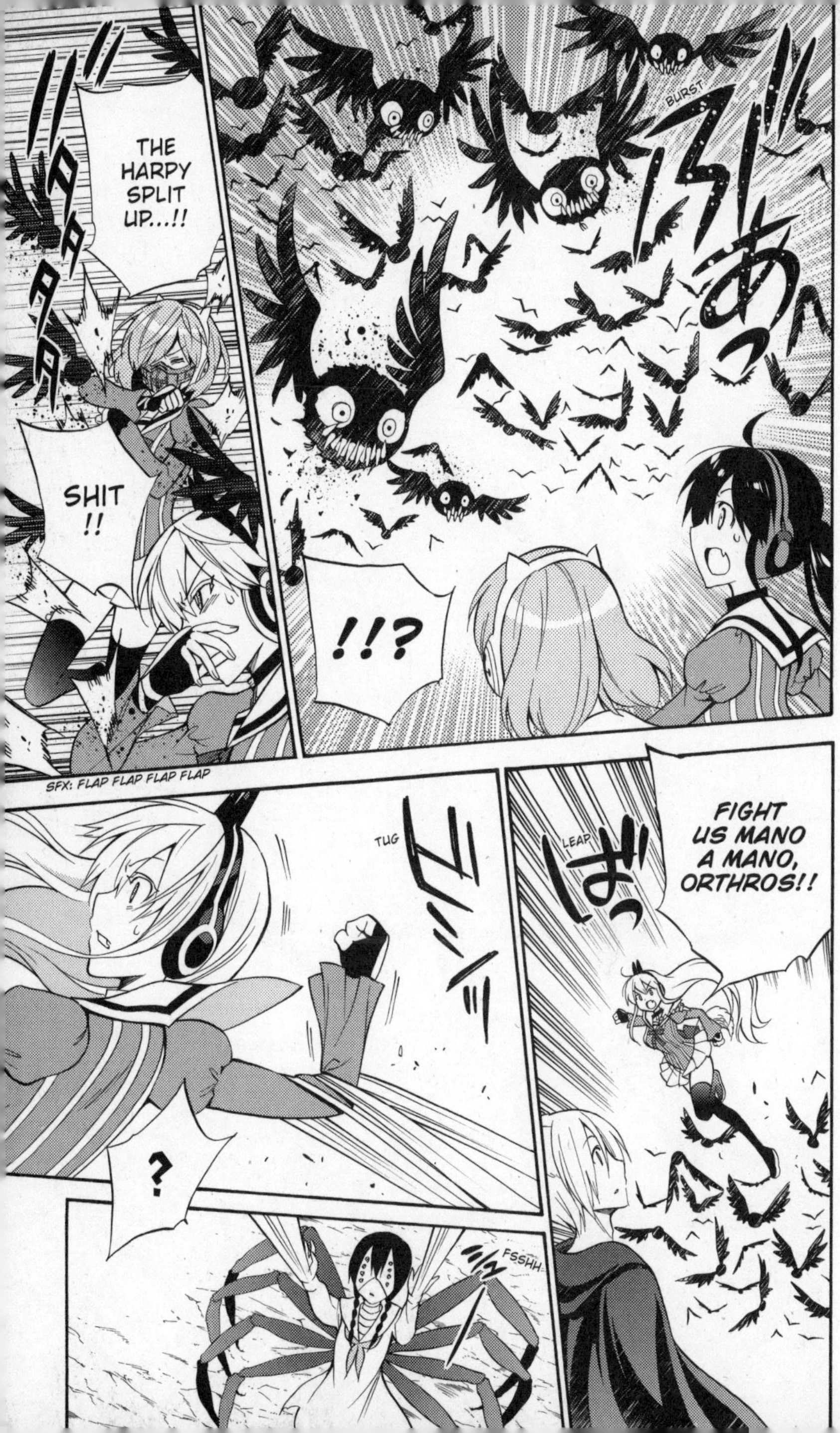
BURST
!!?
THE HARPY SPLIT UP...!!
SHIT!!
SFX: FLAP FLAP FLAP FLAP
LEAP
FIGHT US MANO A MANO, ORTHROS!!
TUG
?
FSSHH

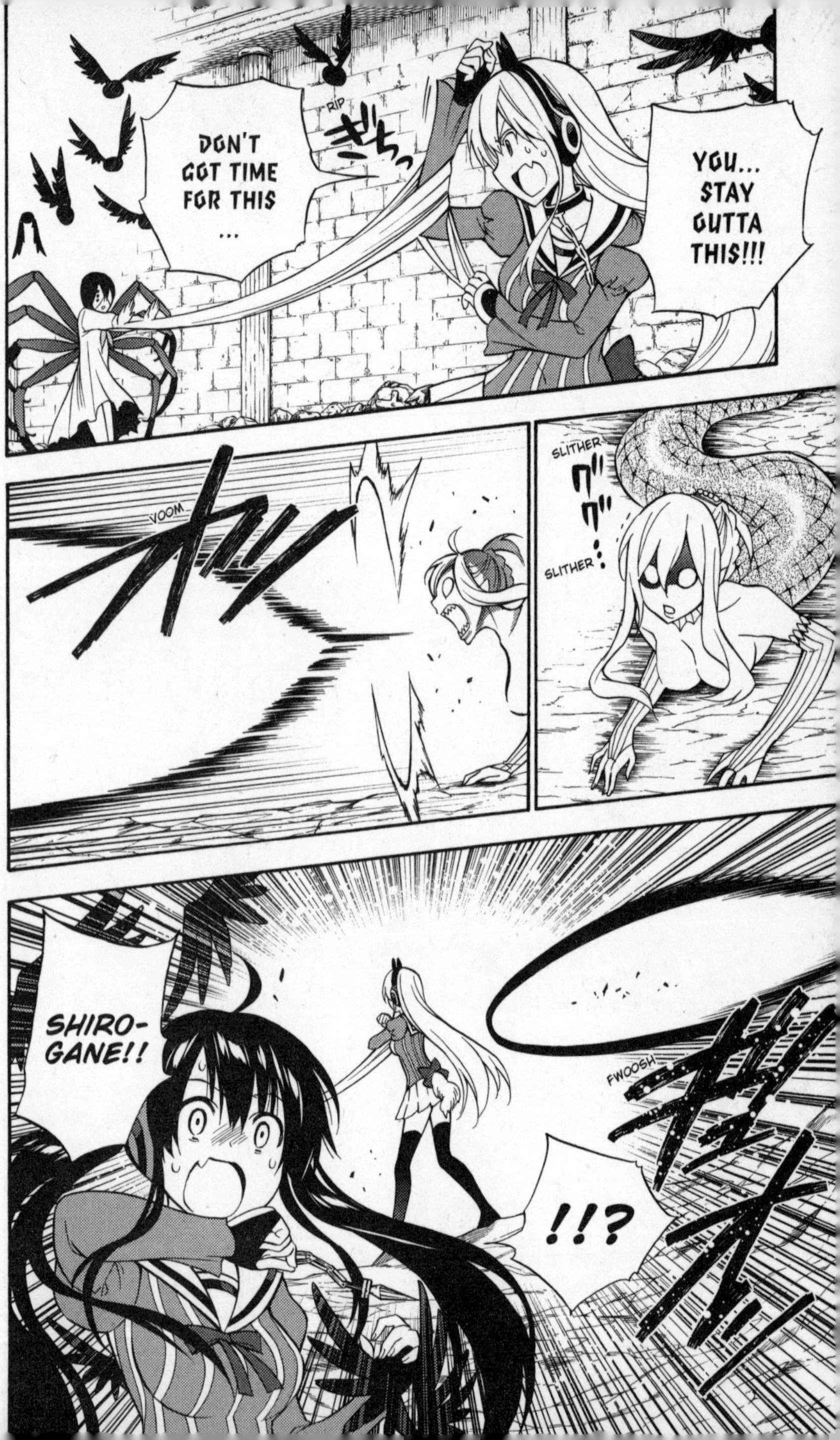
YOU... STAY OUTTA THIS!!!
RIP
DON'T GOT TIME FOR THIS ...
SLITHER
SLITHER
VOOM
FWOOSH
!!?
SHIRO-GANE!!

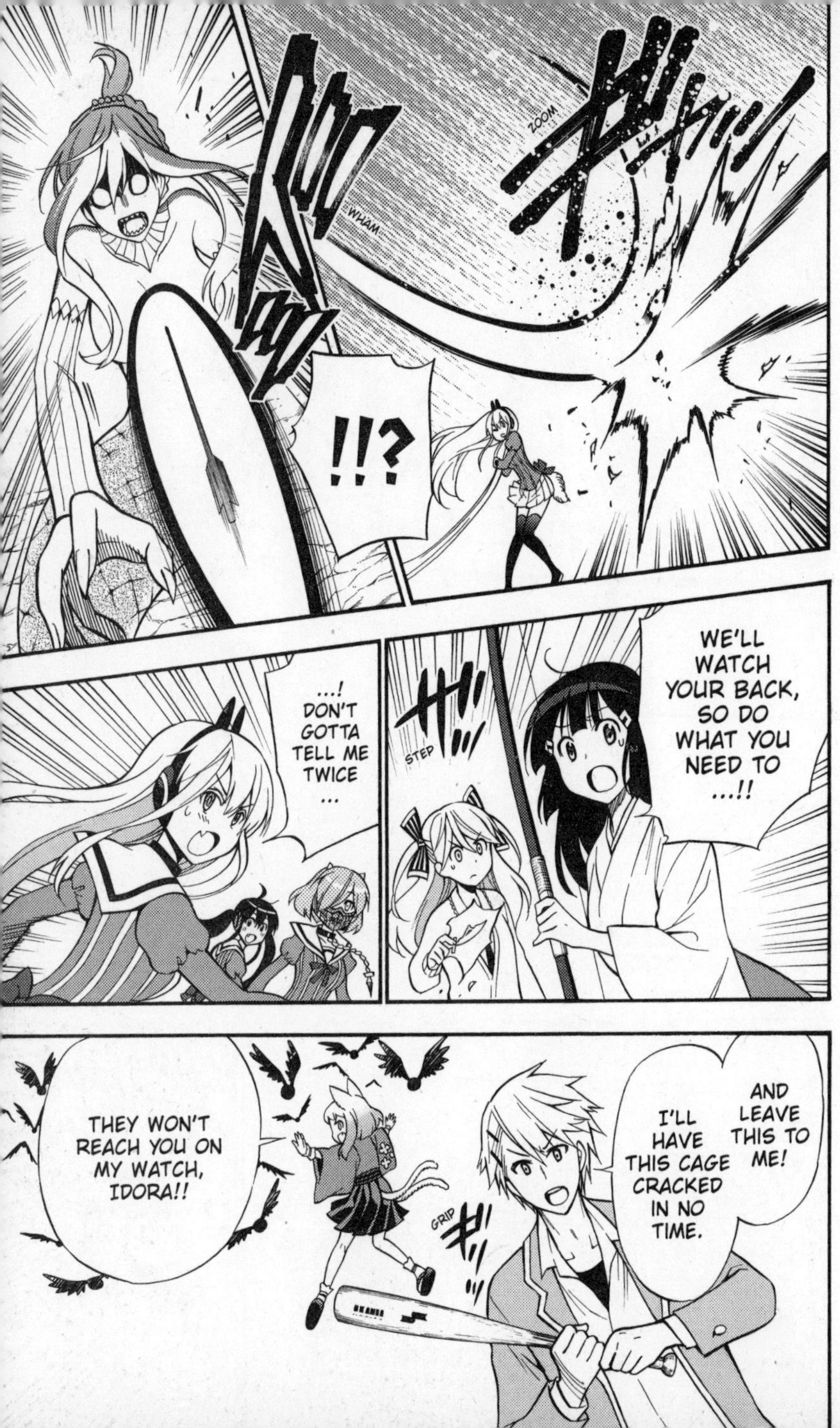
ZOOM
WHAM
!!?
WE'LL WATCH YOUR BACK, SO DO WHAT YOU NEED TO ...!!
STEP
...! DON'T GOTTA TELL ME TWICE ...
AND LEAVE THIS TO ME!
I'LL HAVE THIS CAGE CRACKED IN NO TIME.
GRIP
THEY WON'T REACH YOU ON MY WATCH, IDORA!!

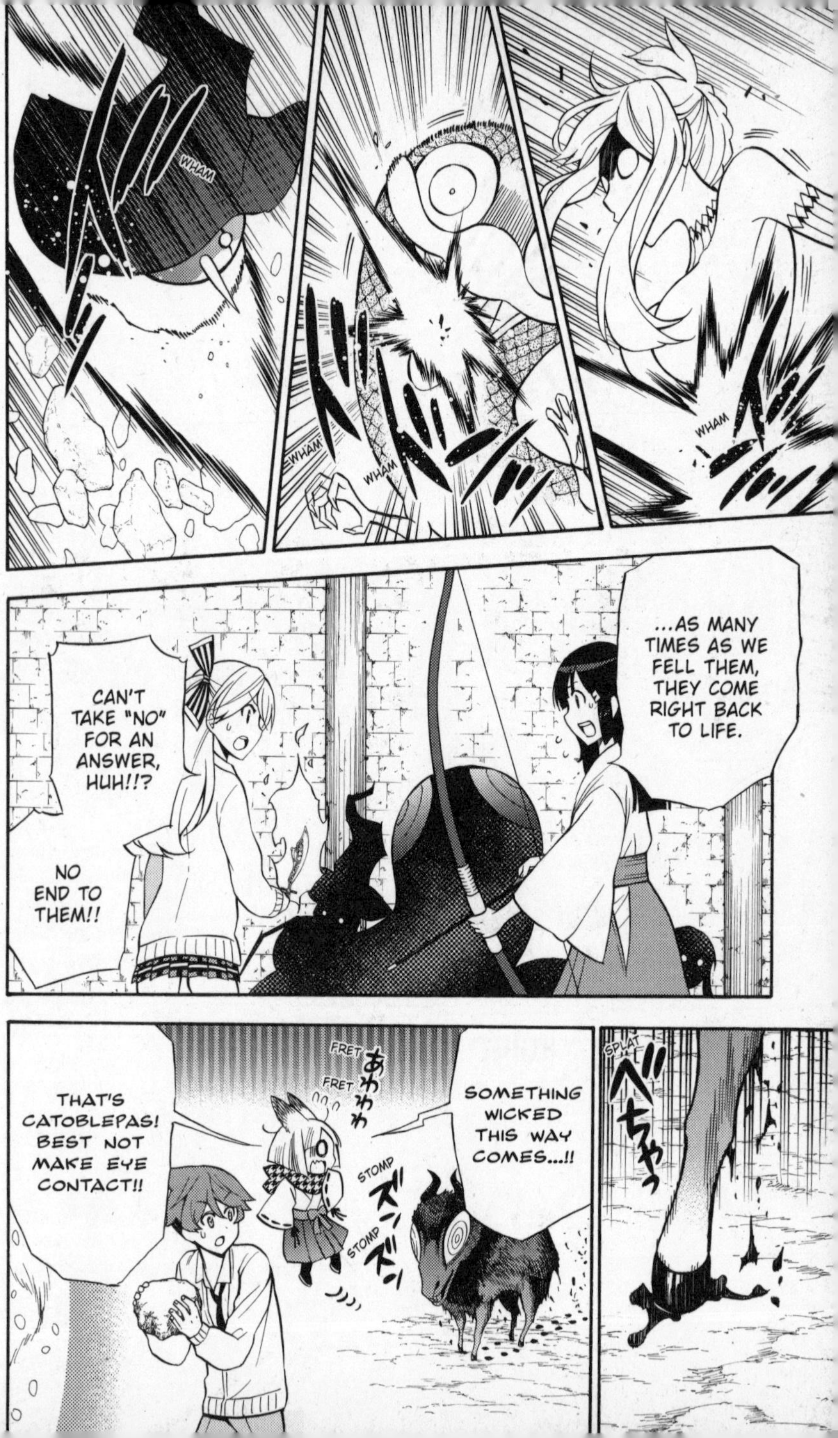
WHAM
WHAM
WHAM
WHAM
...AS MANY TIMES AS WE FELL THEM, THEY COME RIGHT BACK TO LIFE.
CAN'T TAKE "NO" FOR AN ANSWER, HUH!!?
NO END TO THEM!!
SPLAT
SOMETHING WICKED THIS WAY COMES...!!
FRET FRET
STOMP STOMP
THAT'S CATOBLEPAS! BEST NOT MAKE EYE CONTACT!!

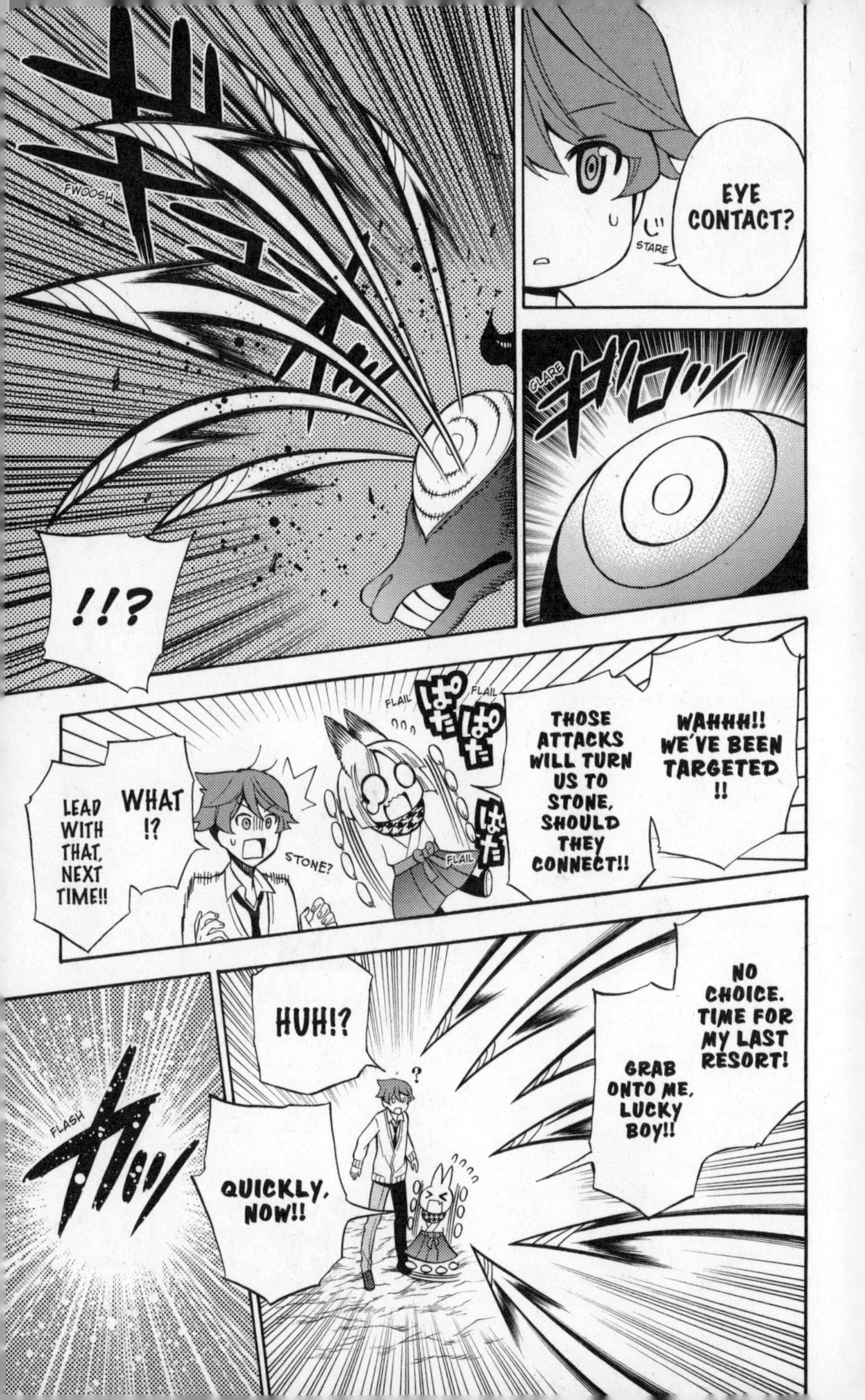

EYE CONTACT?
じ
STARE
GLARE
FWOOSH
!!?
WAHHH!! WE'VE BEEN TARGETED!!
THOSE ATTACKS WILL TURN US TO STONE, SHOULD THEY CONNECT!!
ぱたぱた
FLAIL
FLAIL
FLAIL
STONE?
WHAT!?
LEAD WITH THAT, NEXT TIME!!
NO CHOICE. TIME FOR MY LAST RESORT!
GRAB ONTO ME, LUCKY BOY!!
HUH!?
QUICKLY, NOW!!
FLASH

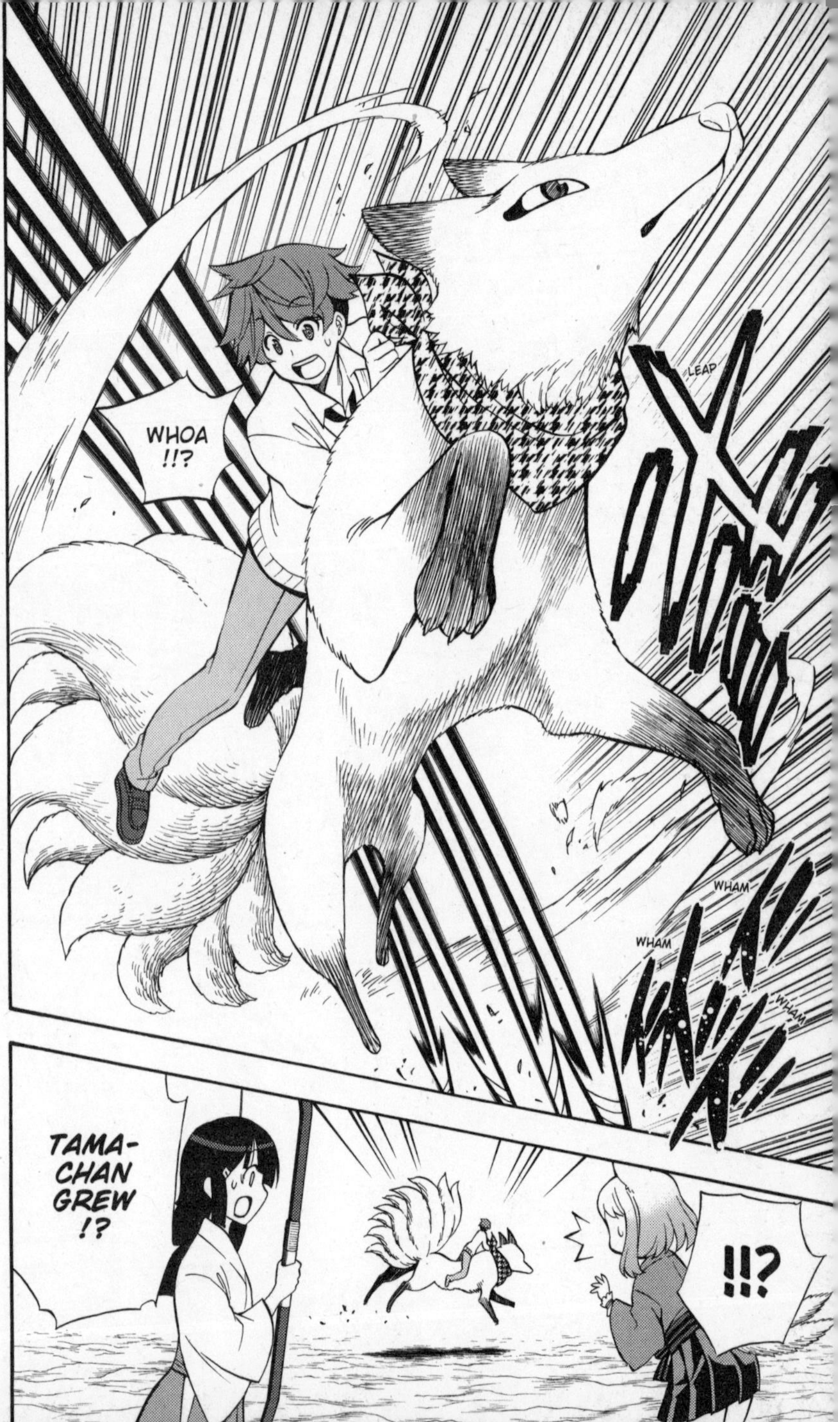
LEAP
WHOA!!?
WHAM
WHAM
WHAM
!!?
TAMA-CHAN GREW!?

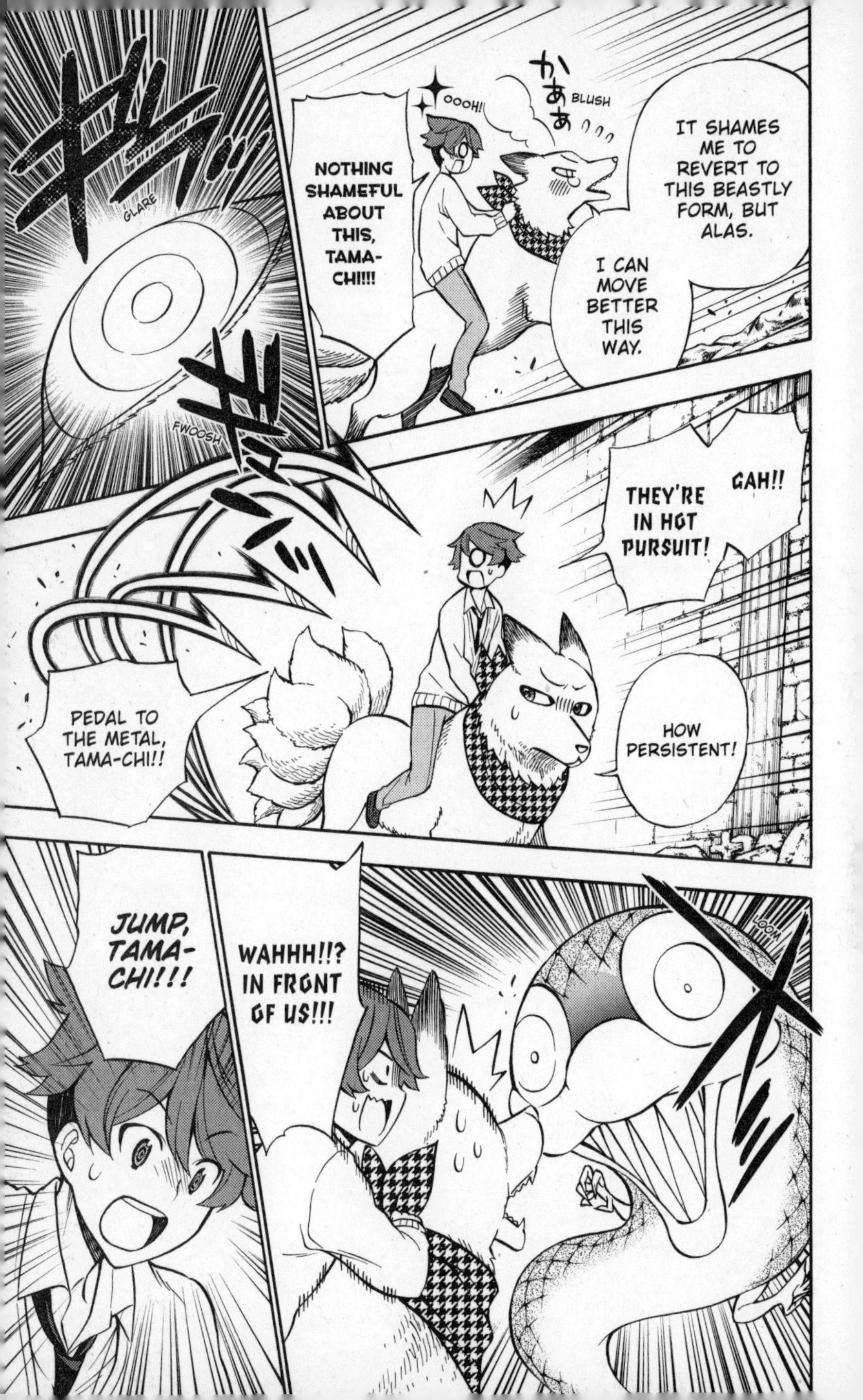
IT SHAMES ME TO REVERT TO THIS BEASTLY FORM, BUT ALAS.
I CAN MOVE BETTER THIS WAY.
かあああ
BLUSH
OOOH!
NOTHING SHAMEFUL ABOUT THIS, TAMA-CHI!!!
GLARE
FWOOSH
GAH!!
THEY'RE IN HOT PURSUIT!
HOW PERSISTENT!
PEDAL TO THE METAL, TAMA-CHI!!
LOOM
WAHHH!!? IN FRONT OF US!!!
JUMP, TAMA-CHI!!!

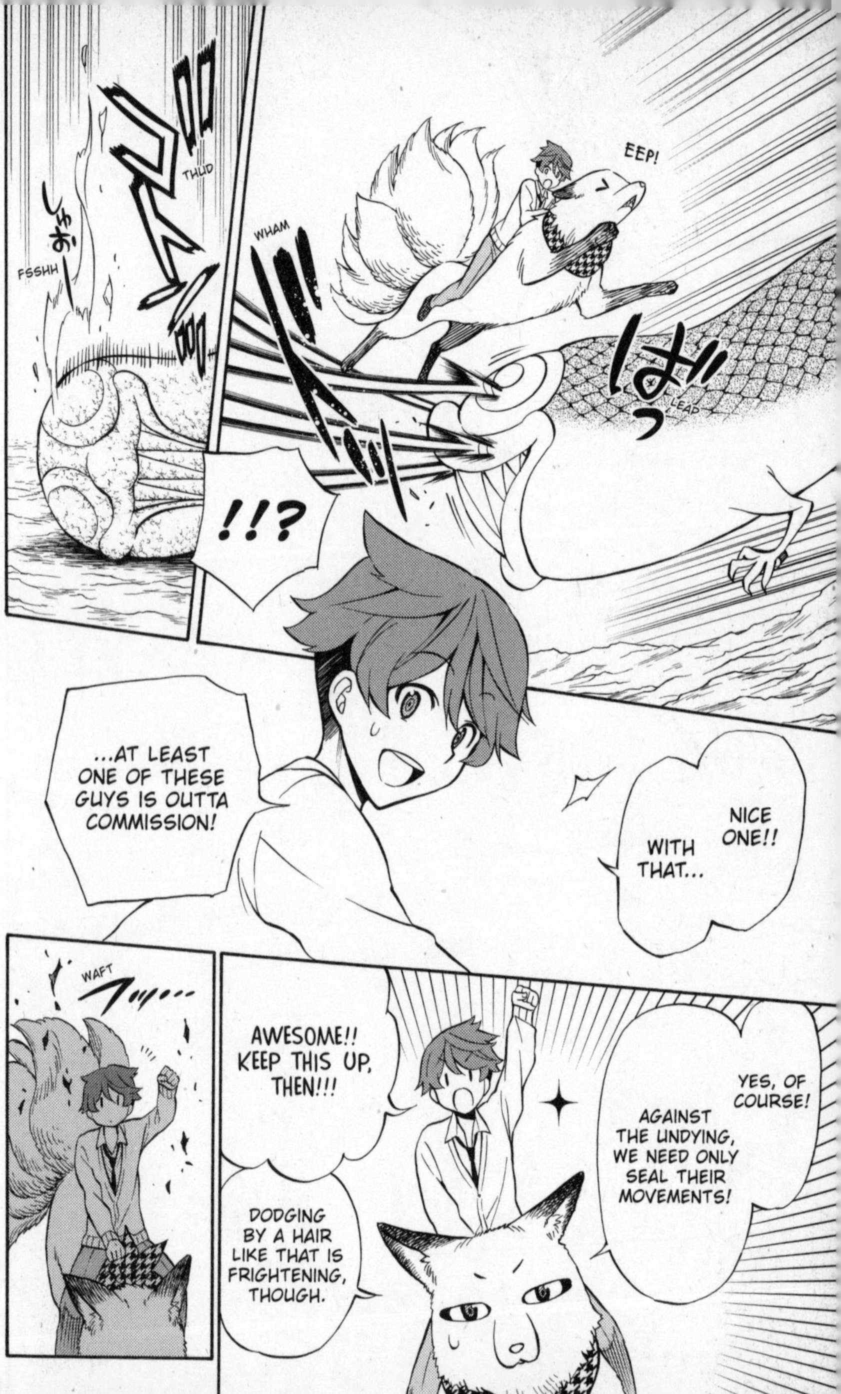
EEP!
ばっ
LEAP
WHAM
THUD
しゅおー
FSSHH
!!?
NICE ONE!!
WITH THAT...
...AT LEAST ONE OF THESE GUYS IS OUTTA COMMISSION!
YES, OF COURSE!
AGAINST THE UNDYING, WE NEED ONLY SEAL THEIR MOVEMENTS!
AWESOME!! KEEP THIS UP, THEN!!!
DODGING BY A HAIR LIKE THAT IS FRIGHTENING, THOUGH.
WAFT

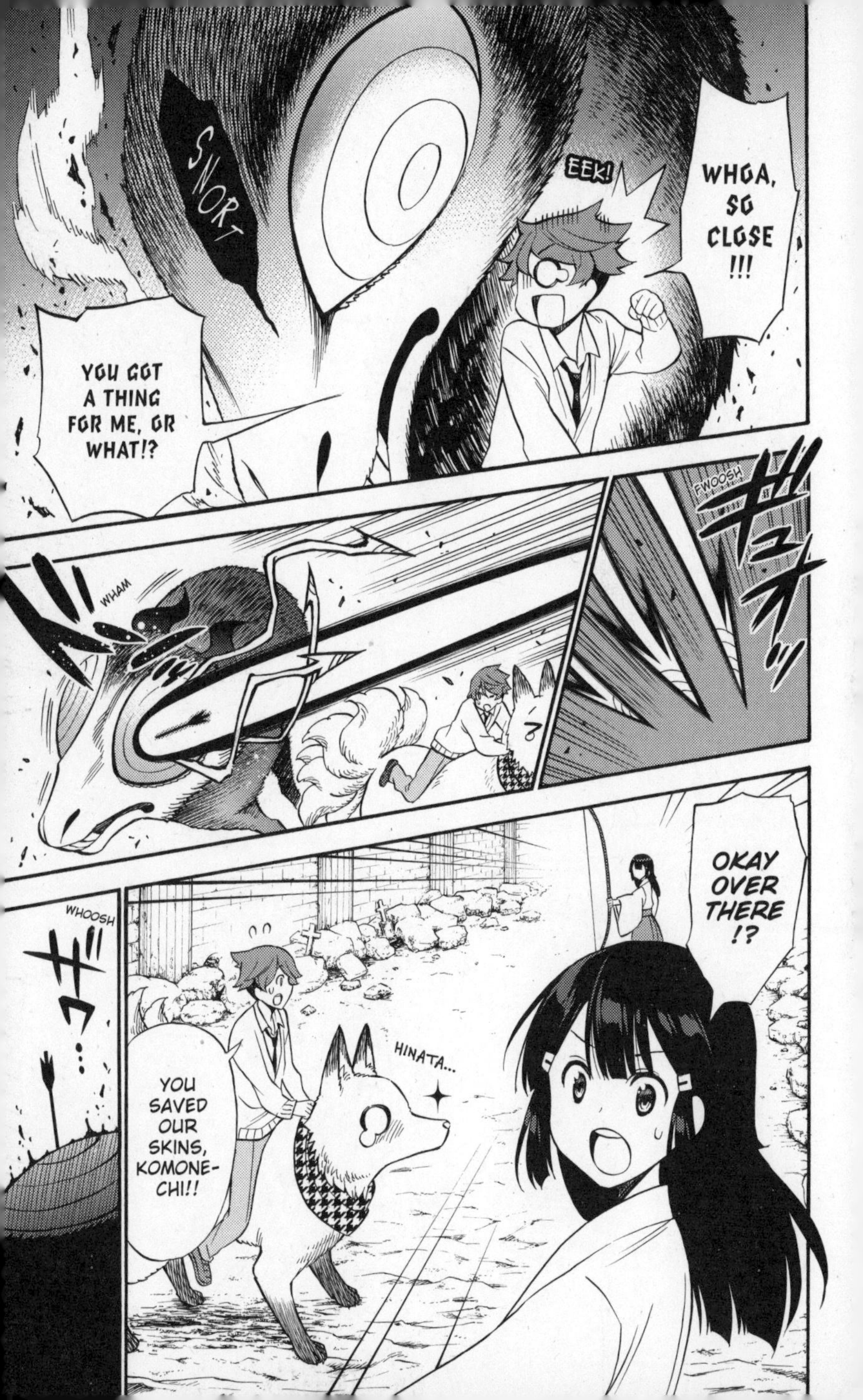
WHOA, SO CLOSE!!!
EEK!
SNORT
YOU GOT A THING FOR ME, OR WHAT!?
FWOOSH
WHAM
OKAY OVER THERE!?
HINATA...
YOU SAVED OUR SKINS, KOMONE-CHI!!
WHOOSH

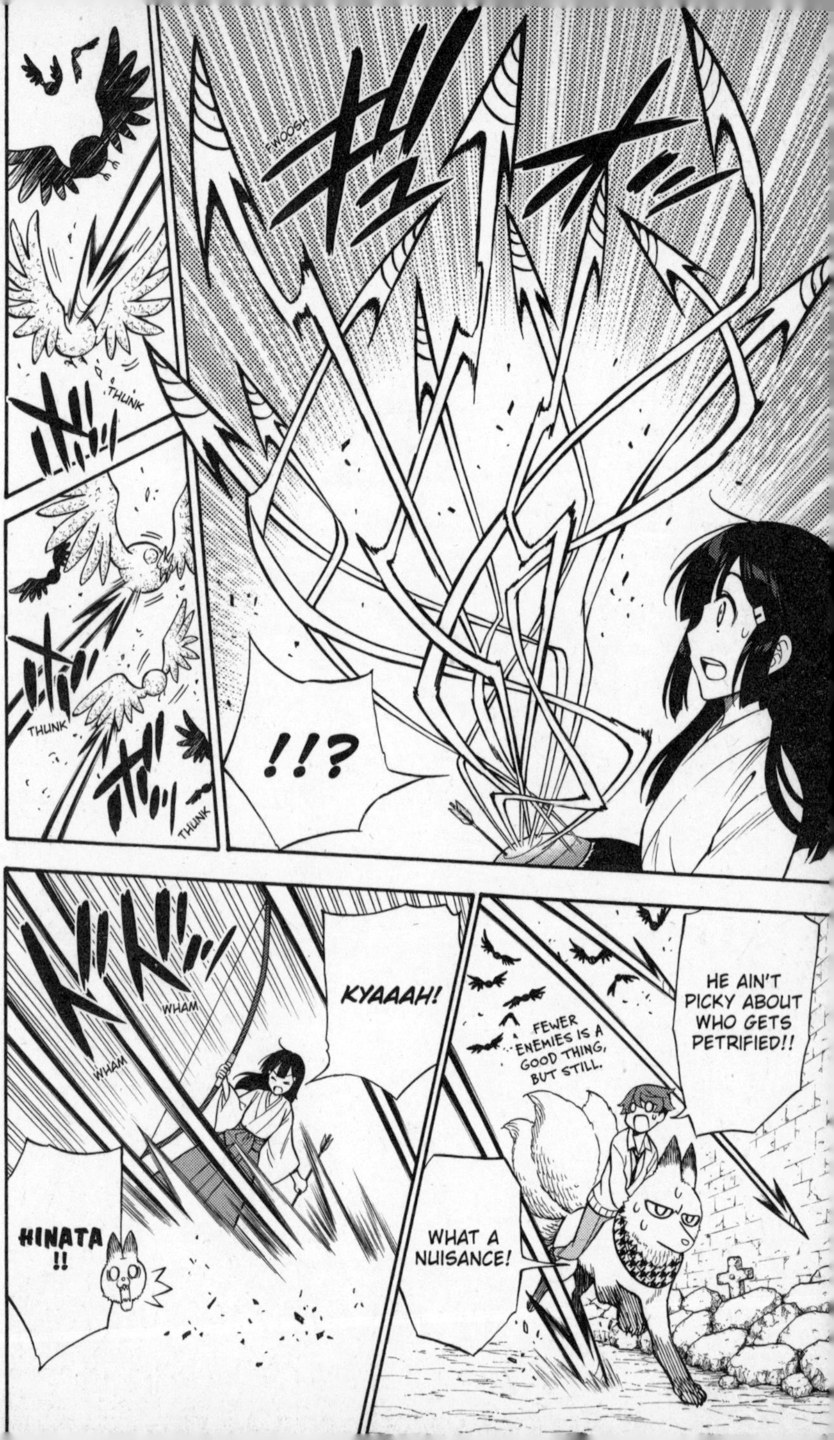
FWOOSH
!!?
THUNK
THUNK
THUNK
HE AIN'T PICKY ABOUT WHO GETS PETRIFIED!!
FEWER ENEMIES IS A GOOD THING, BUT STILL.
WHAT A NUISANCE!
KYAAAH!
WHAM
WHAM
HINATA !!

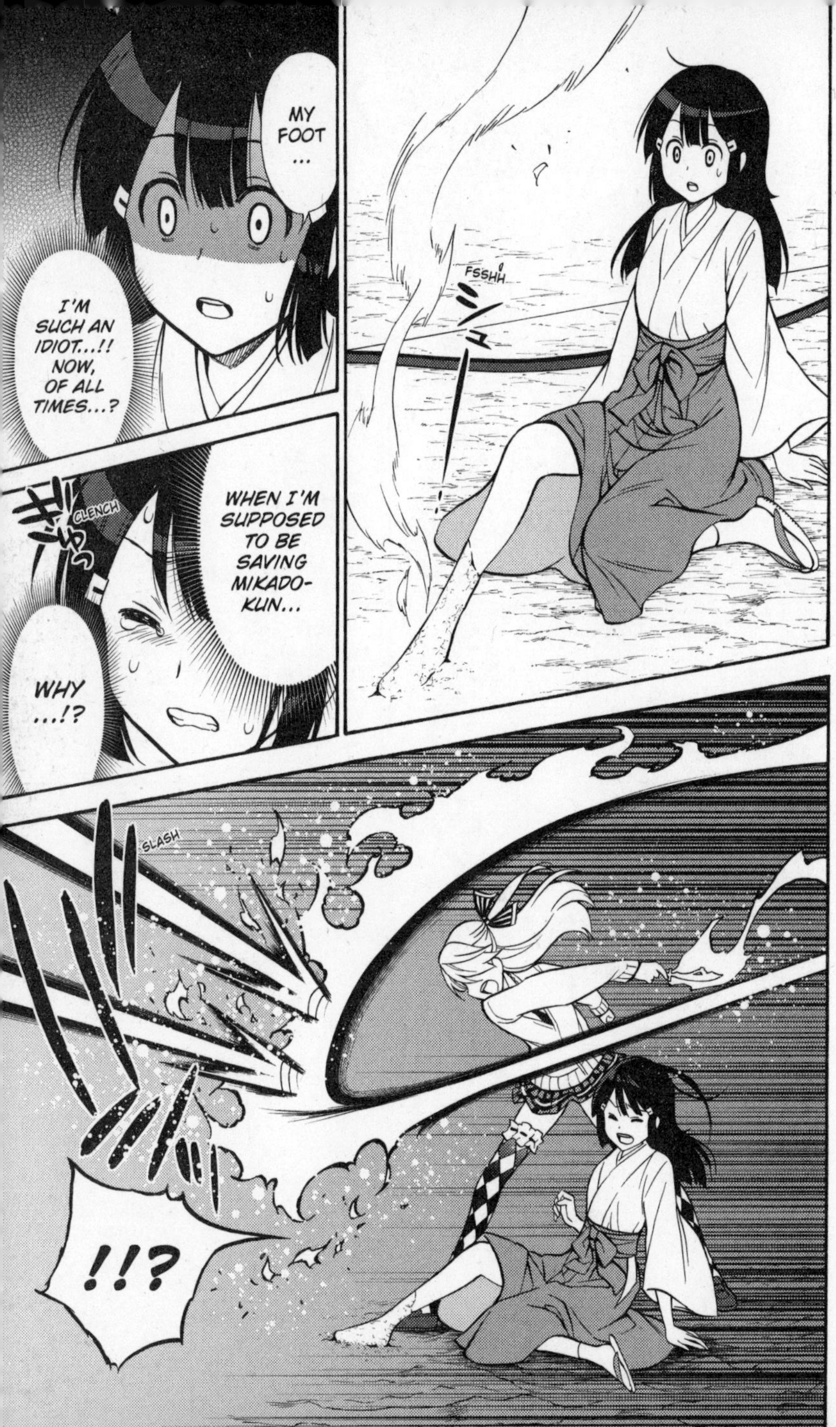
FSSHH
MY FOOT ...
I'M SUCH AN IDIOT...!! NOW, OF ALL TIMES...?
CLENCH
WHEN I'M SUPPOSED TO BE SAVING MIKADO-KUN...
WHY ...!?
SLASH
!!?

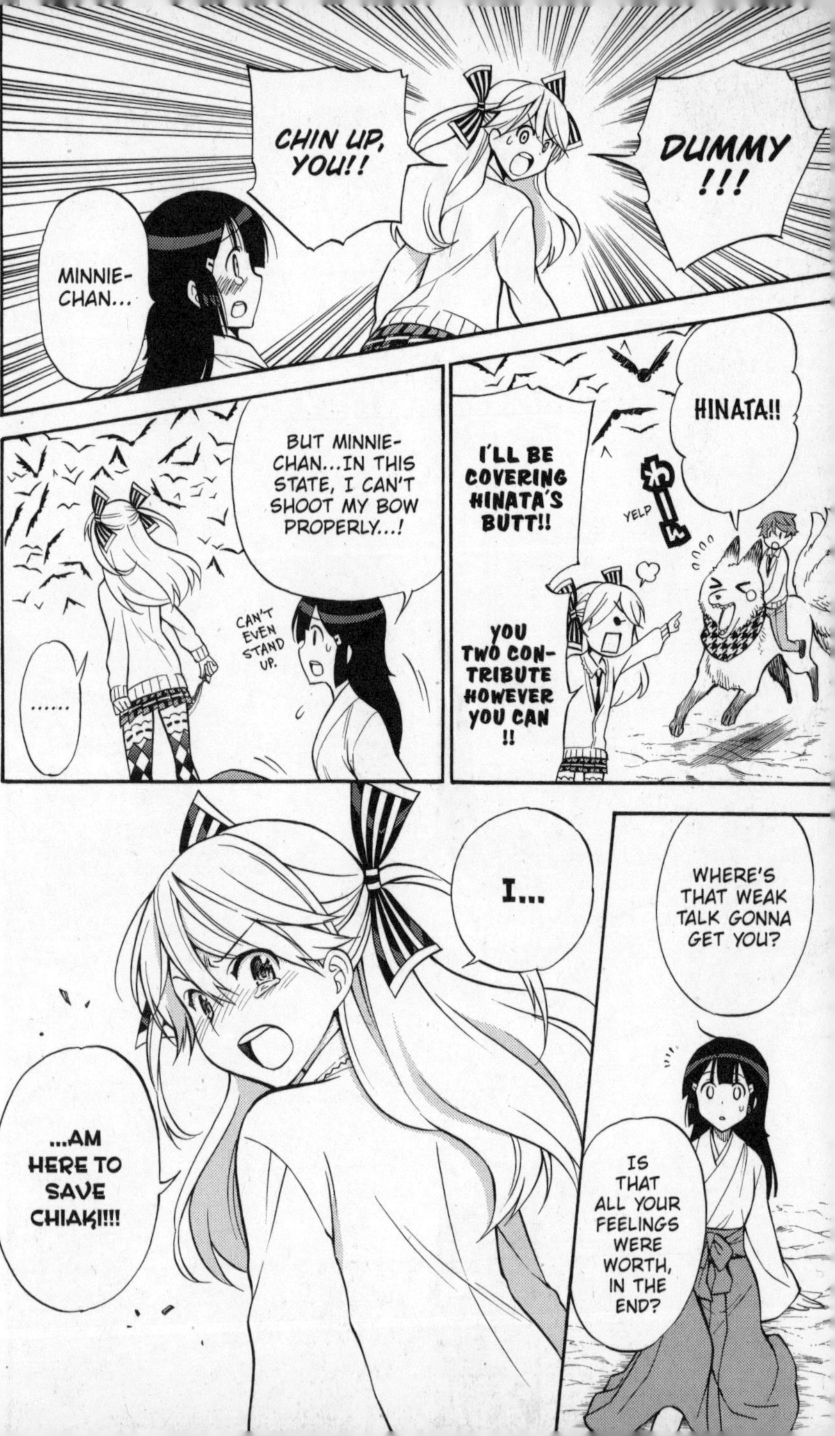
DUMMY !!!
CHIN UP, YOU!!
MINNIE-CHAN...
HINATA!!
YELP
I'LL BE COVERING HINATA'S BUTT!!
YOU TWO CON-TRIBUTE HOWEVER YOU CAN !!
BUT MINNIE-CHAN...IN THIS STATE, I CAN'T SHOOT MY BOW PROPERLY...!
CAN'T EVEN STAND UP.
......
WHERE'S THAT WEAK TALK GONNA GET YOU?
IS THAT ALL YOUR FEELINGS WERE WORTH, IN THE END?
I...
...AM HERE TO SAVE CHIAKI!!!!

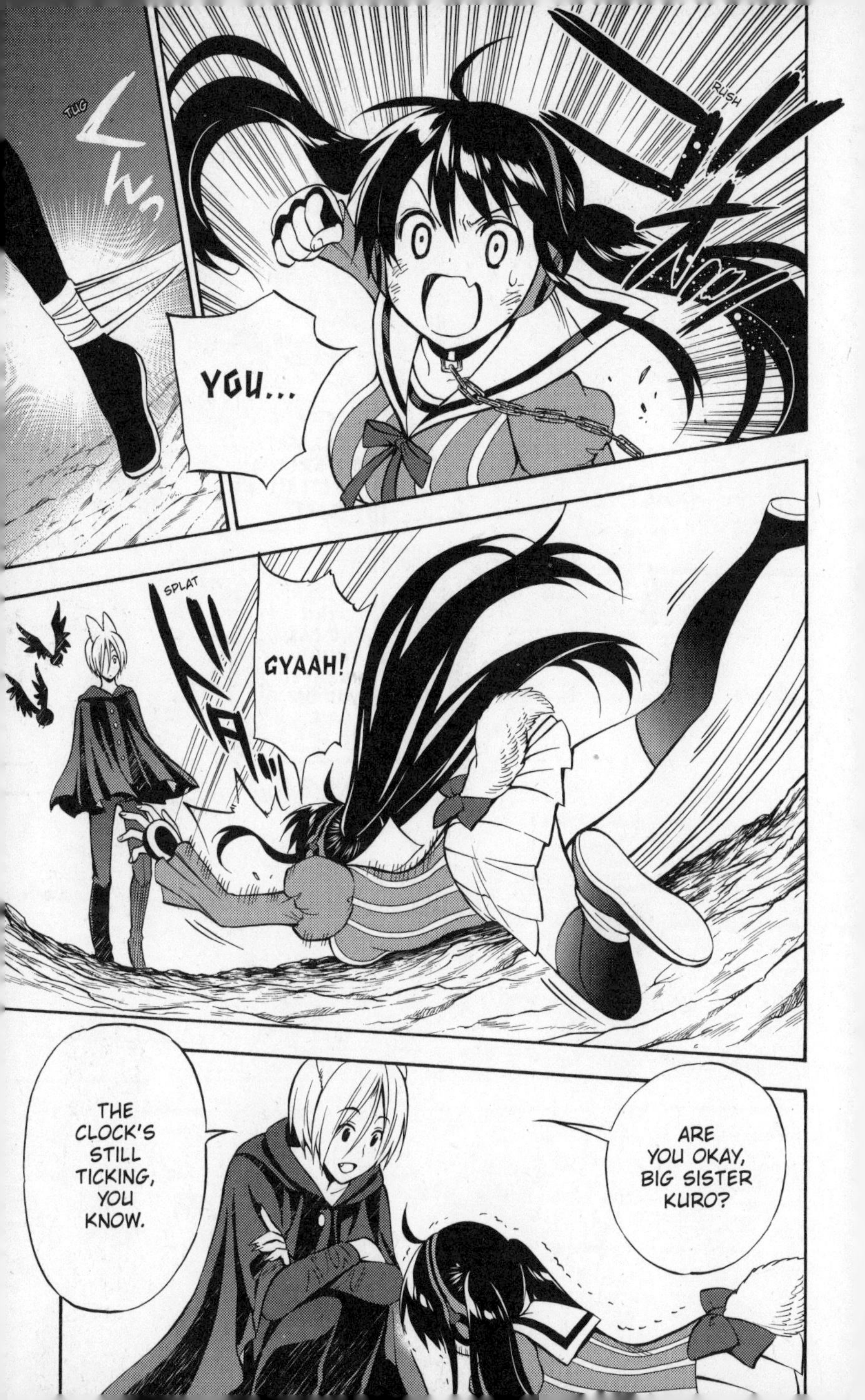
RUSH
YOU...
TUG
GYAAH!
SPLAT
ARE YOU OKAY, BIG SISTER KURO?
THE CLOCK'S STILL TICKING, YOU KNOW.

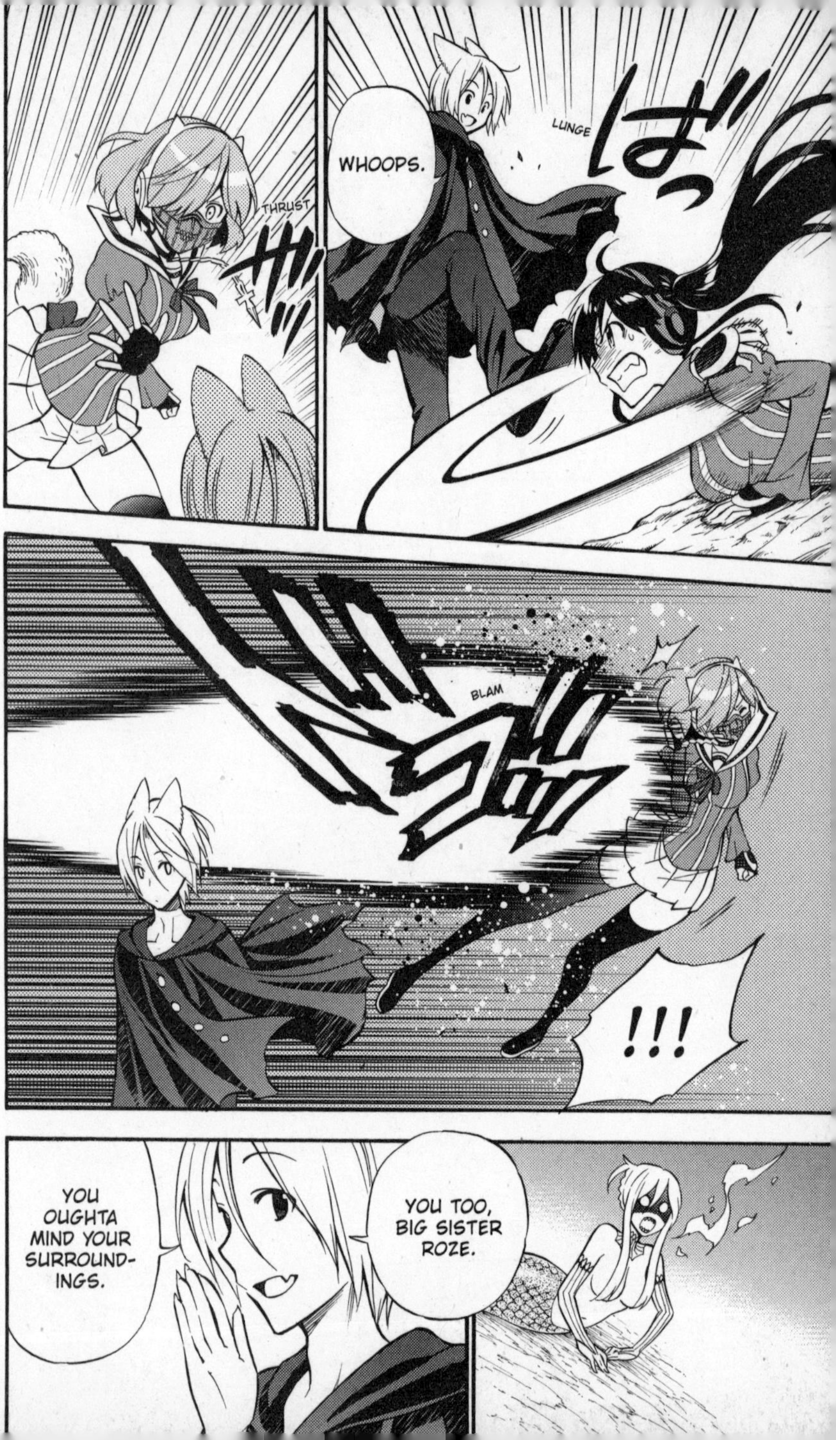

WHOOPS.
LUNGE
ばっ
THRUST
BLAM
!!!
YOU OUGHTA MIND YOUR SURROUNDINGS.
YOU TOO, BIG SISTER ROZE.

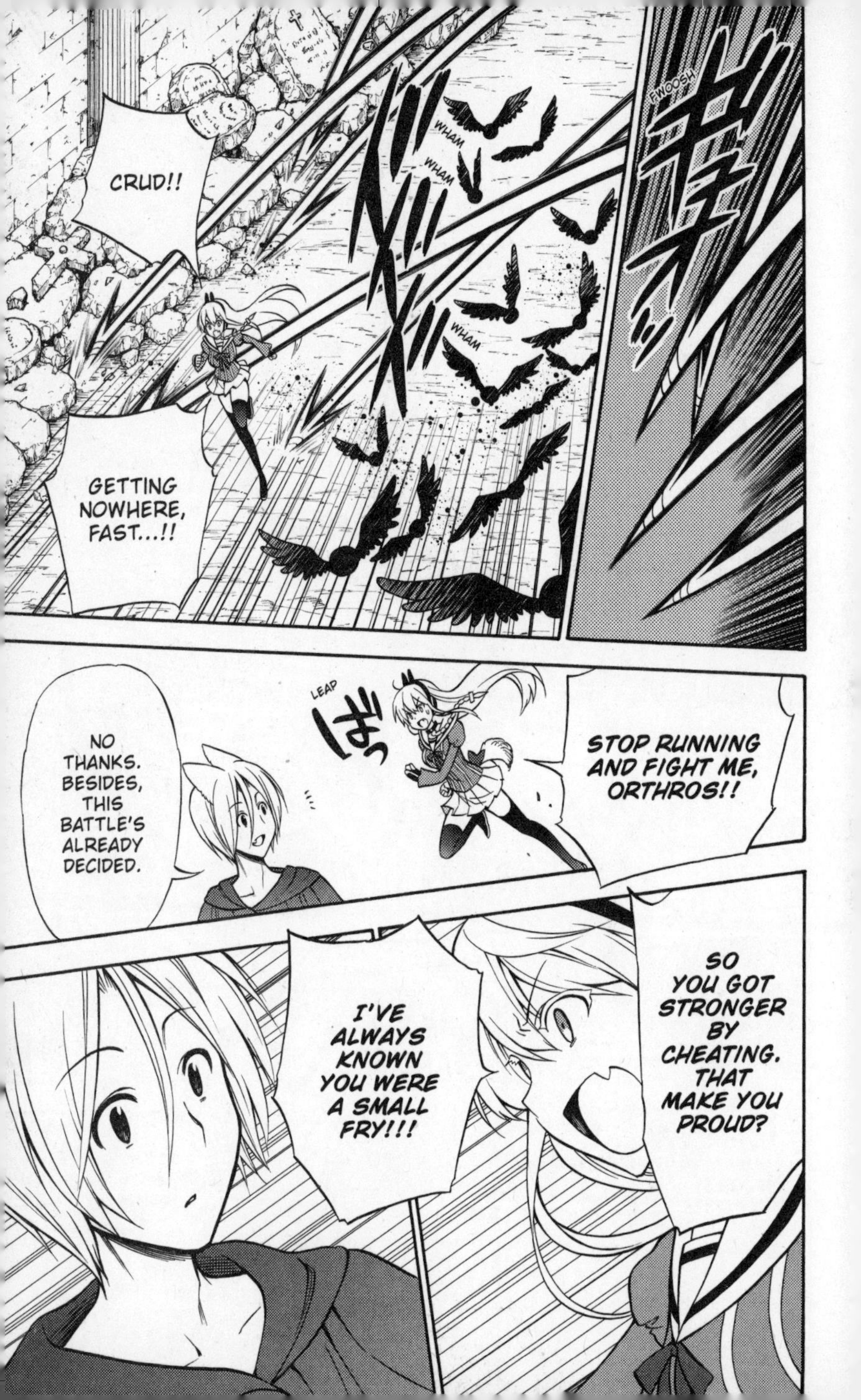
FWOOSH
WHAM
WHAM
WHAM
CRUD!!
GETTING NOWHERE, FAST...!!
STOP RUNNING AND FIGHT ME, ORTHROS!!
LEAP
NO THANKS. BESIDES, THIS BATTLE'S ALREADY DECIDED.
SO YOU GOT STRONGER BY CHEATING. THAT MAKE YOU PROUD?
I'VE ALWAYS KNOWN YOU WERE A SMALL FRY!!!

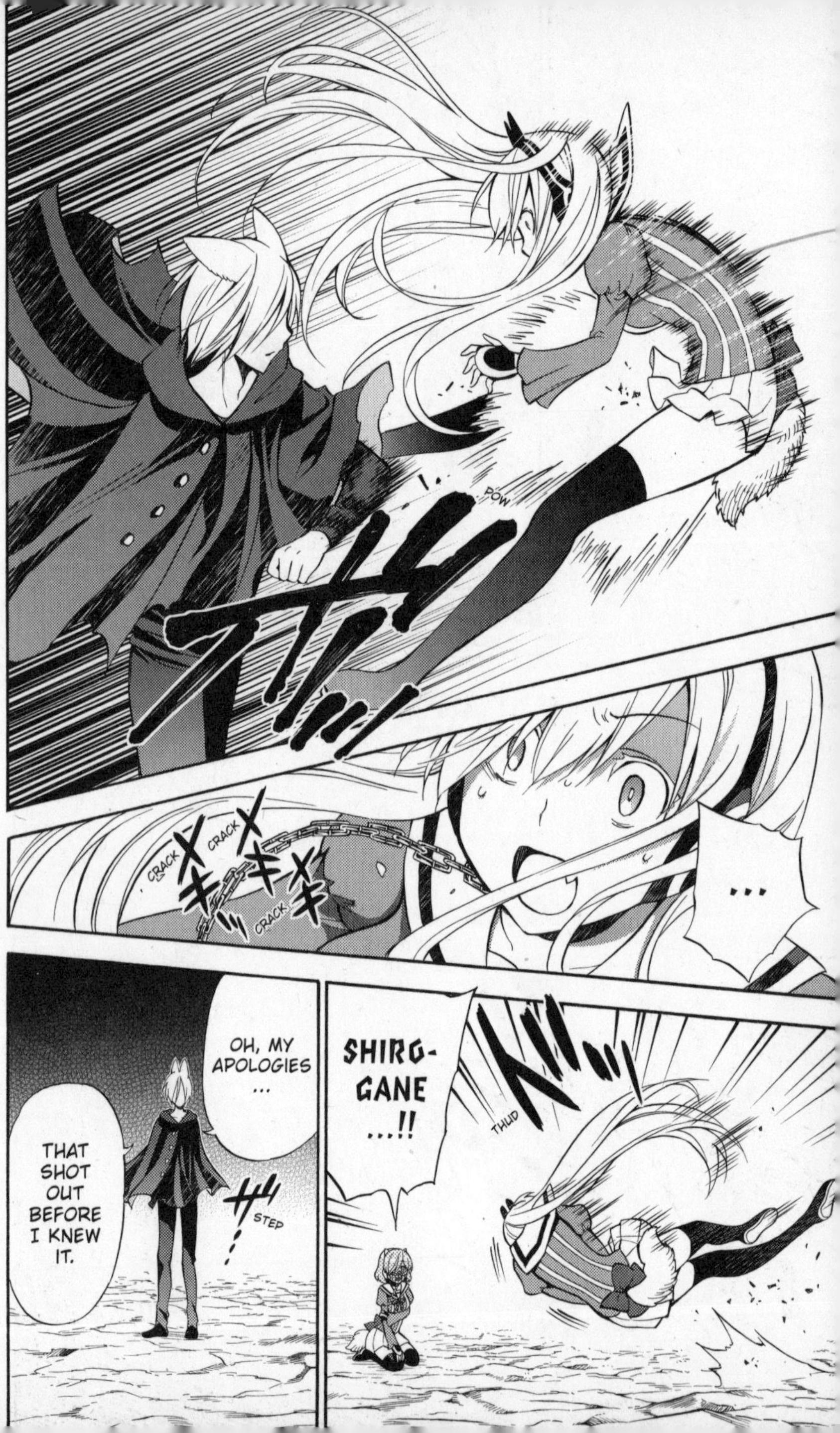
POW
...
CRACK
CRACK
CRACK
CRACK
THUD
SHIRO-GANE ...!!
OH, MY APOLOGIES ...
THAT SHOT OUT BEFORE I KNEW IT.
STEP

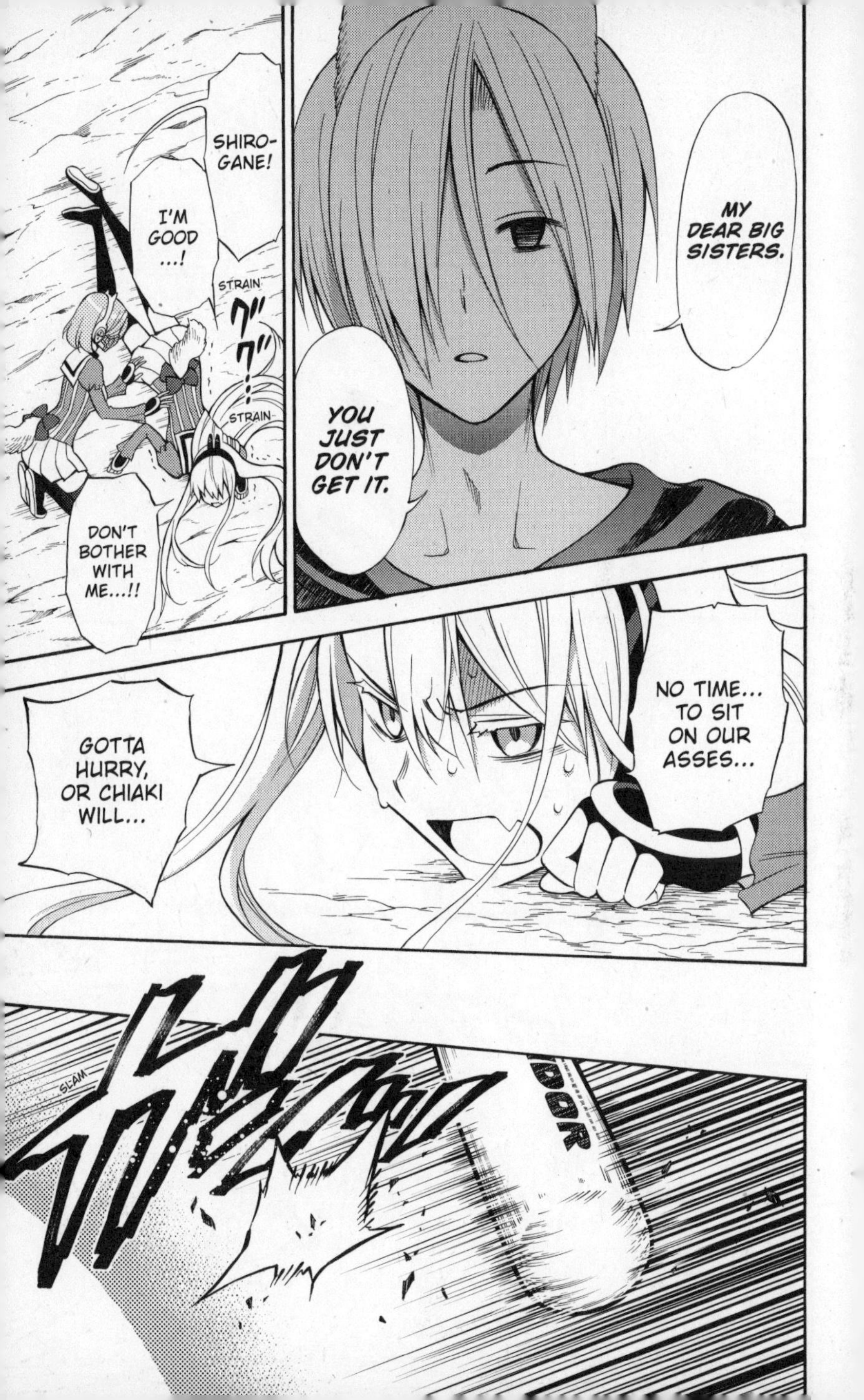
MY DEAR BIG SISTERS.
YOU JUST DON'T GET IT.
SHIRO-GANE!
I'M GOOD ...!
STRAIN
STRAIN
DON'T BOTHER WITH ME...!!
NO TIME... TO SIT ON OUR ASSES...
GOTTA HURRY, OR CHIAKI WILL...
SLAM

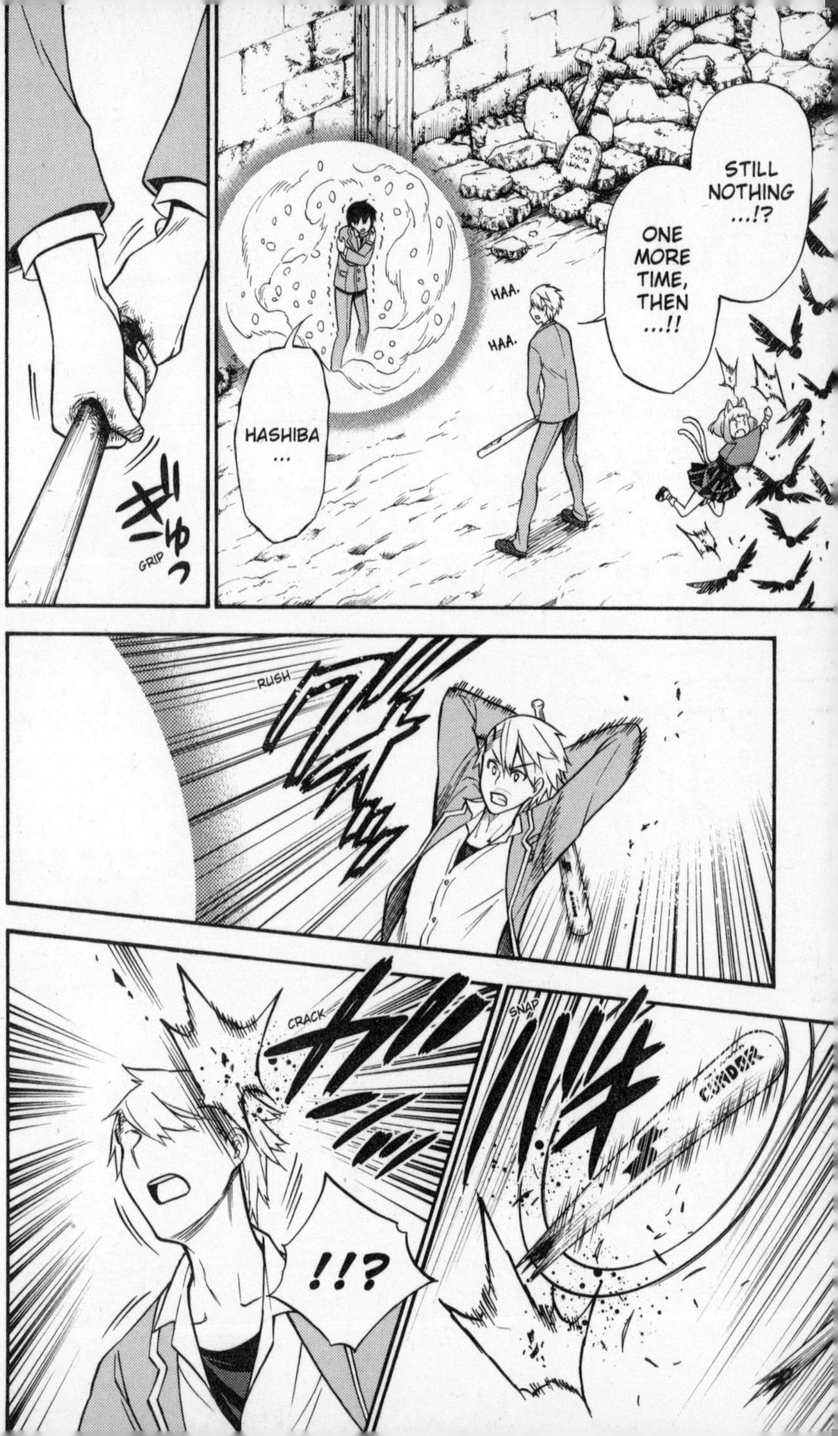
STILL NOTHING ...!?
ONE MORE TIME, THEN ...!!
HAA.
HAA.
HASHIBA ...
ぎゅっ
GRIP
RUSH
SNAP
CRACK
!!?

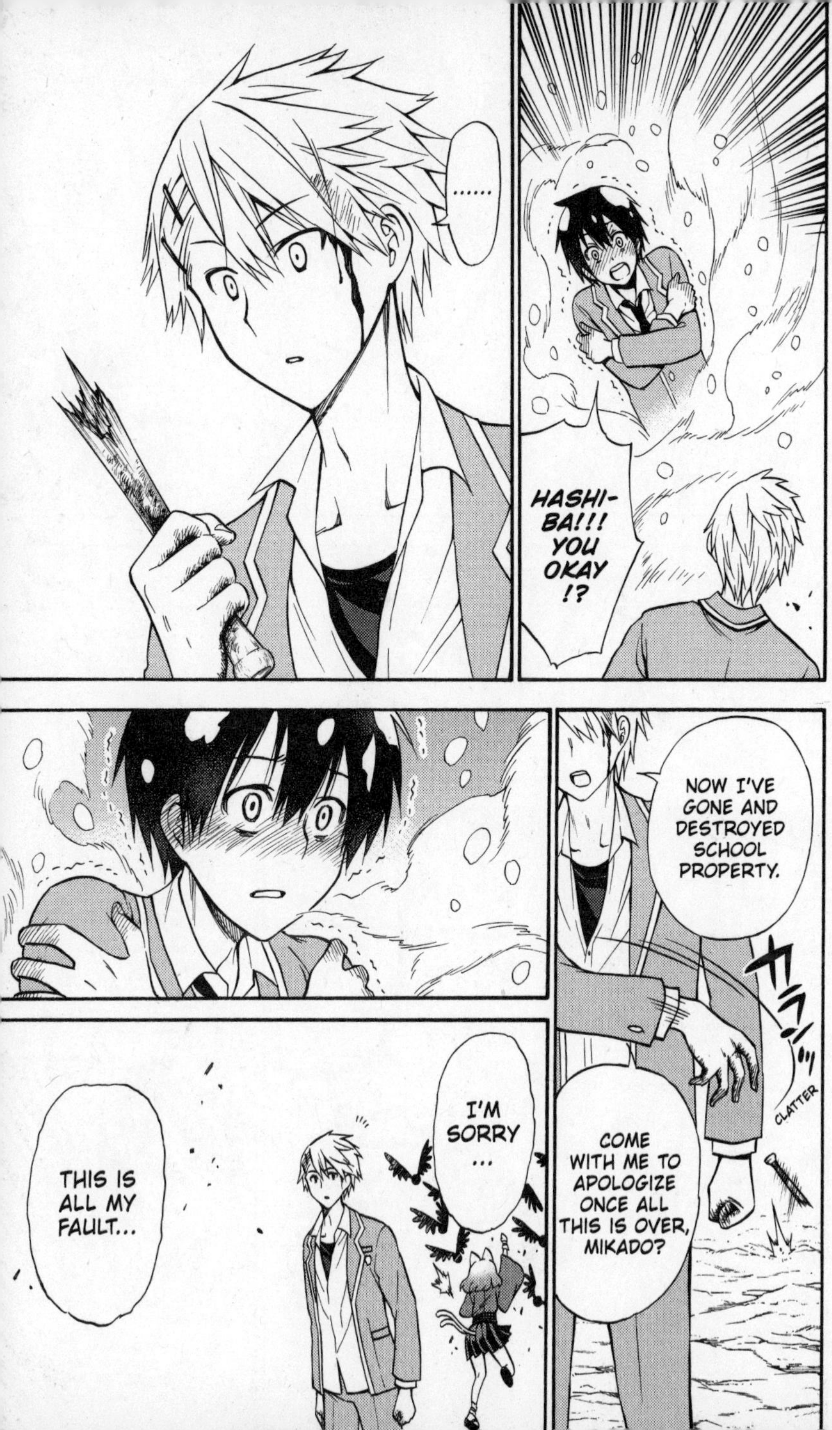
HASHIBA!!! YOU OKAY!?
......
NOW I'VE GONE AND DESTROYED SCHOOL PROPERTY.
CLATTER
COME WITH ME TO APOLOGIZE ONCE ALL THIS IS OVER, MIKADO?
I'M SORRY...
THIS IS ALL MY FAULT...

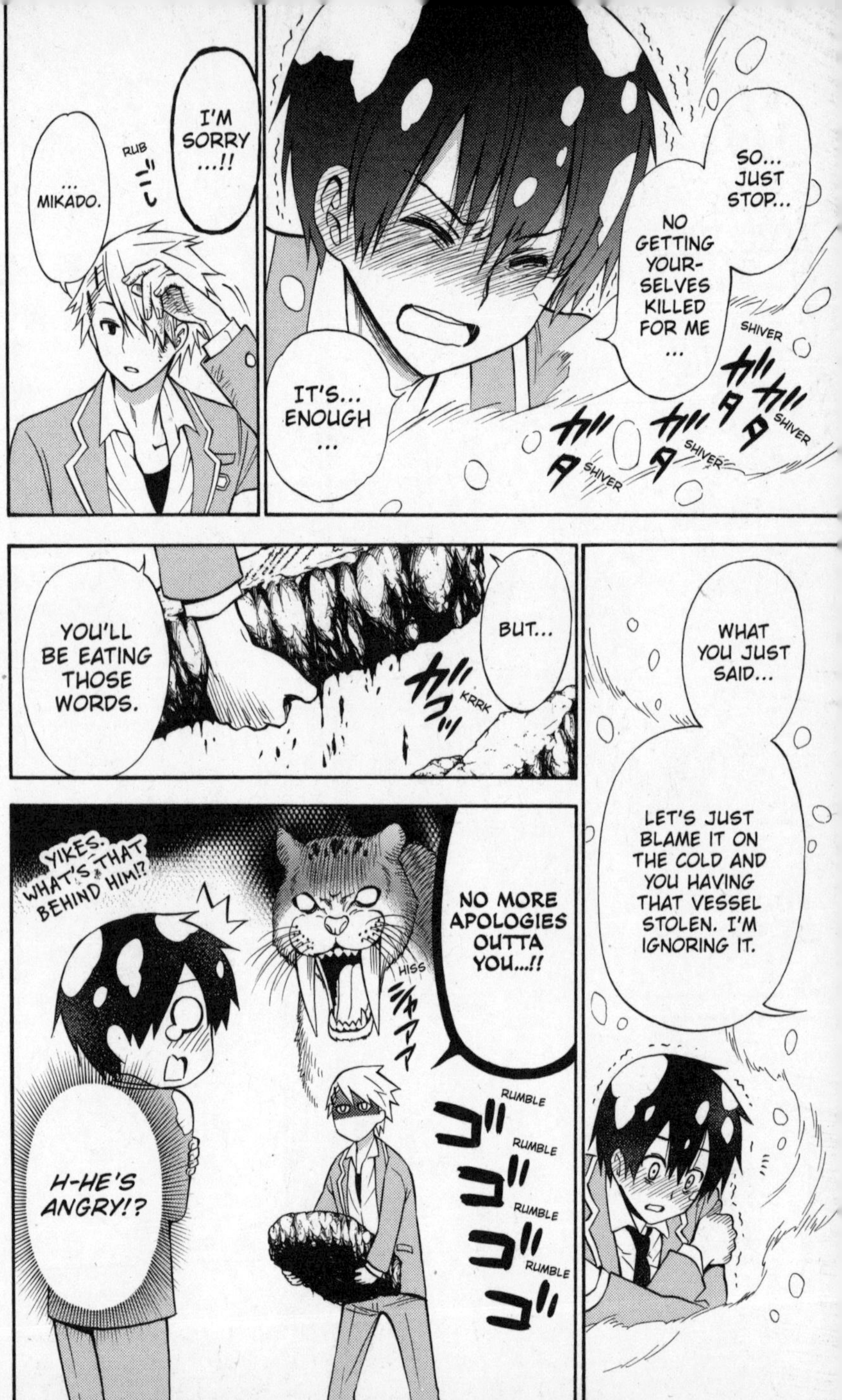
SO... JUST STOP...
NO GETTING YOUR-SELVES KILLED FOR ME ...
IT'S... ENOUGH ...
SHIVER
SHIVER
SHIVER
SHIVER
I'M SORRY ...!!
RUB
... MIKADO.
WHAT YOU JUST SAID...
LET'S JUST BLAME IT ON THE COLD AND YOU HAVING THAT VESSEL STOLEN. I'M IGNORING IT.
BUT...
KRRK
YOU'LL BE EATING THOSE WORDS.
NO MORE APOLOGIES OUTTA YOU...!!
HISS
RUMBLE
RUMBLE
RUMBLE
RUMBLE
YIKES. WHAT'S THAT BEHIND HIM!?
H-HE'S ANGRY!?

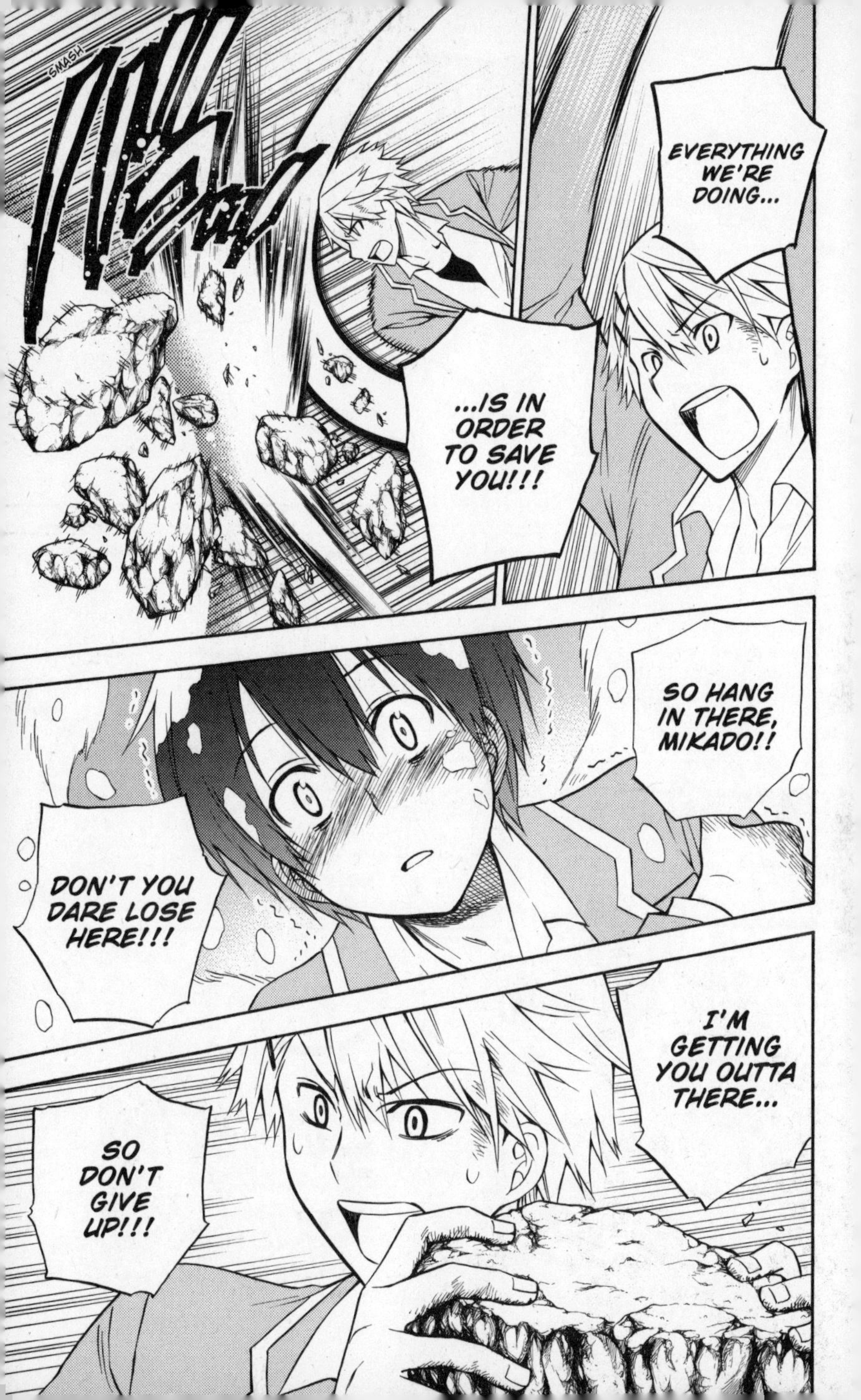
EVERYTHING WE'RE DOING...
...IS IN ORDER TO SAVE YOU!!!
SMASH
SO HANG IN THERE, MIKADO!!
DON'T YOU DARE LOSE HERE!!!
I'M GETTING YOU OUTTA THERE...
SO DON'T GIVE UP!!!

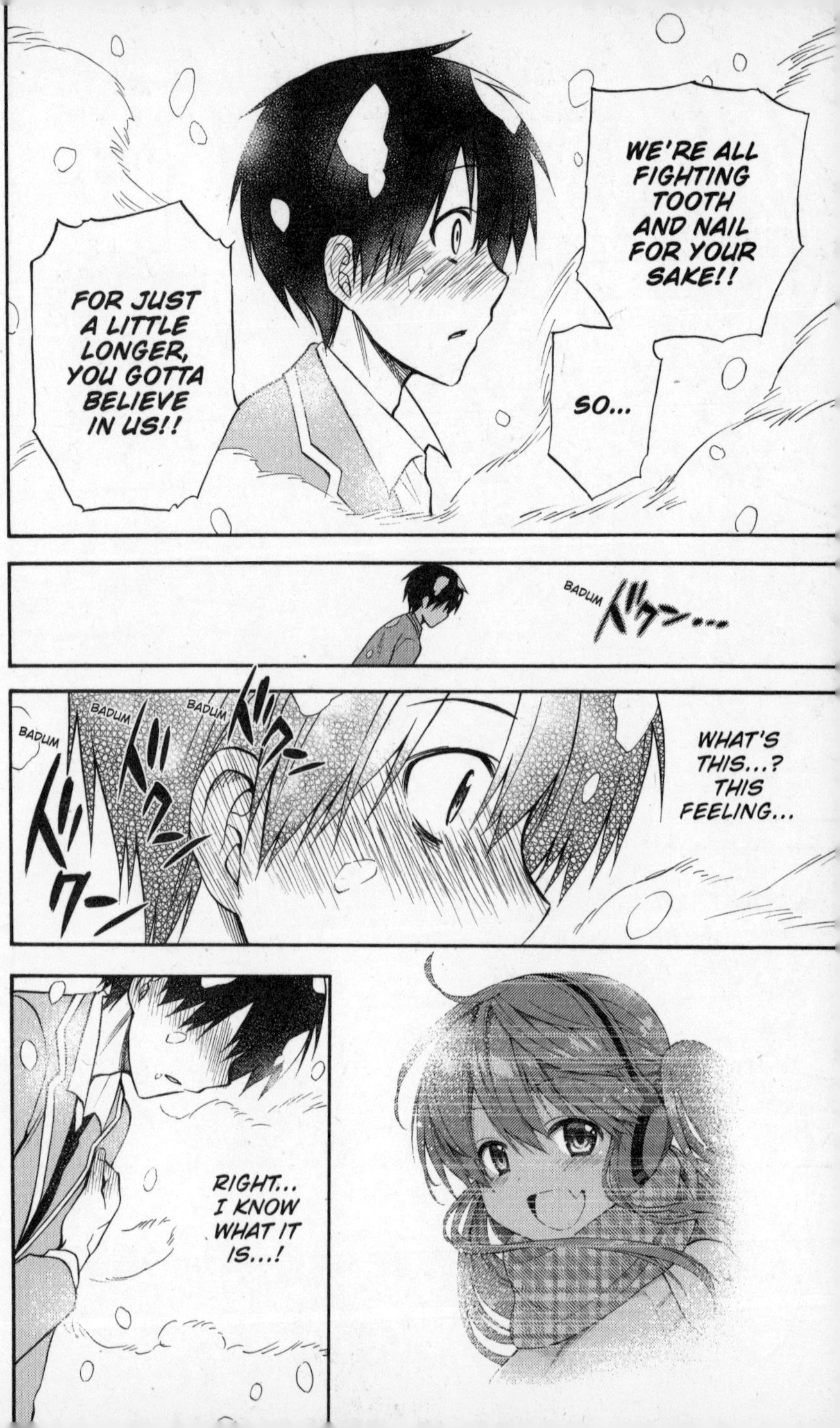
WE'RE ALL FIGHTING TOOTH AND NAIL FOR YOUR SAKE!!
SO...
FOR JUST A LITTLE LONGER, YOU GOTTA BELIEVE IN US!!
BADUM
WHAT'S THIS...? THIS FEELING...
BADUM
BADUM
BADUM
RIGHT... I KNOW WHAT IT IS...!

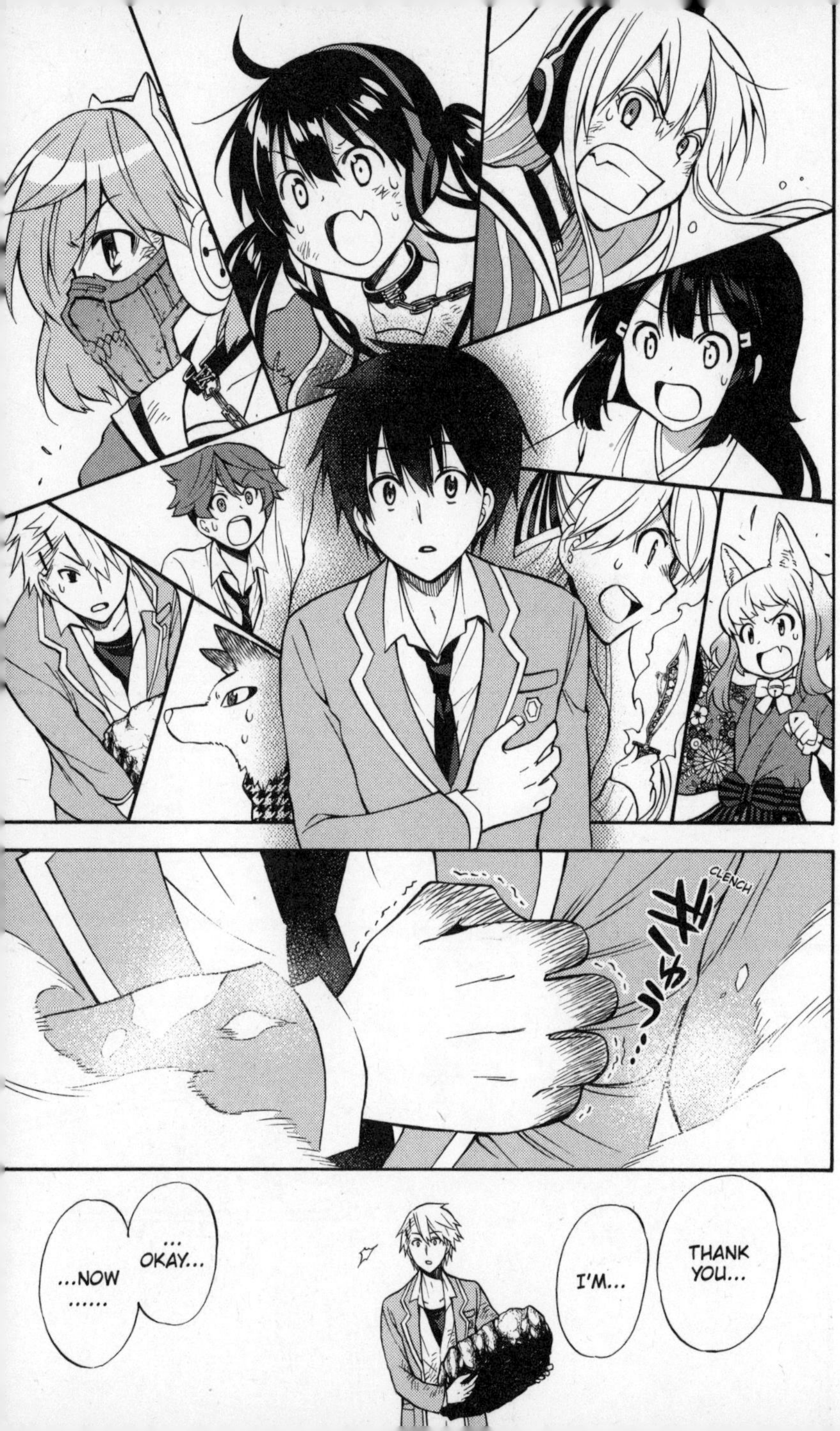
CLENCH
THANK YOU...
I'M...
... OKAY...
...NOW
......

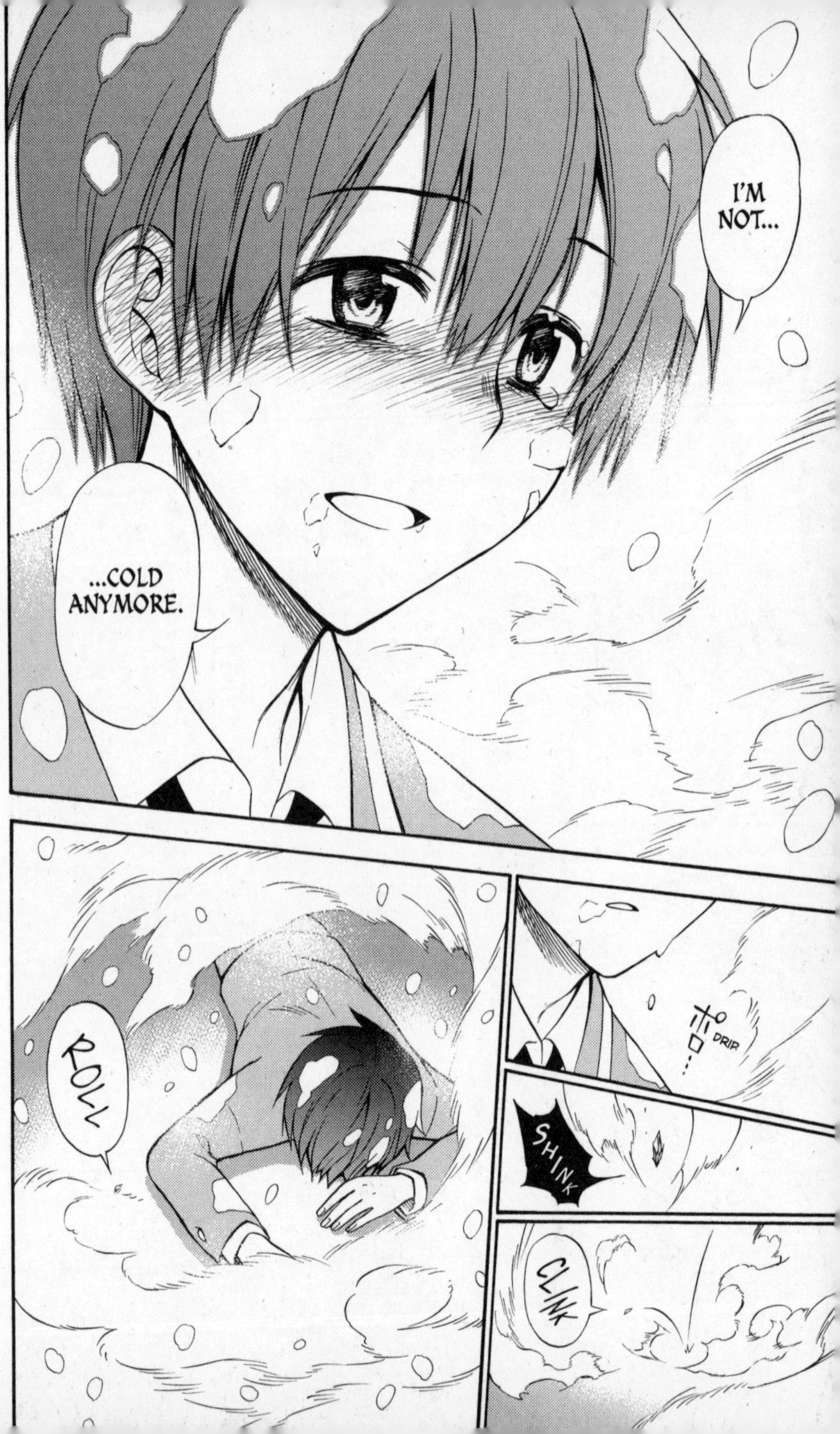
I'M NOT...
...COLD ANYMORE.
DRIP
SHINK
CLINK
ROLL

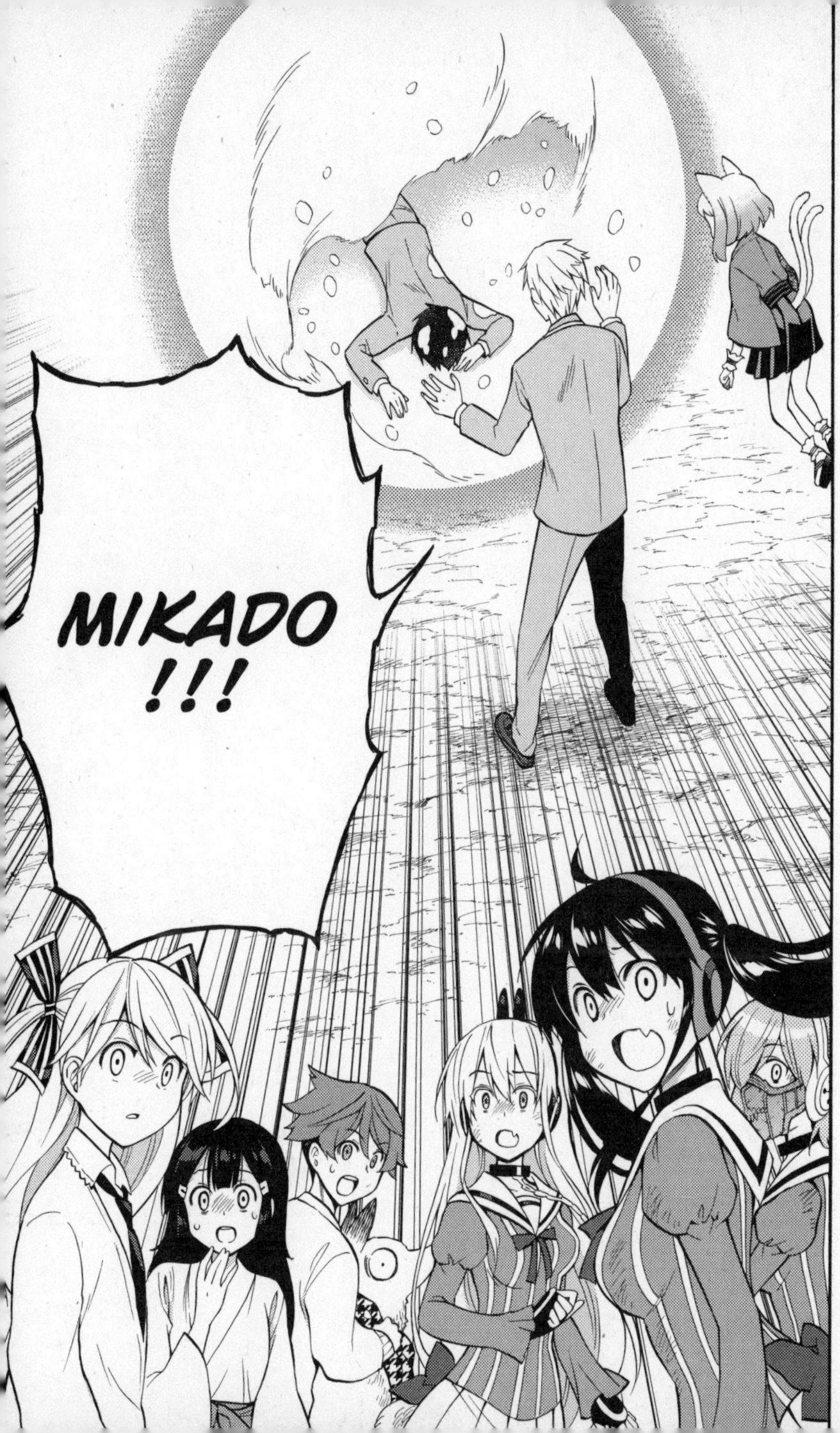
MIKADO !!!

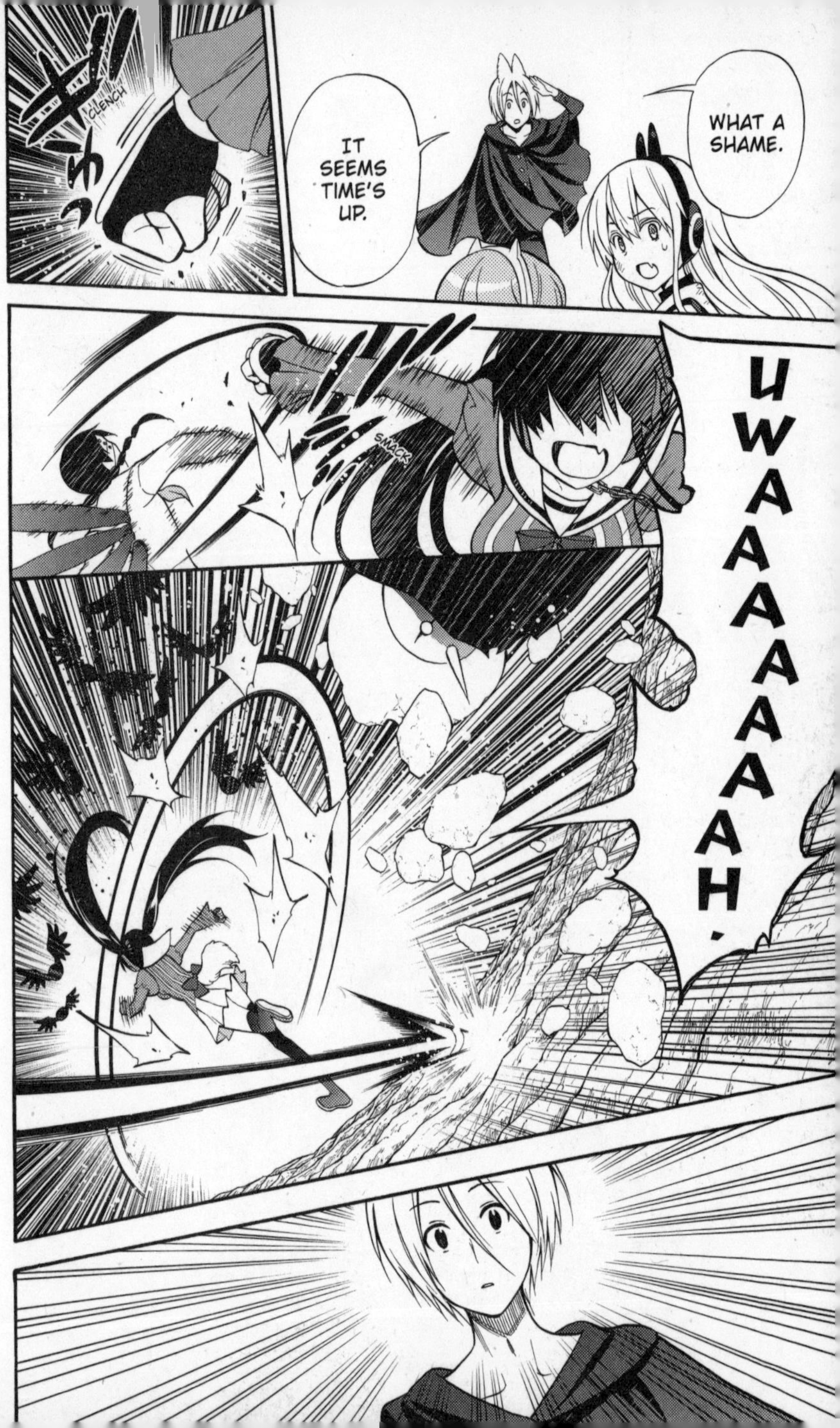
WHAT A SHAME.
IT SEEMS TIME'S UP.
CLENCH
UWAAAAAAAH.
SMACK

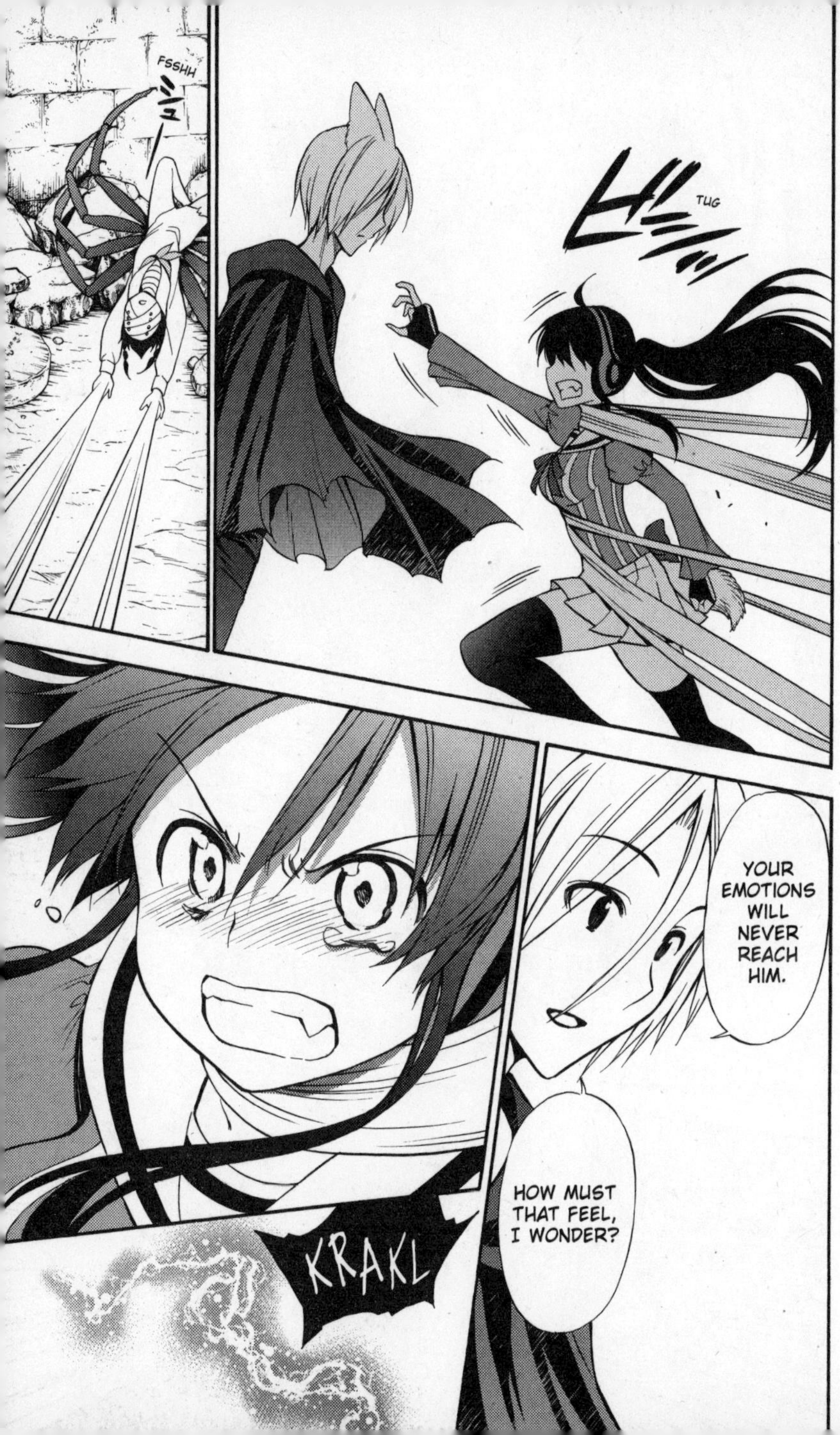
TUG
FSSHH
YOUR EMOTIONS WILL NEVER REACH HIM.
HOW MUST THAT FEEL, I WONDER?
KRAKL

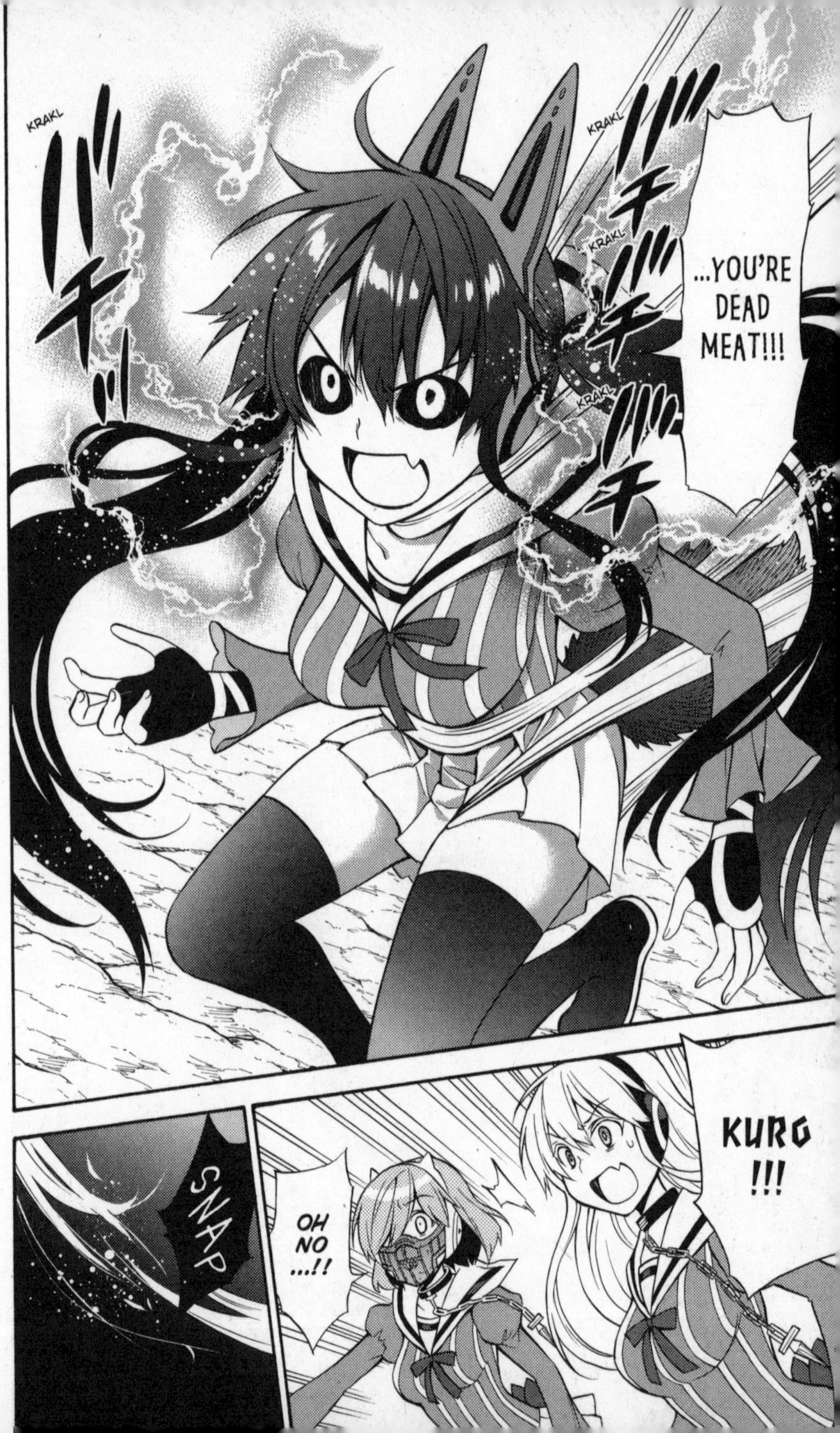
KRAKL
KRAKL
KRAKL
KRAKL
...YOU'RE DEAD MEAT!!!
KURG !!!
OH NO ...!!
SNAP

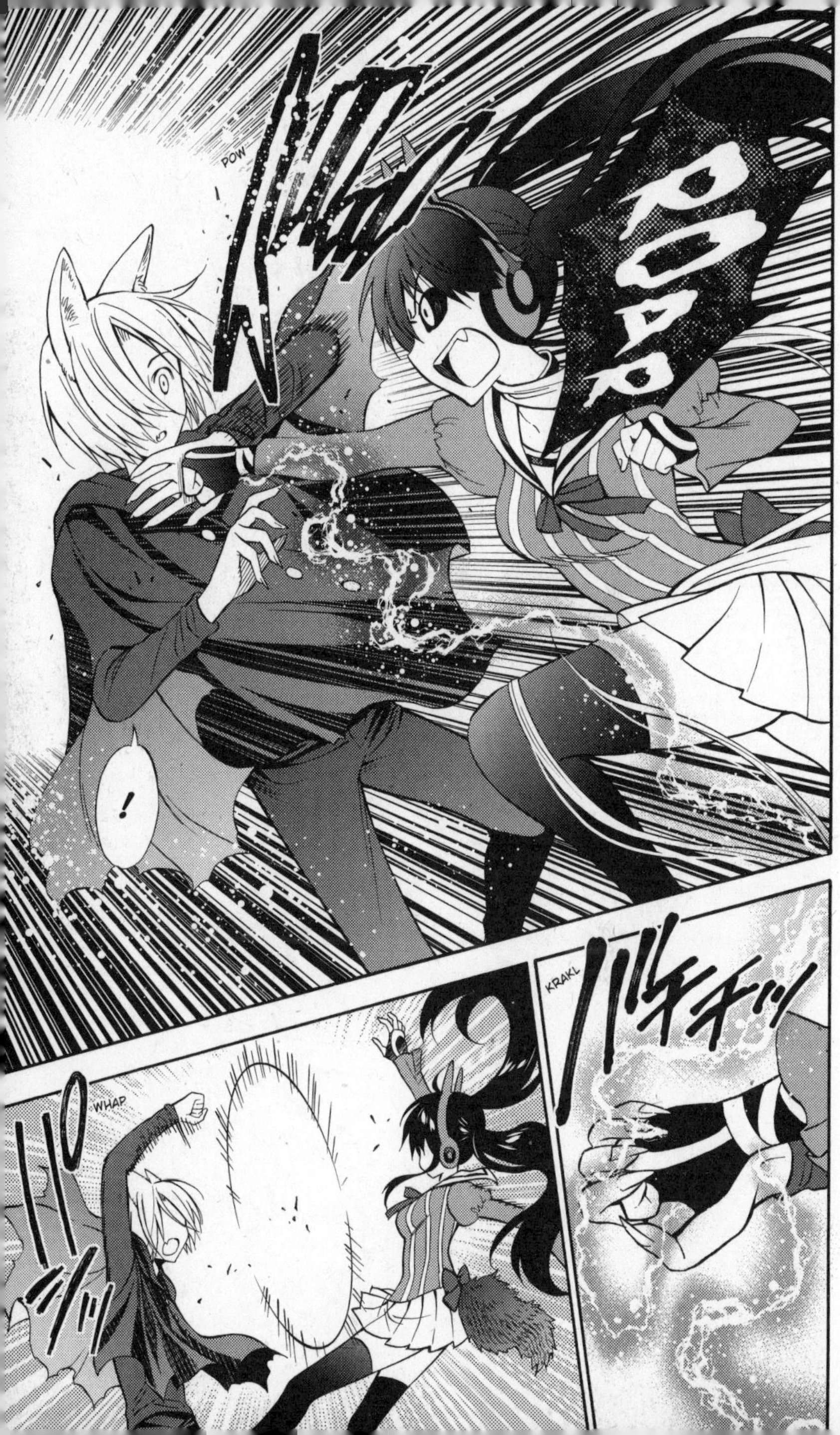
ROAR
POW
!
KRAKL
WHAP

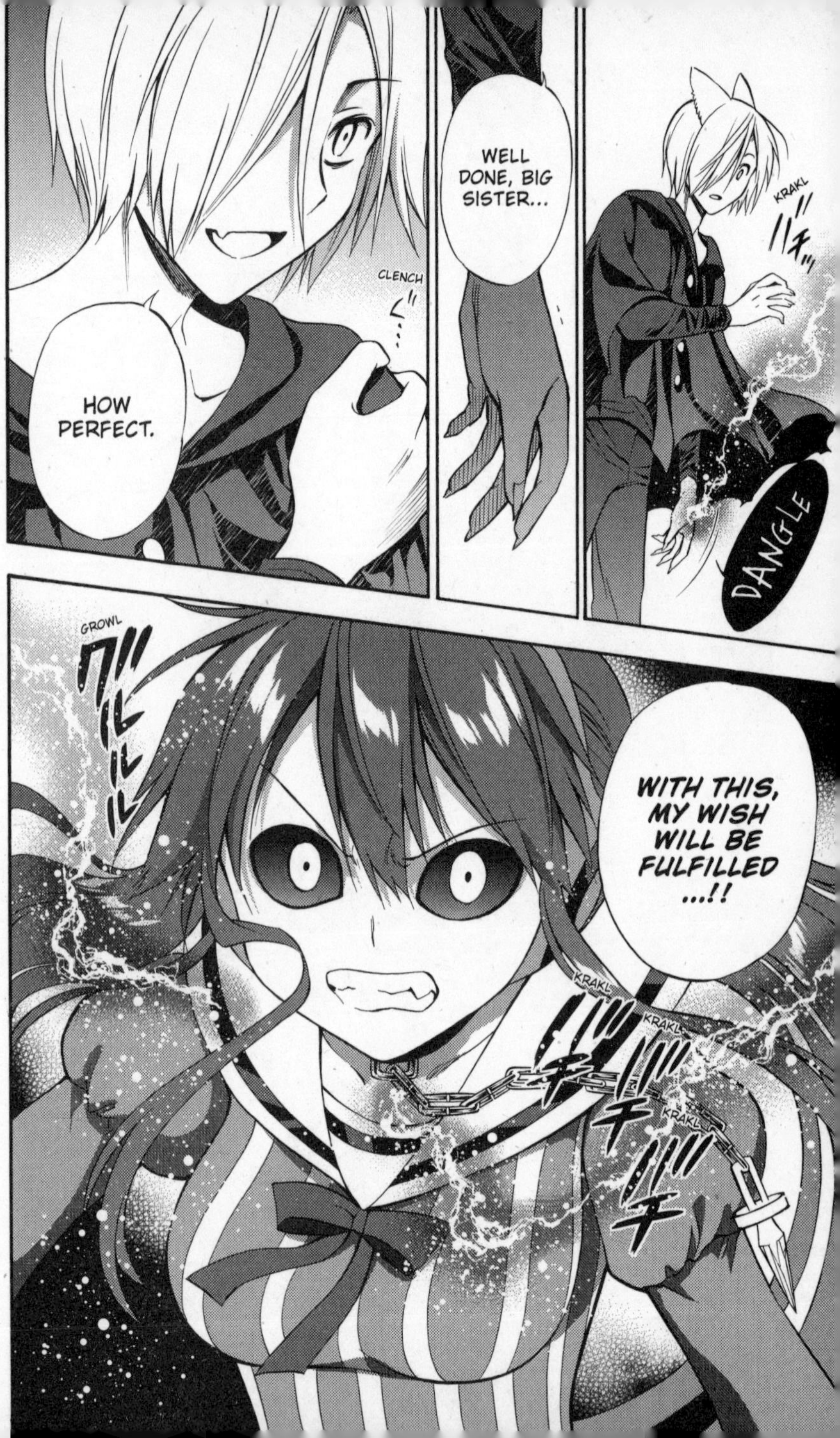

KRAKL
DANGLE
WELL DONE, BIG SISTER...
CLENCH
HOW PERFECT.
GROWL
WITH THIS, MY WISH WILL BE FULFILLED ...!!
KRAKL
KRAKL
KRAKL

🐾 TODAY'S CERBERUS

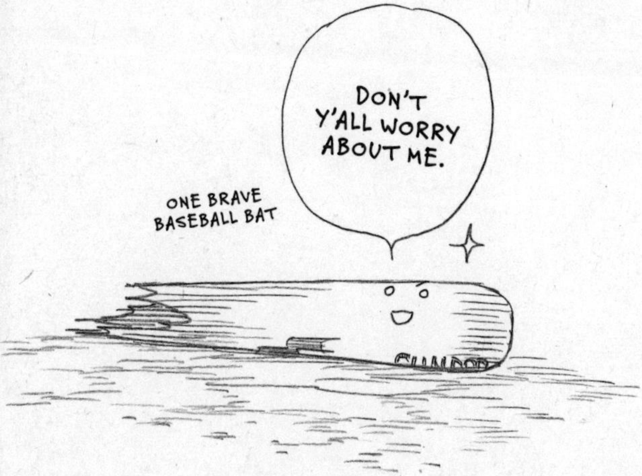
DON'T Y'ALL WORRY ABOUT ME.
ONE BRAVE BASEBALL BAT

TODAY'S CERBERUS

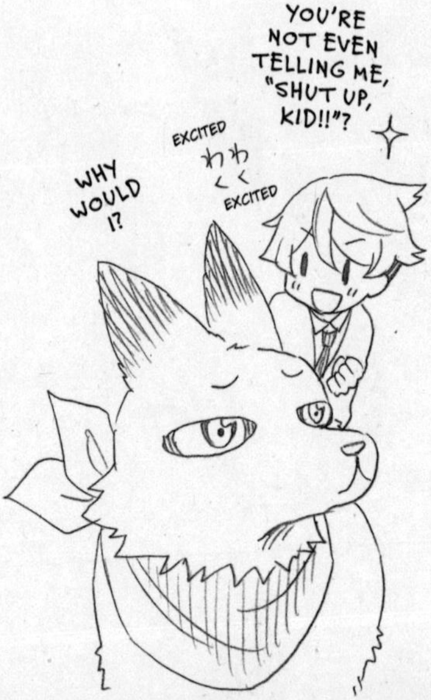
YOU'RE NOT EVEN TELLING ME, "SHUT UP, KID!!"?
EXCITED
わく
わく
EXCITED
WHY WOULD I?

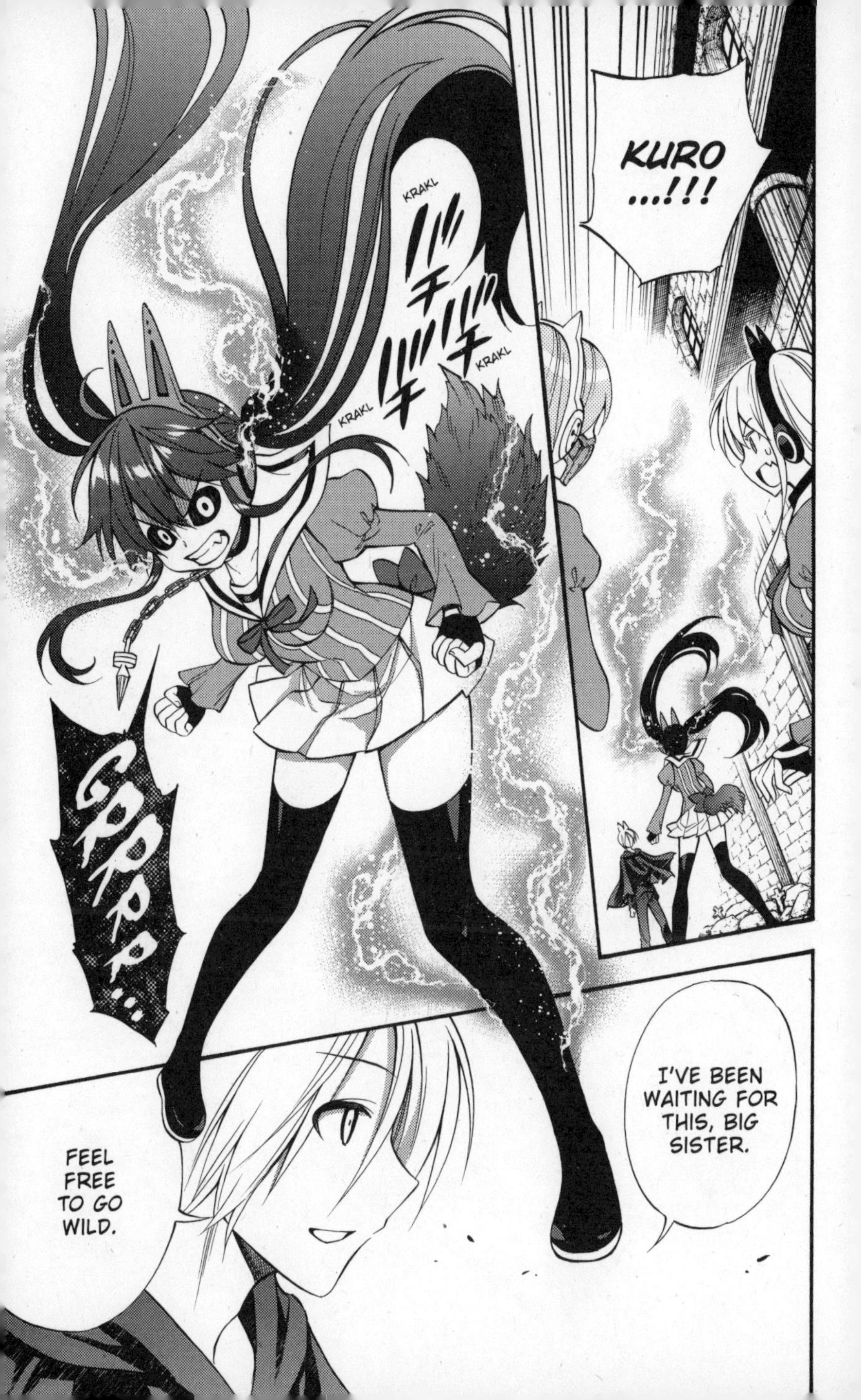
KURO ...!!!
KRAKL
KRAKL
KRAKL
GRRRR...
I'VE BEEN WAITING FOR THIS, BIG SISTER.
FEEL FREE TO GO WILD.

CHAPTER 53: PRAYER

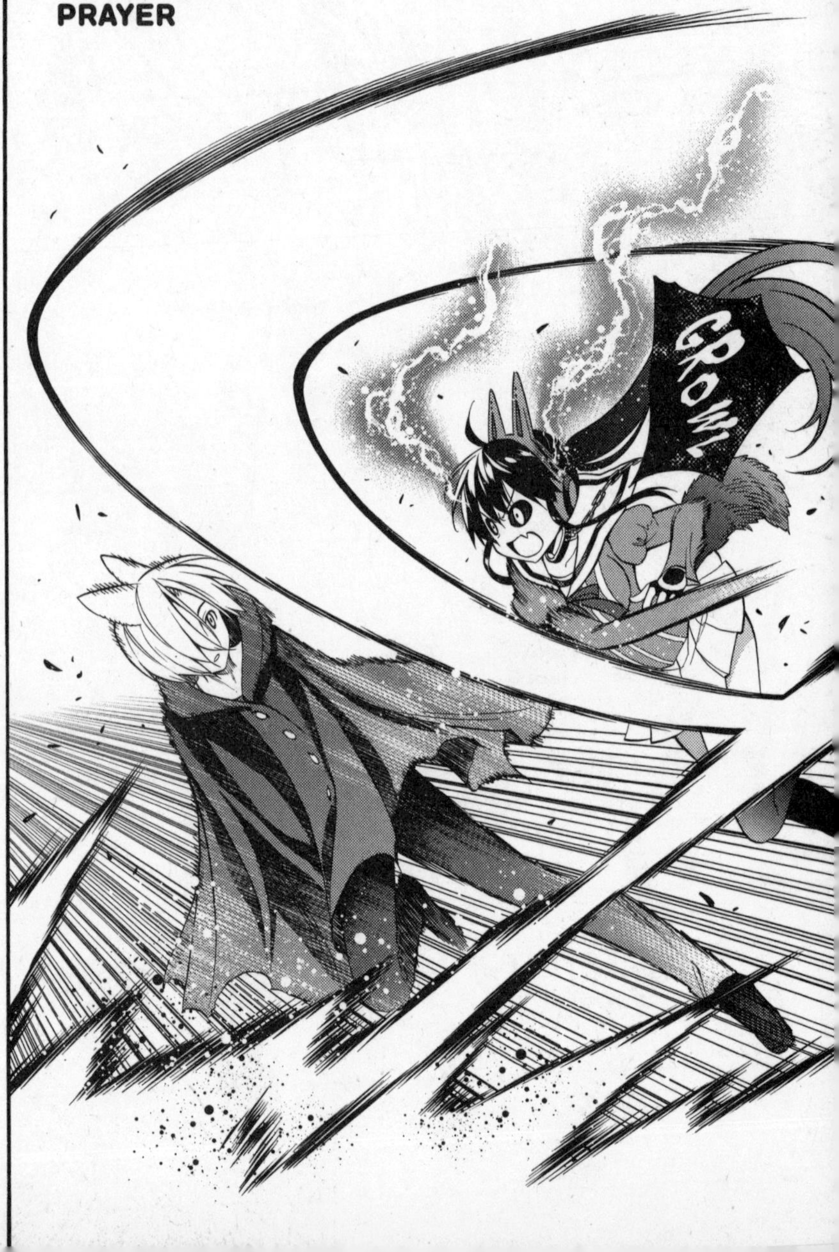
GROWL

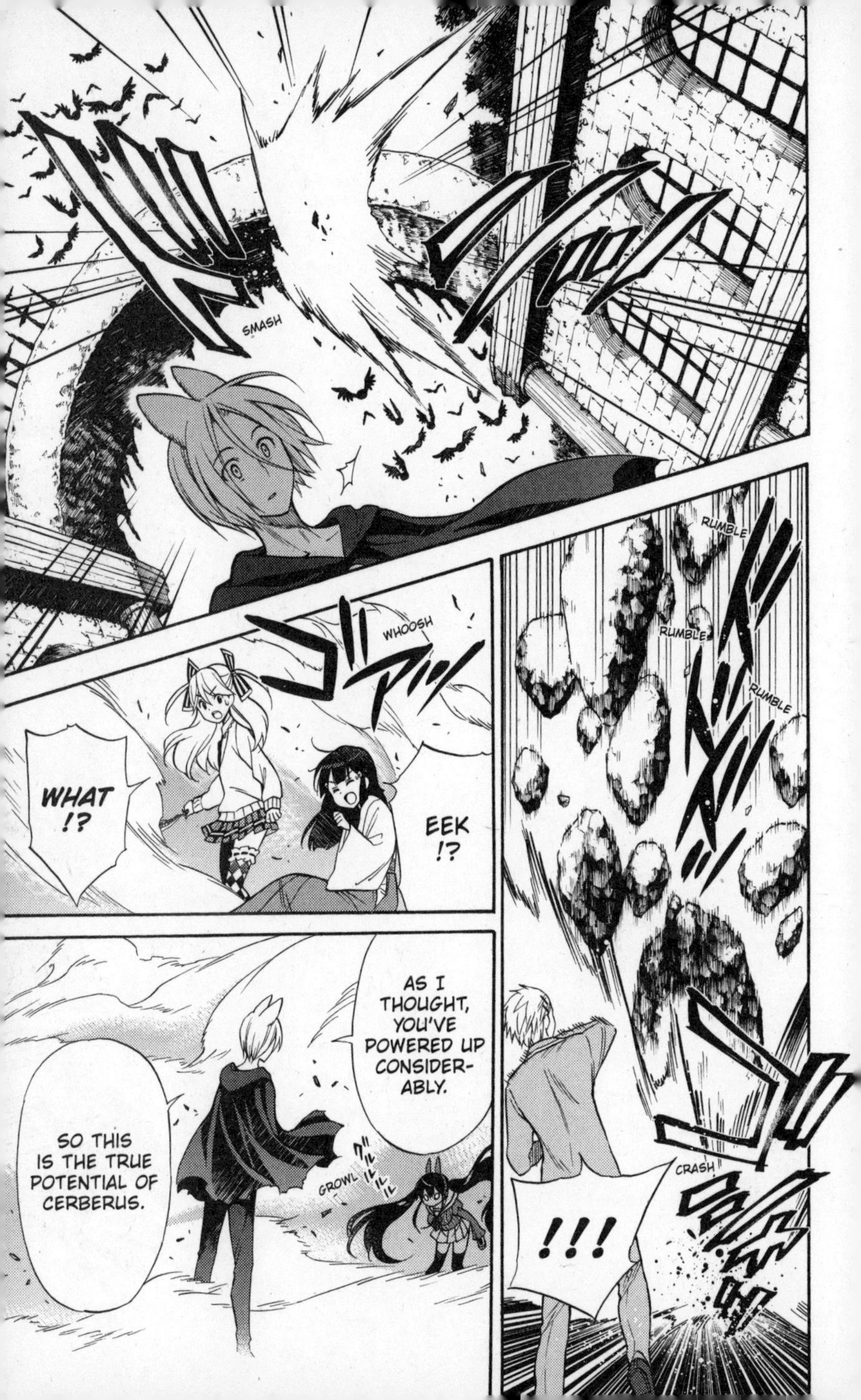
SMASH
RUMBLE
RUMBLE
RUMBLE
CRASH
!!!
WHOOSH
EEK !?
WHAT !?
AS I THOUGHT, YOU'VE POWERED UP CONSIDER-ABLY.
GROWL
SO THIS IS THE TRUE POTENTIAL OF CERBERUS.

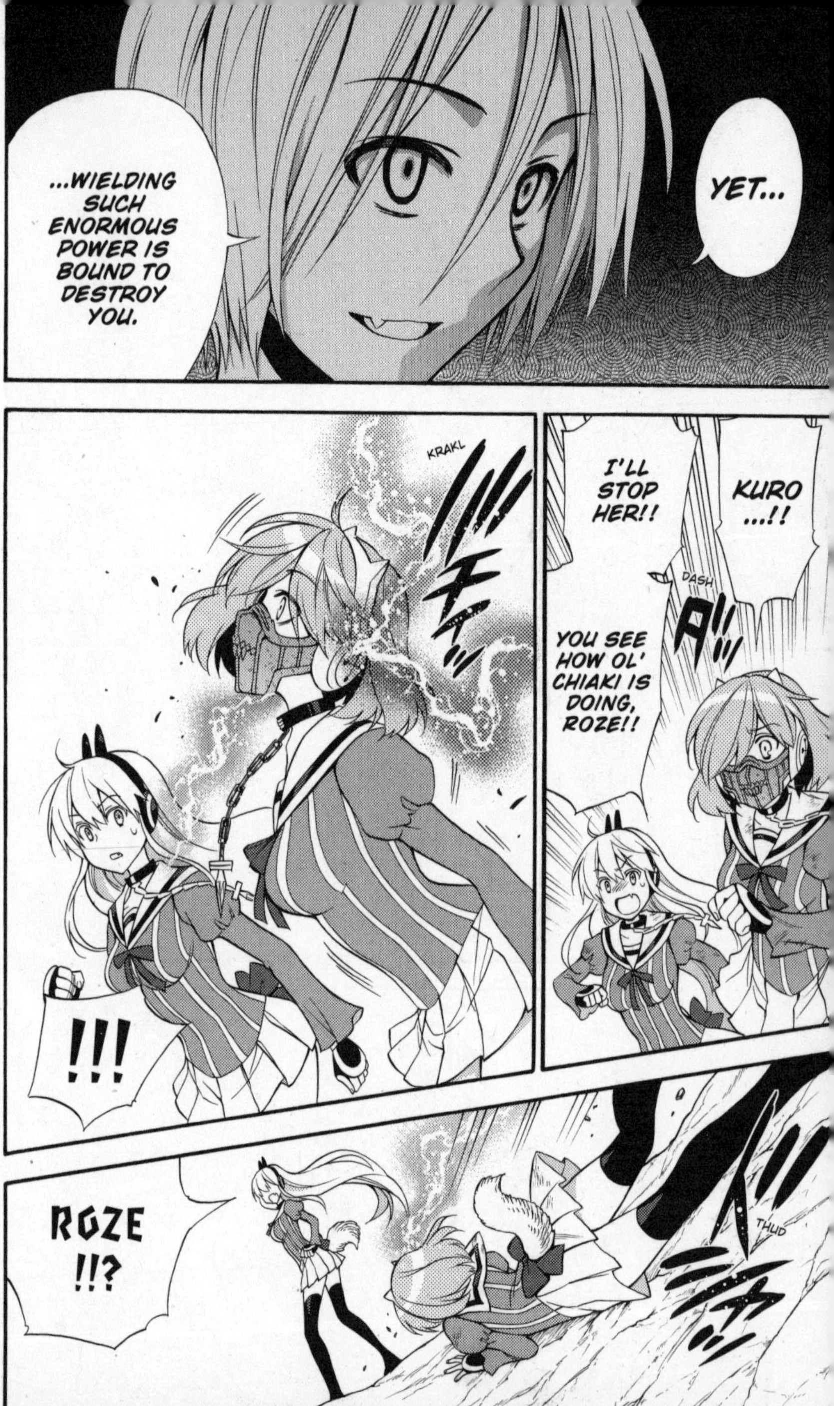
YET...
...WIELDING SUCH ENORMOUS POWER IS BOUND TO DESTROY YOU.
KURO ...!!
I'LL STOP HER!!
DASH
YOU SEE HOW OL' CHIAKI IS DOING, ROZE!!
KRAKL
!!!
THUD
ROZE !!?

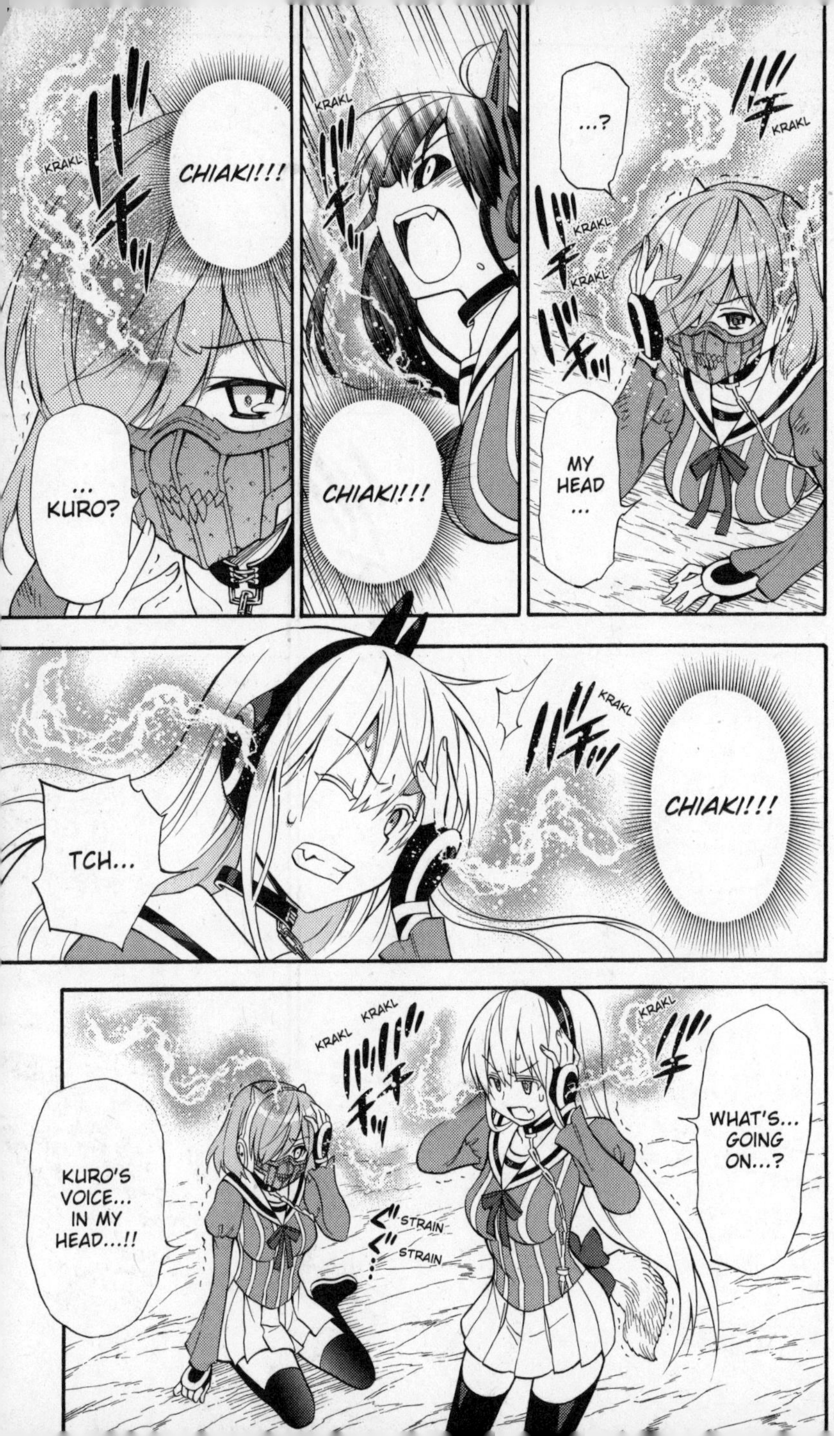
KRAKL
...?
KRAKL
KRAKL
MY HEAD ...
KRAKL
CHIAKI!!!
CHIAKI!!!
KRAKL
... KURO?
KRAKL
CHIAKI!!!
TCH...
KRAKL
WHAT'S... GOING ON...?
KRAKL KRAKL
STRAIN
STRAIN
KURO'S VOICE... IN MY HEAD...!!

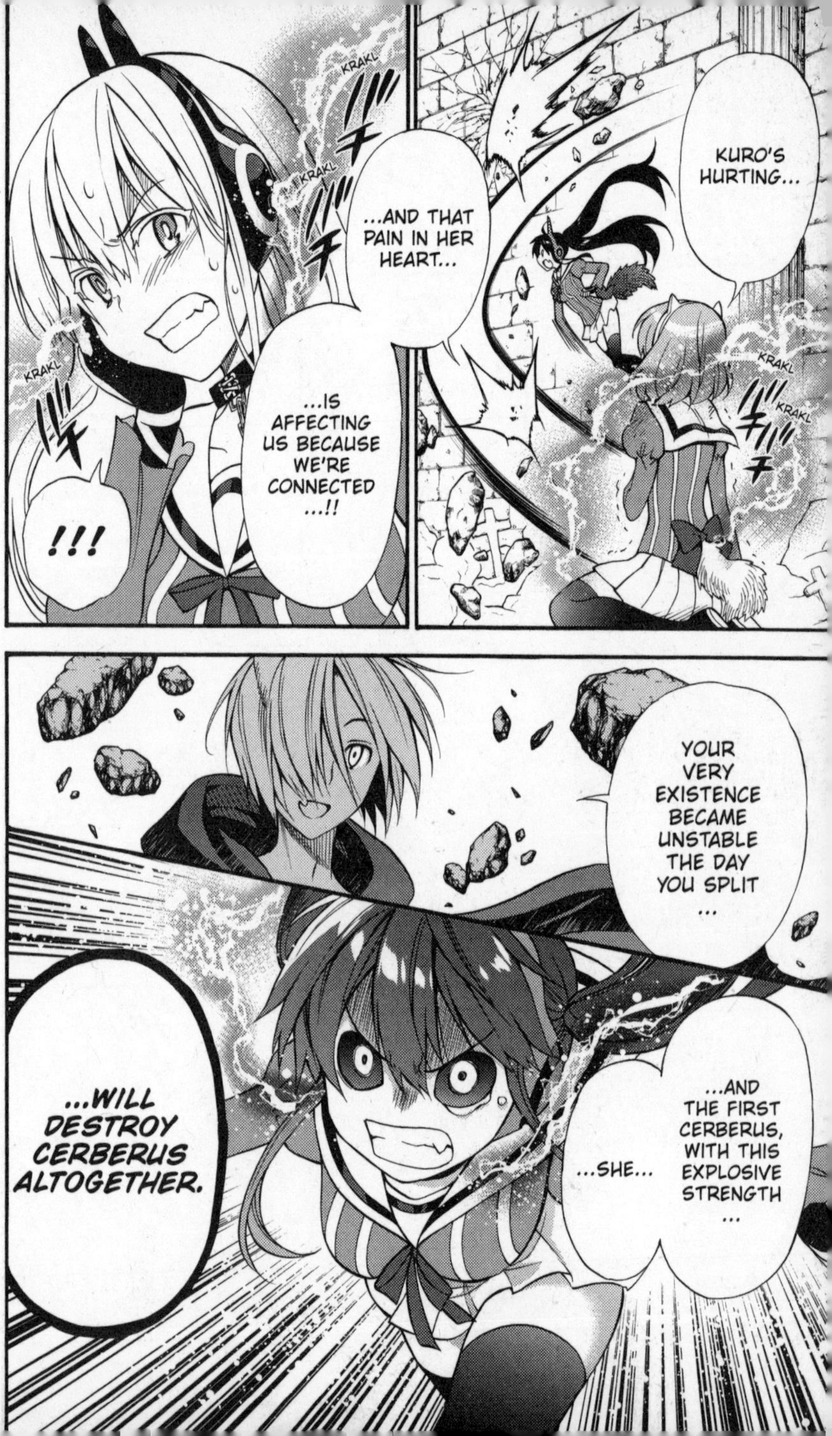
KURO'S HURTING...
KRAKL
KRAKL
...AND THAT PAIN IN HER HEART...
KRAKL
KRAKL
...IS AFFECTING US BECAUSE WE'RE CONNECTED ...!!
KRAKL
!!!
YOUR VERY EXISTENCE BECAME UNSTABLE THE DAY YOU SPLIT ...
...AND THE FIRST CERBERUS, WITH THIS EXPLOSIVE STRENGTH ...
...SHE...
...WILL DESTROY CERBERUS ALTOGETHER.

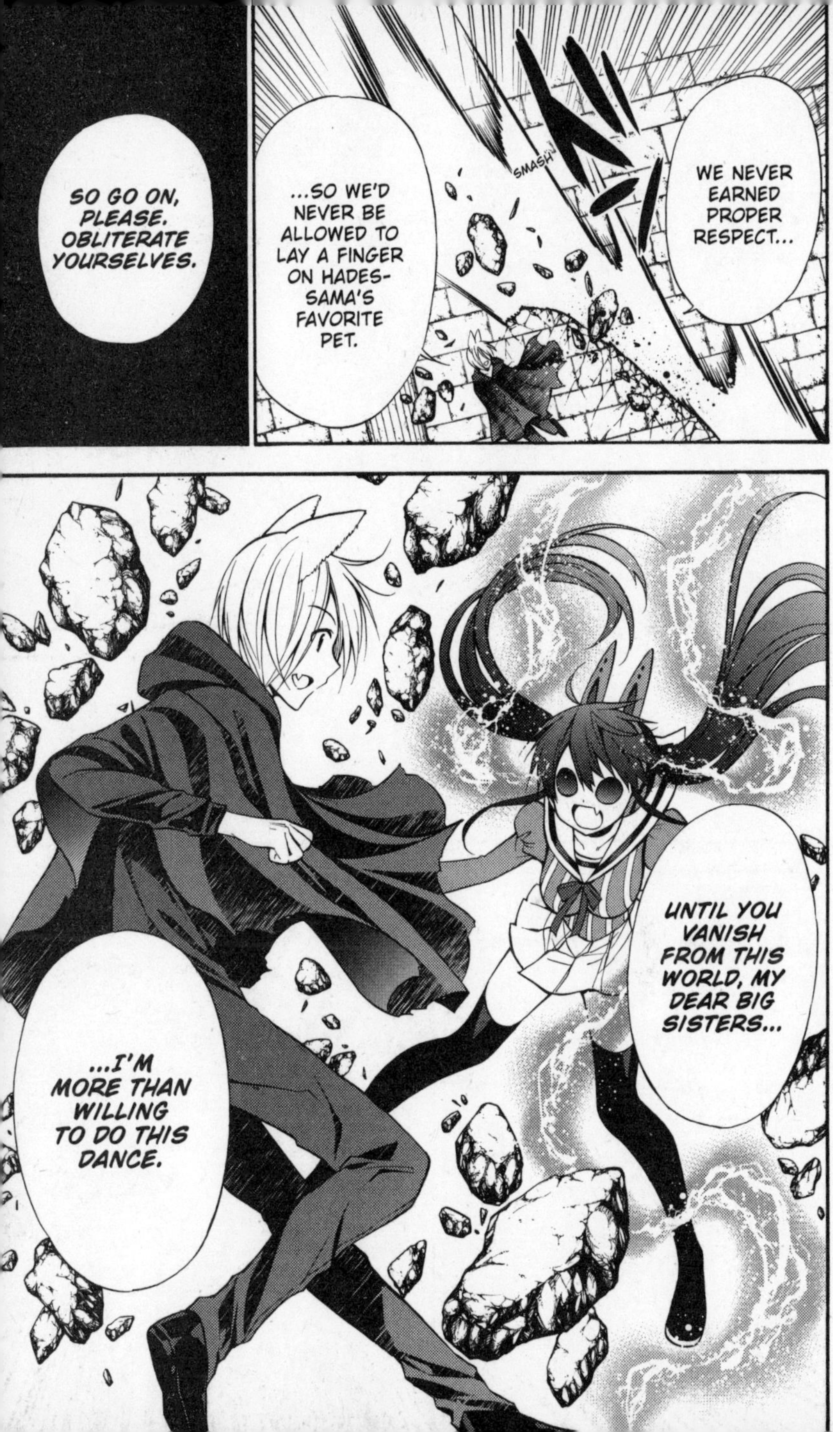
WE NEVER EARNED PROPER RESPECT...
SMASH
...SO WE'D NEVER BE ALLOWED TO LAY A FINGER ON HADES-SAMA'S FAVORITE PET.
SO GO ON, PLEASE. OBLITERATE YOURSELVES.
UNTIL YOU VANISH FROM THIS WORLD, MY DEAR BIG SISTERS...
...I'M MORE THAN WILLING TO DO THIS DANCE.

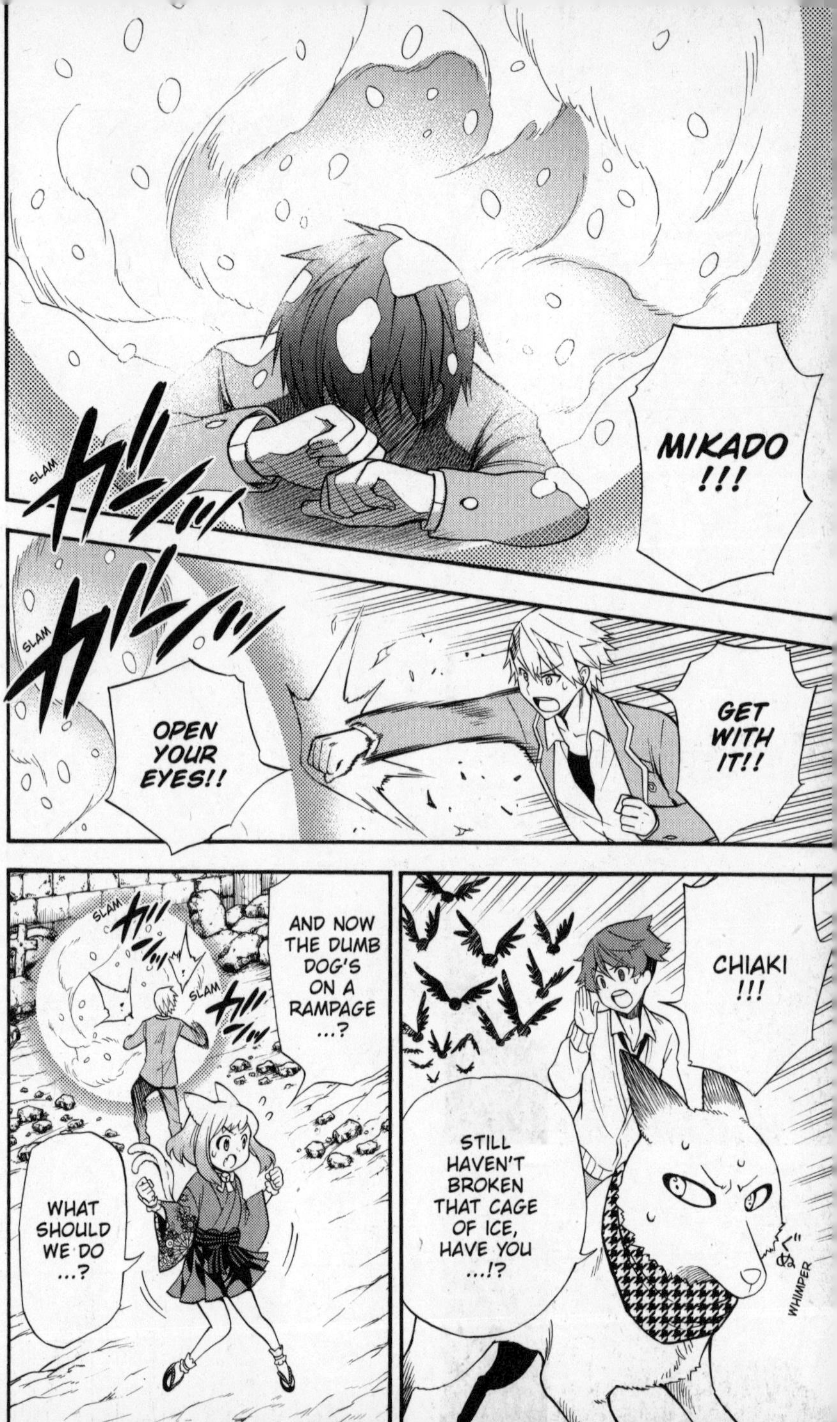
MIKADO!!!
SLAM
GET WITH IT!!
OPEN YOUR EYES!!
SLAM
CHIAKI!!!
STILL HAVEN'T BROKEN THAT CAGE OF ICE, HAVE YOU...!?
WHIMPER
AND NOW THE DUMB DOG'S ON A RAMPAGE...?
SLAM
SLAM
WHAT SHOULD WE DO...?

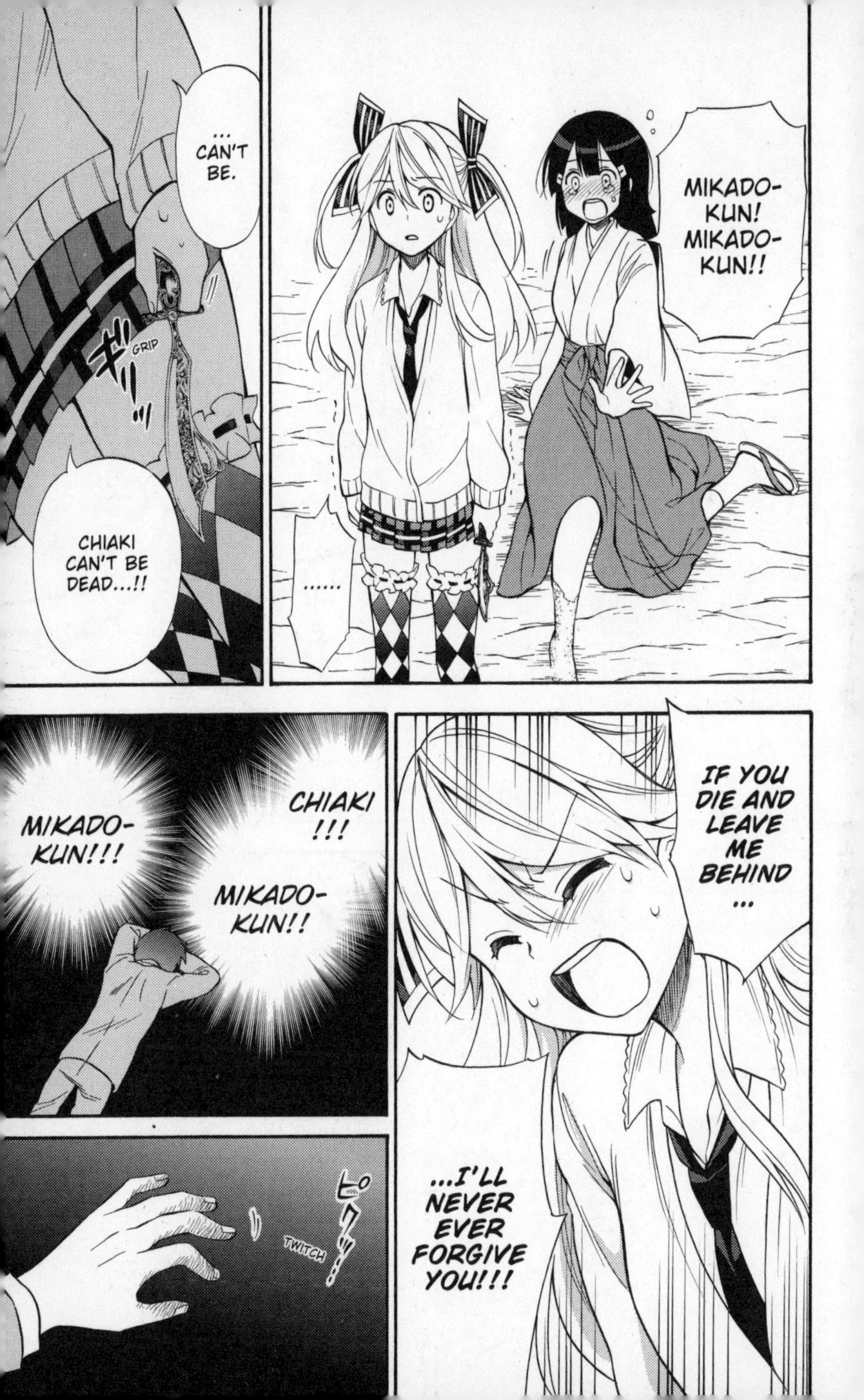
MIKADO-KUN! MIKADO-KUN!!
......
... CAN'T BE.
GRIP
CHIAKI CAN'T BE DEAD...!!
IF YOU DIE AND LEAVE ME BEHIND ...
...I'LL NEVER EVER FORGIVE YOU!!!
CHIAKI !!!
MIKADO-KUN!!!
MIKADO-KUN!!
TWITCH

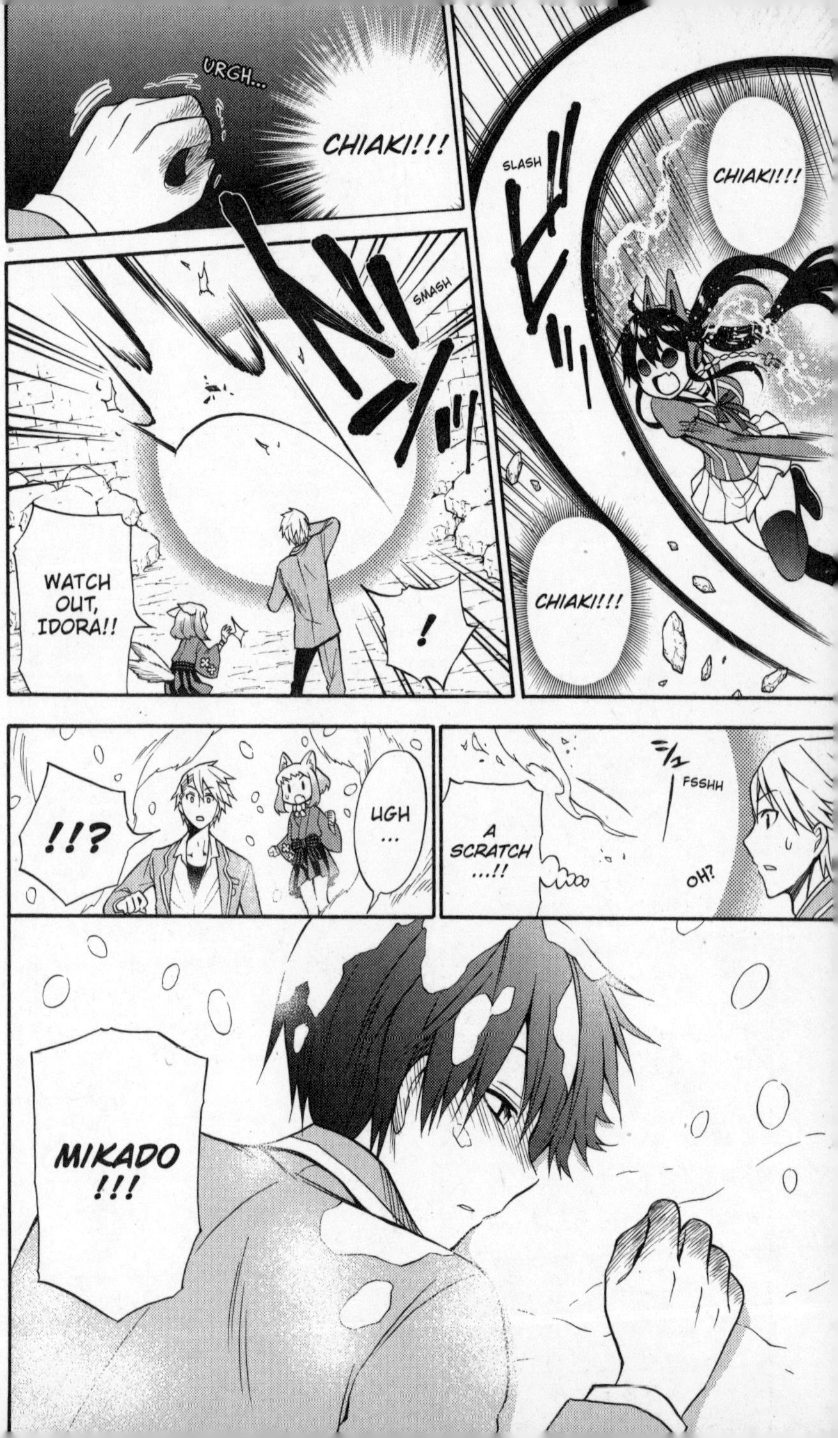
CHIAKI!!!
SLASH
CHIAKI!!!
URGH...
CHIAKI!!!
SMASH
!
WATCH OUT, IDORA!!
FSSHH
OH?
A SCRATCH ...!!
UGH ...
!!?
MIKADO !!!

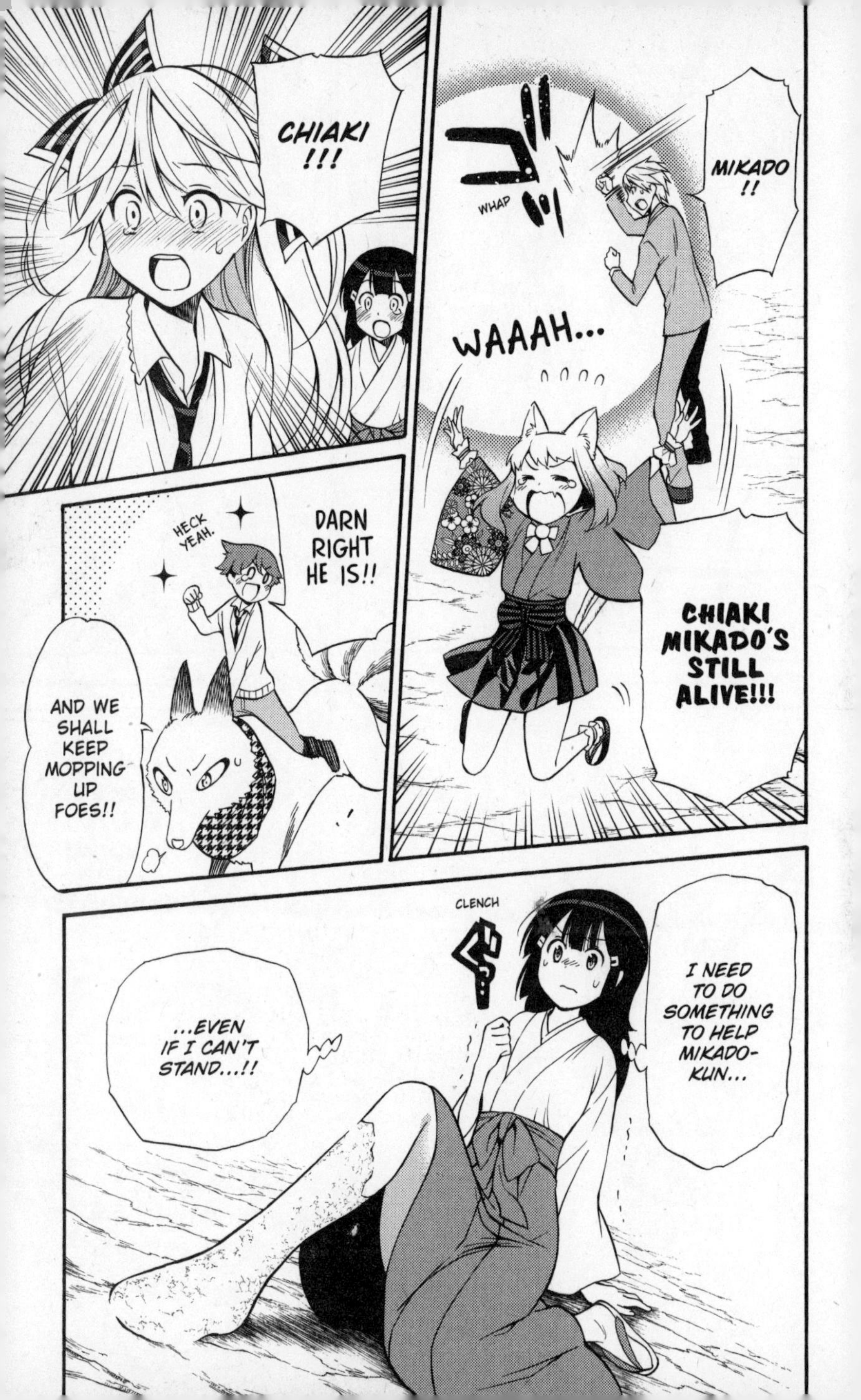
MIKADO!!
WHAP
WAAAH...
CHIAKI MIKADO'S STILL ALIVE!!!
CHIAKI!!!
DARN RIGHT HE IS!!
HECK YEAH.
AND WE SHALL KEEP MOPPING UP FOES!!
I NEED TO DO SOMETHING TO HELP MIKADO-KUN...
CLENCH
...EVEN IF I CAN'T STAND...!!

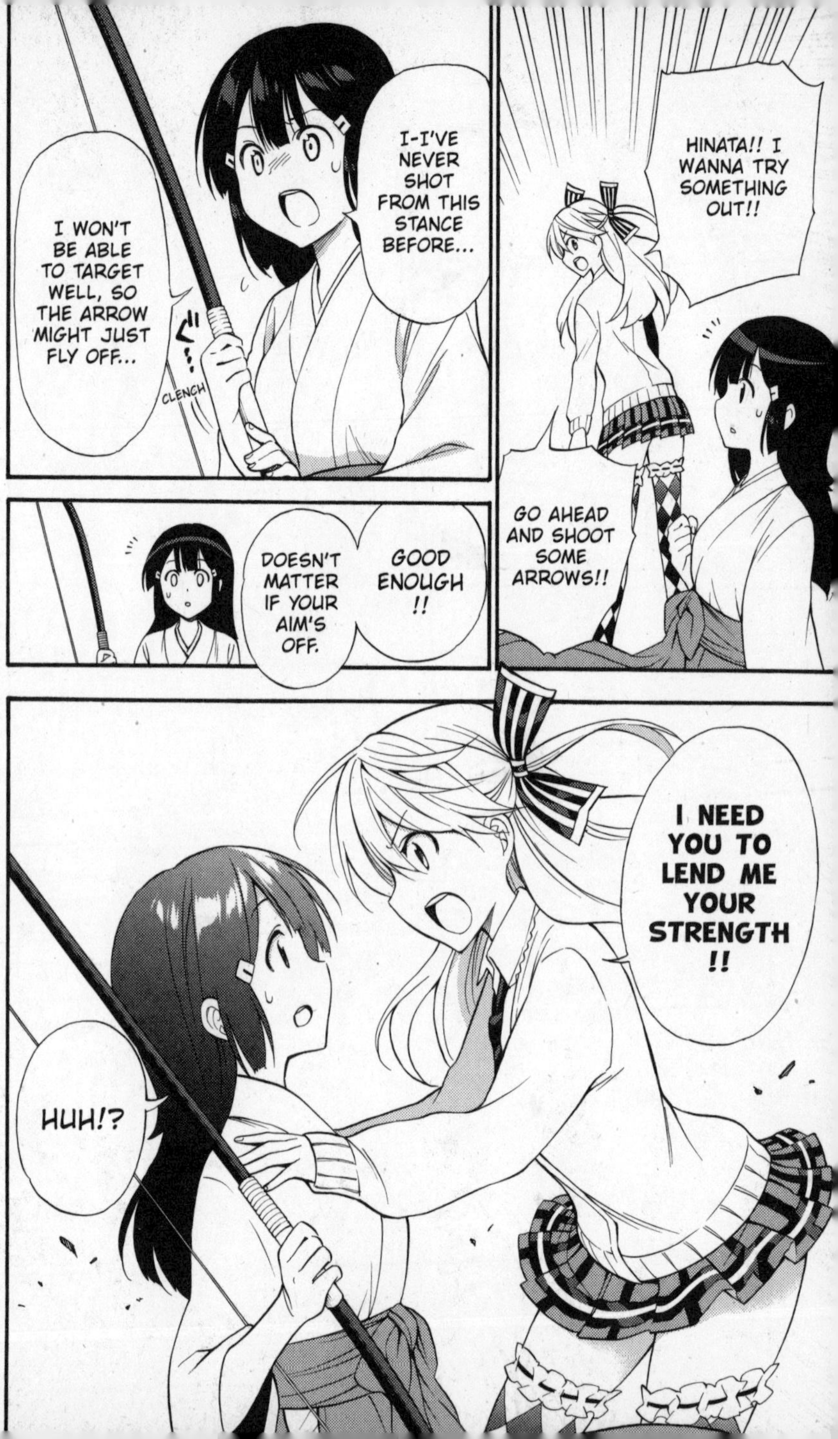
HINATA!! I WANNA TRY SOMETHING OUT!!
GO AHEAD AND SHOOT SOME ARROWS!!
I-I'VE NEVER SHOT FROM THIS STANCE BEFORE...
I WON'T BE ABLE TO TARGET WELL, SO THE ARROW MIGHT JUST FLY OFF...
CLENCH
GOOD ENOUGH!!
DOESN'T MATTER IF YOUR AIM'S OFF.
I NEED YOU TO LEND ME YOUR STRENGTH!!
HUH!?

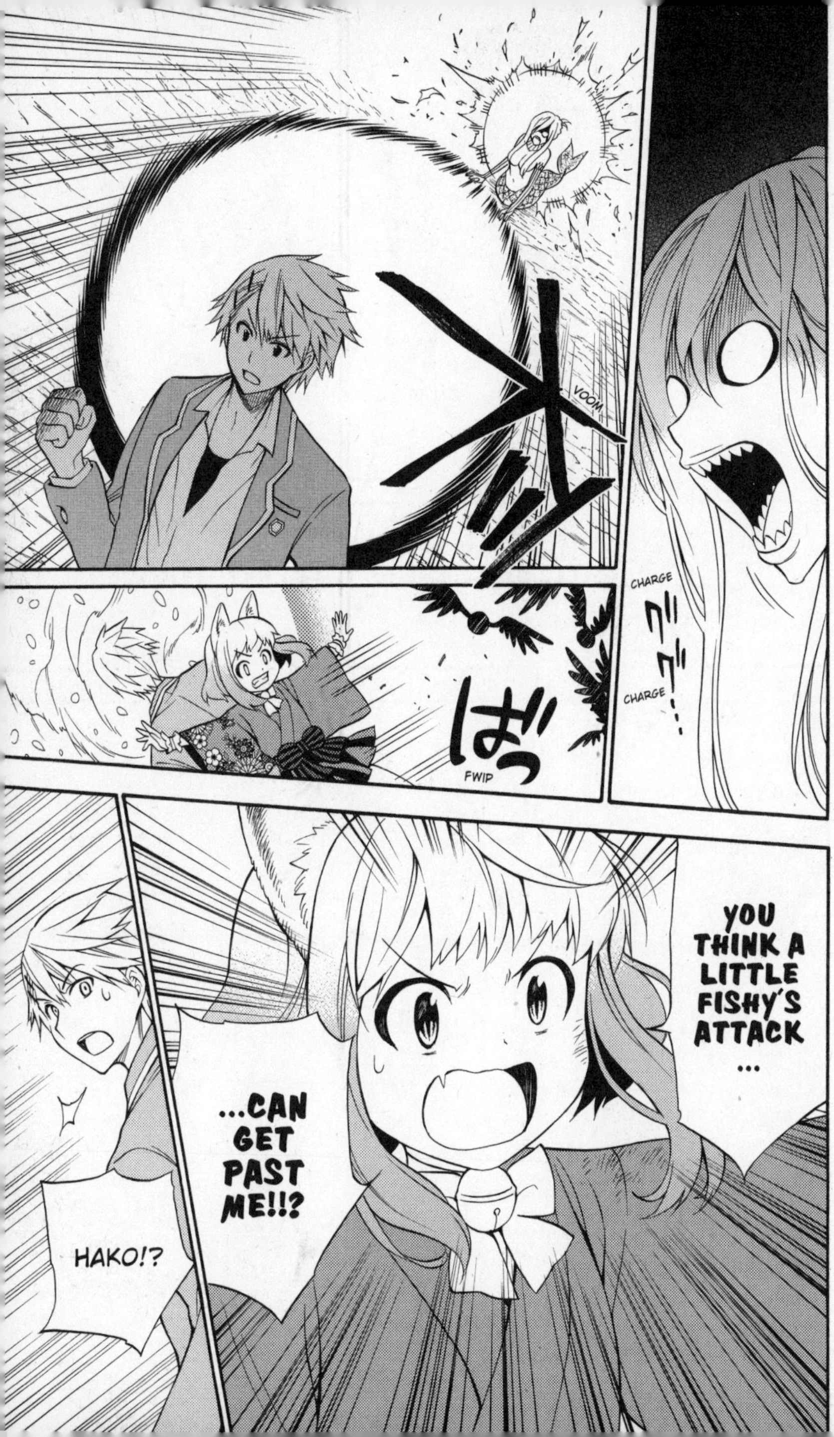
CHARGE
CHARGE
VOOM
ばっ
FWIP
YOU THINK A LITTLE FISHY'S ATTACK ...
...CAN GET PAST ME!!?
HAKO!?

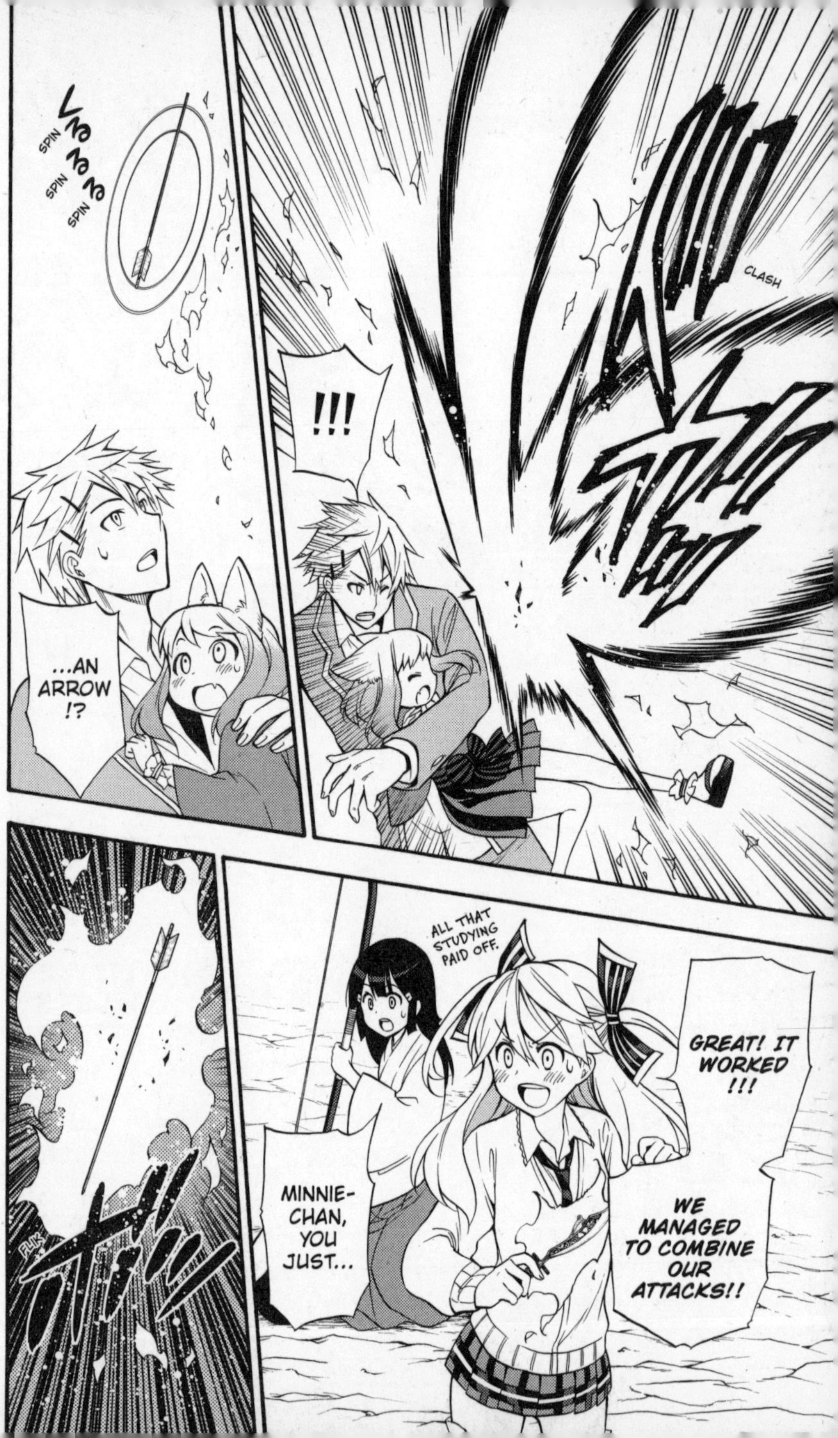
CLASH
!!!
SPIN SPIN SPIN
...AN ARROW!?
GREAT! IT WORKED!!!
ALL THAT STUDYING PAID OFF.
WE MANAGED TO COMBINE OUR ATTACKS!!
MINNIE-CHAN, YOU JUST...
FLIK

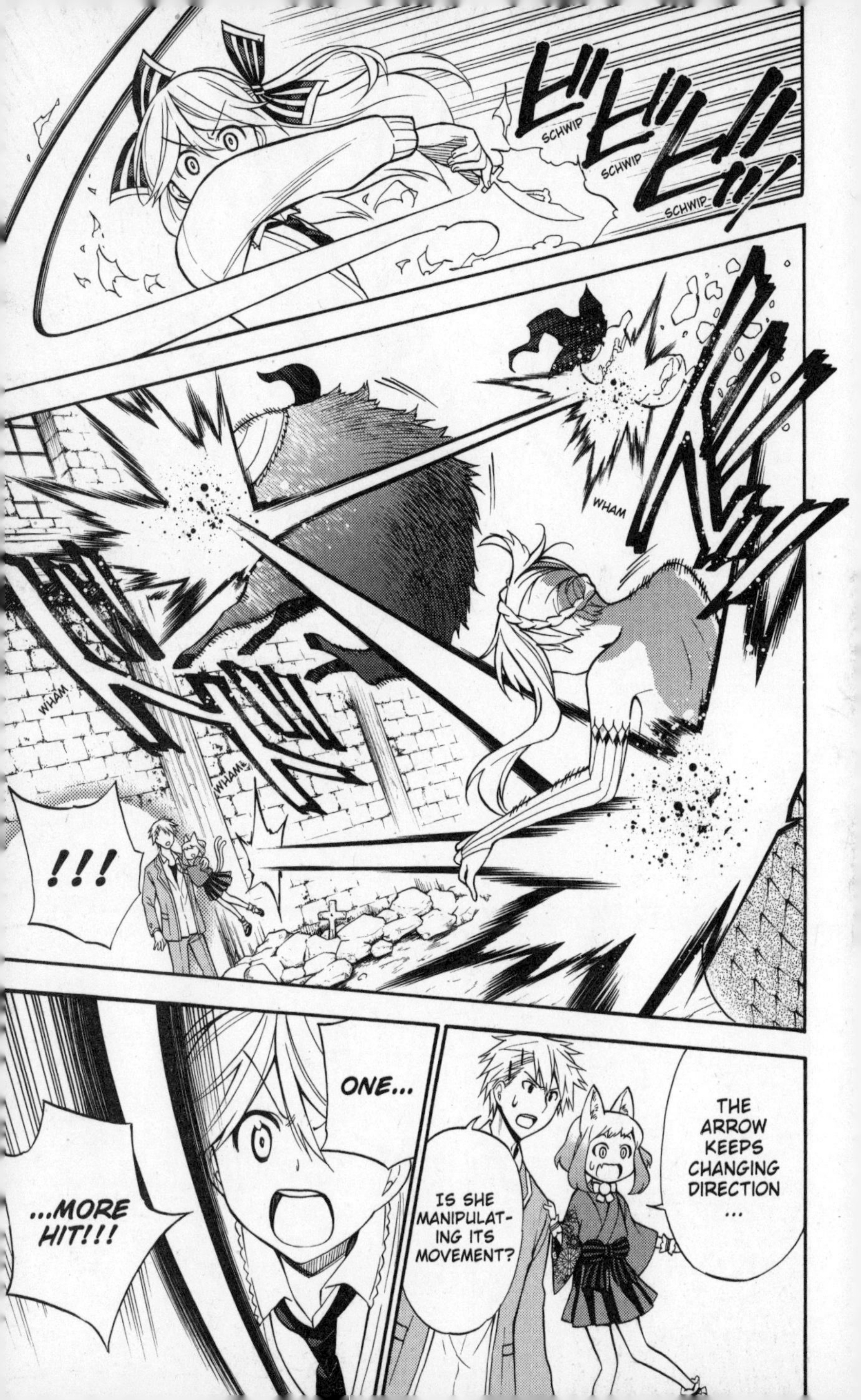
SCHWIP
SCHWIP
SCHWIP
WHAM
WHAM
WHAM
!!!
THE ARROW KEEPS CHANGING DIRECTION ...
IS SHE MANIPULATING ITS MOVEMENT?
ONE...
...MORE HIT!!!

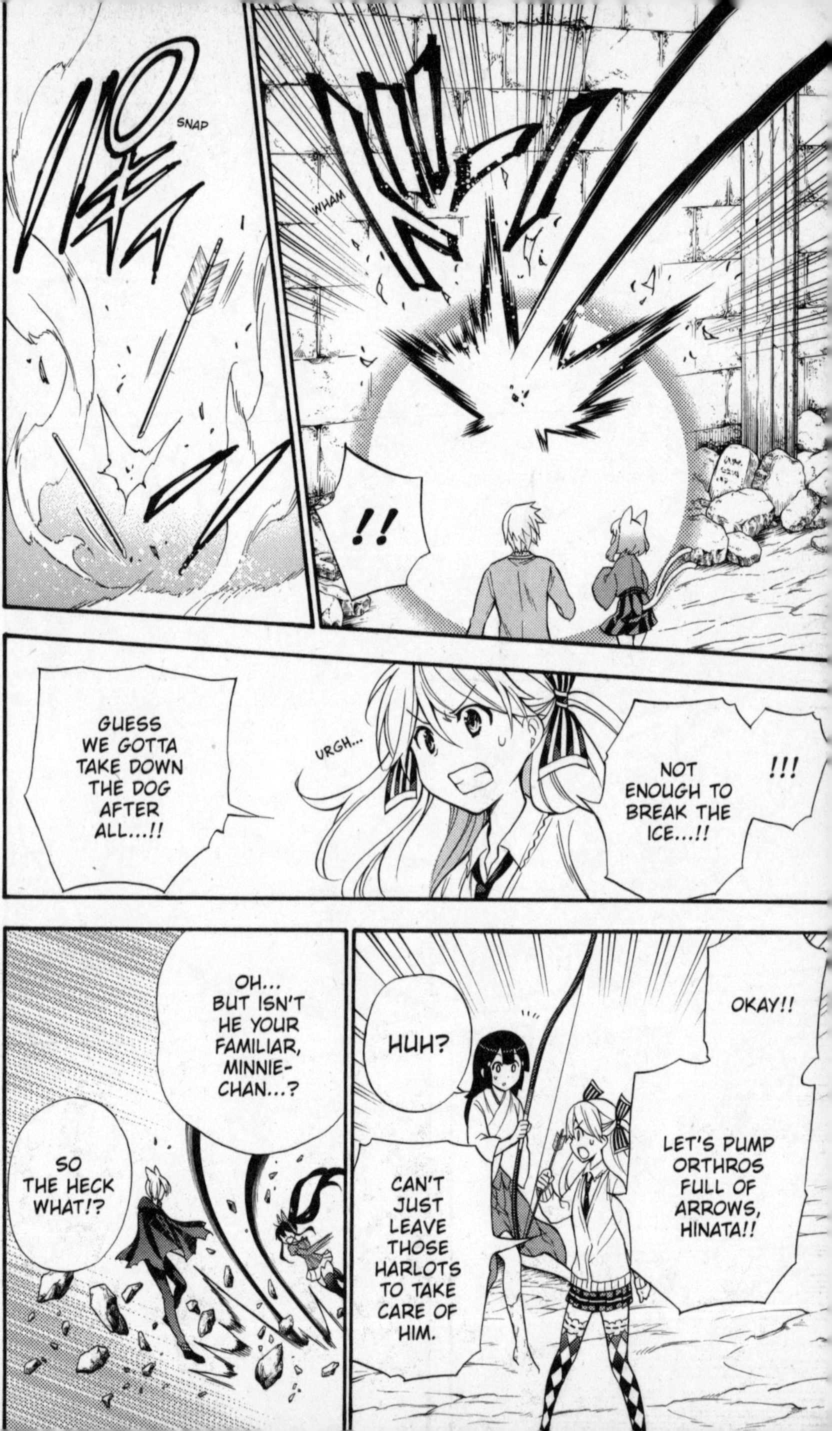
WHAM
!!
SNAP
!!!
NOT ENOUGH TO BREAK THE ICE...!!
URGH...
GUESS WE GOTTA TAKE DOWN THE DOG AFTER ALL...!!
OKAY!!
LET'S PUMP ORTHROS FULL OF ARROWS, HINATA!!
HUH?
CAN'T JUST LEAVE THOSE HARLOTS TO TAKE CARE OF HIM.
OH... BUT ISN'T HE YOUR FAMILIAR, MINNIE-CHAN...?
SO THE HECK WHAT!?

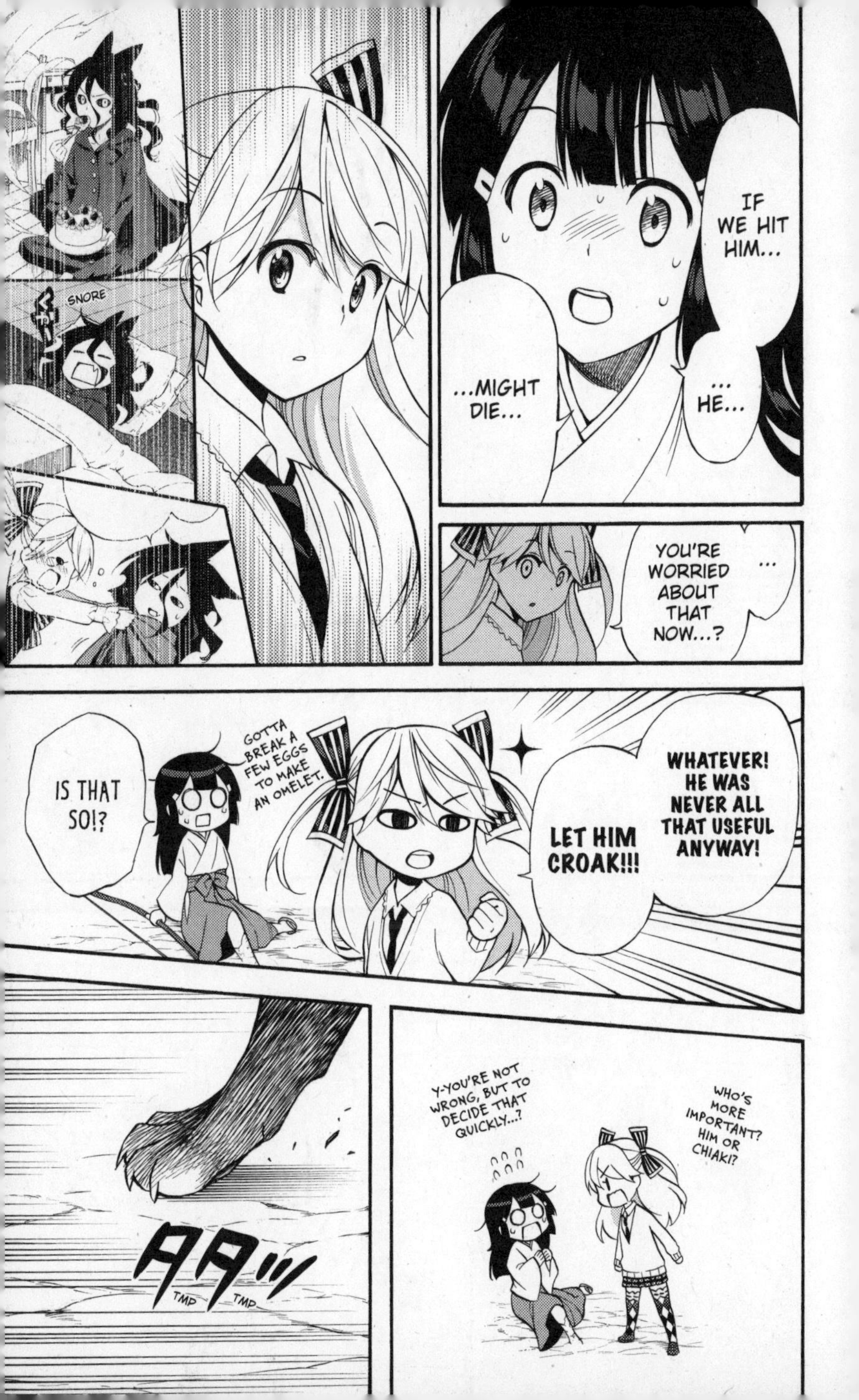
IF WE HIT HIM...
... HE...
...MIGHT DIE...
YOU'RE WORRIED ABOUT THAT NOW...?
...
SNORE
WHATEVER! HE WAS NEVER ALL THAT USEFUL ANYWAY!
LET HIM CROAK!!!
GOTTA BREAK A FEW EGGS TO MAKE AN OMELET.
IS THAT SO!?
WHO'S MORE IMPORTANT? HIM OR CHIAKI?
Y-YOU'RE NOT WRONG, BUT TO DECIDE THAT QUICKLY...?
タタッ
TMP TMP

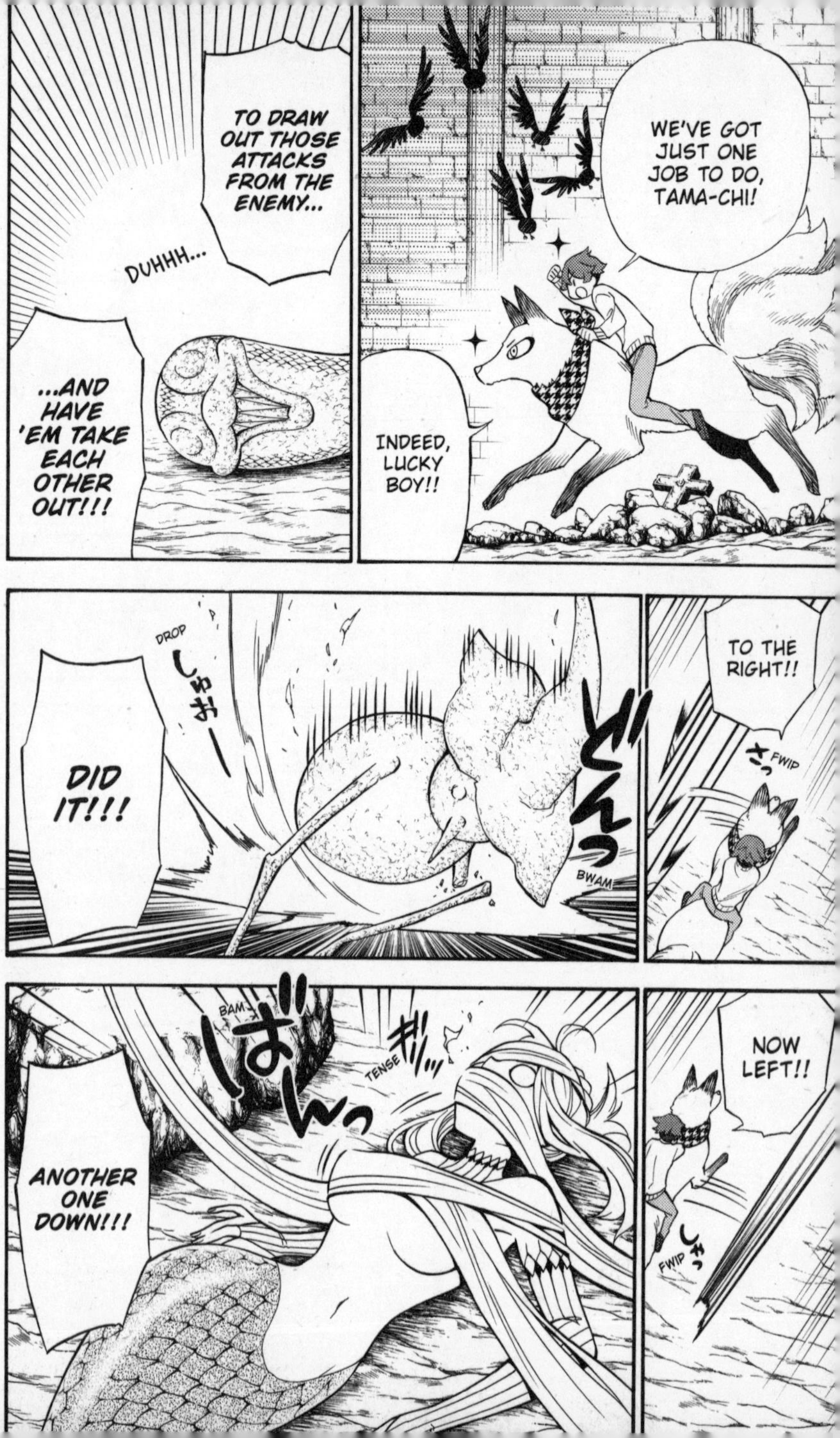
WE'VE GOT JUST ONE JOB TO DO, TAMA-CHI!
INDEED, LUCKY BOY!!
TO DRAW OUT THOSE ATTACKS FROM THE ENEMY...
DUHHH...
...AND HAVE 'EM TAKE EACH OTHER OUT!!!
TO THE RIGHT!!
さっ
FWIP
どんっ
BWAM
しゅおー
DROP
DID IT!!!
NOW LEFT!!
しゅっ
FWIP
ギリッ
TENSE
ばんっ
BAM
ANOTHER ONE DOWN!!!

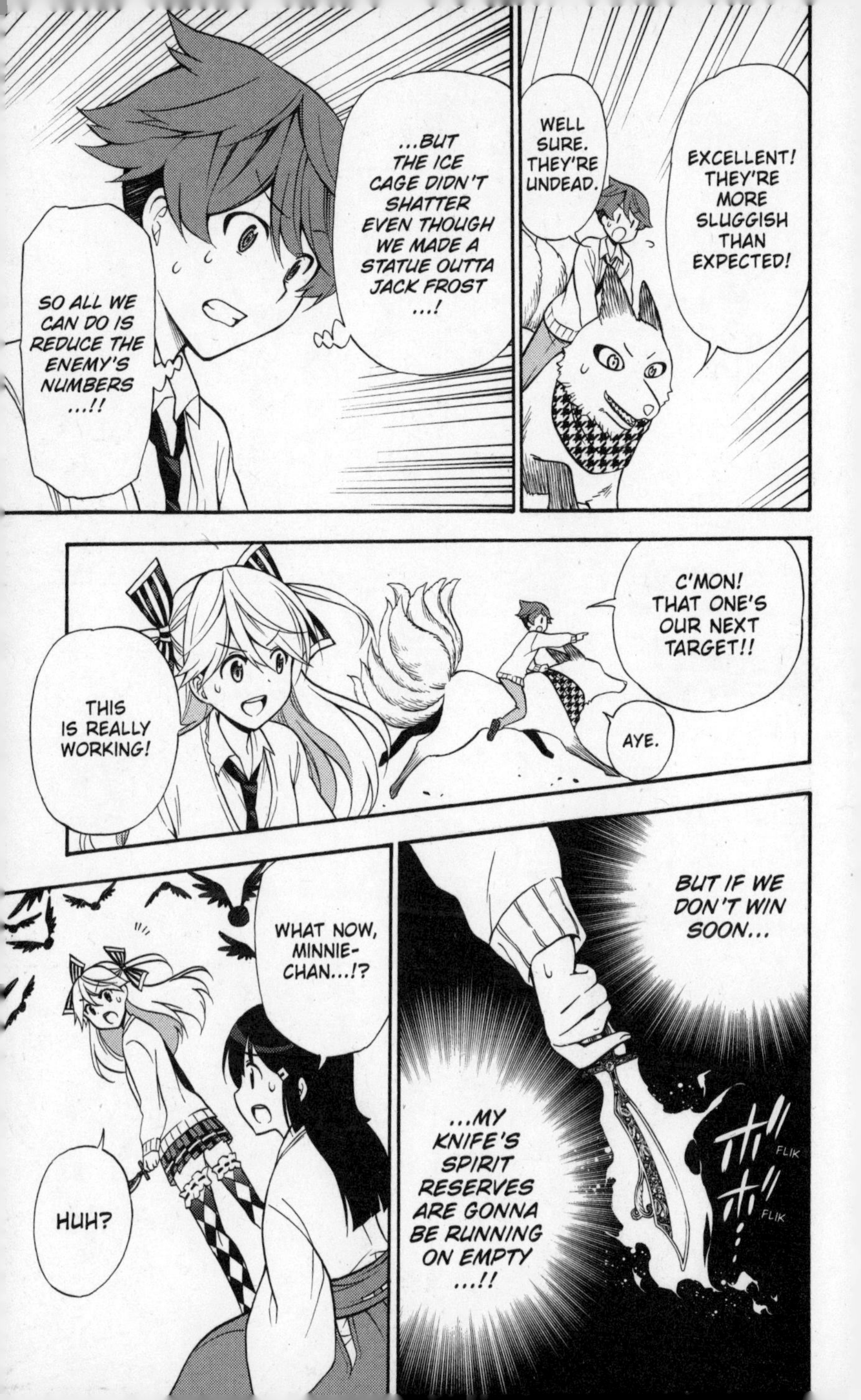
EXCELLENT! THEY'RE MORE SLUGGISH THAN EXPECTED!
WELL SURE. THEY'RE UNDEAD.
...BUT THE ICE CAGE DIDN'T SHATTER EVEN THOUGH WE MADE A STATUE OUTTA JACK FROST ...!
SO ALL WE CAN DO IS REDUCE THE ENEMY'S NUMBERS ...!!
C'MON! THAT ONE'S OUR NEXT TARGET!!
AYE.
THIS IS REALLY WORKING!
BUT IF WE DON'T WIN SOON...
...MY KNIFE'S SPIRIT RESERVES ARE GONNA BE RUNNING ON EMPTY ...!!
FLIK
FLIK
WHAT NOW, MINNIE-CHAN...!?
HUH?

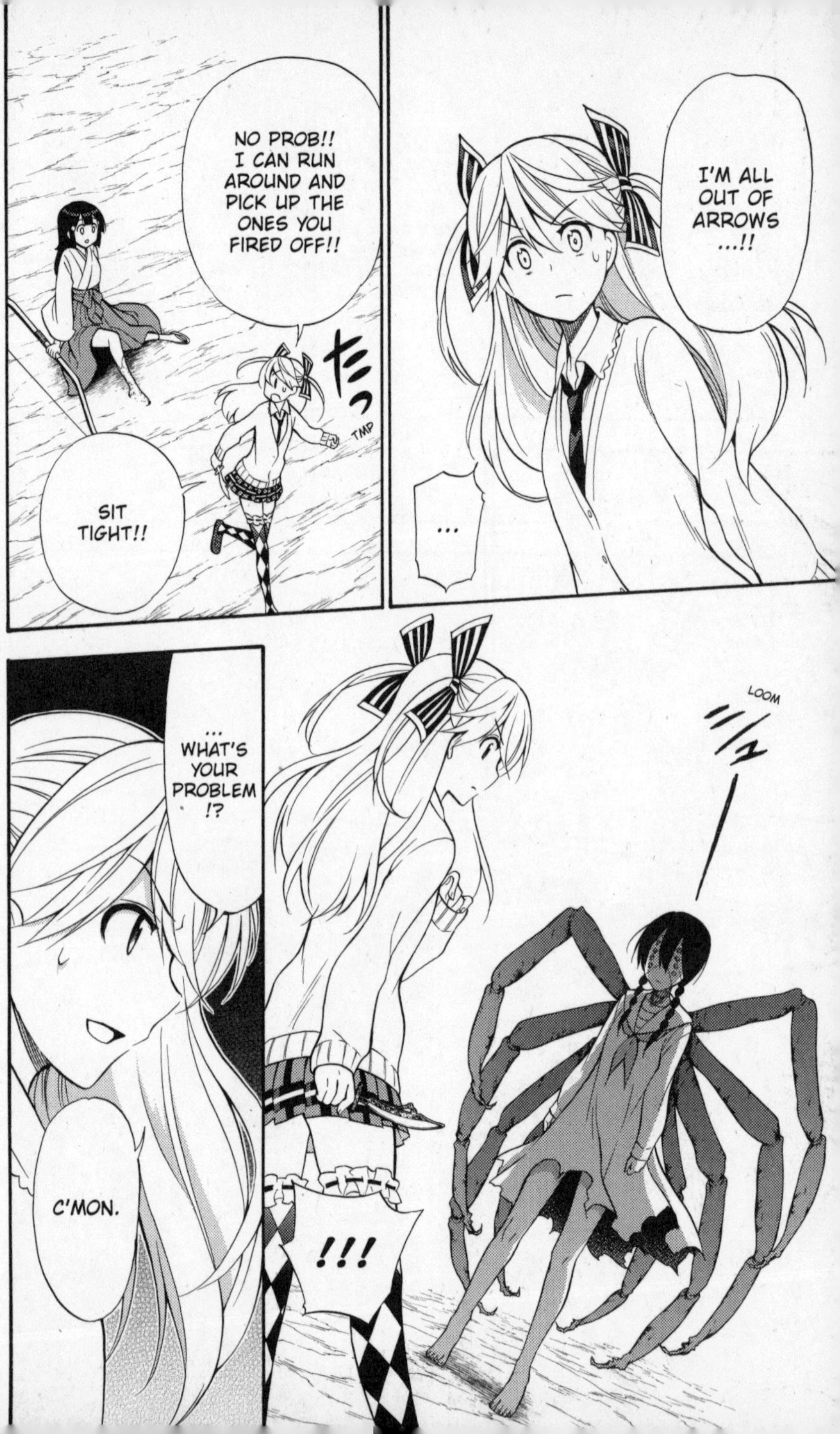
I'M ALL OUT OF ARROWS ...!!
...
NO PROB!! I CAN RUN AROUND AND PICK UP THE ONES YOU FIRED OFF!!
TMP
SIT TIGHT!!
LOOM
!!!
... WHAT'S YOUR PROBLEM !?
C'MON.

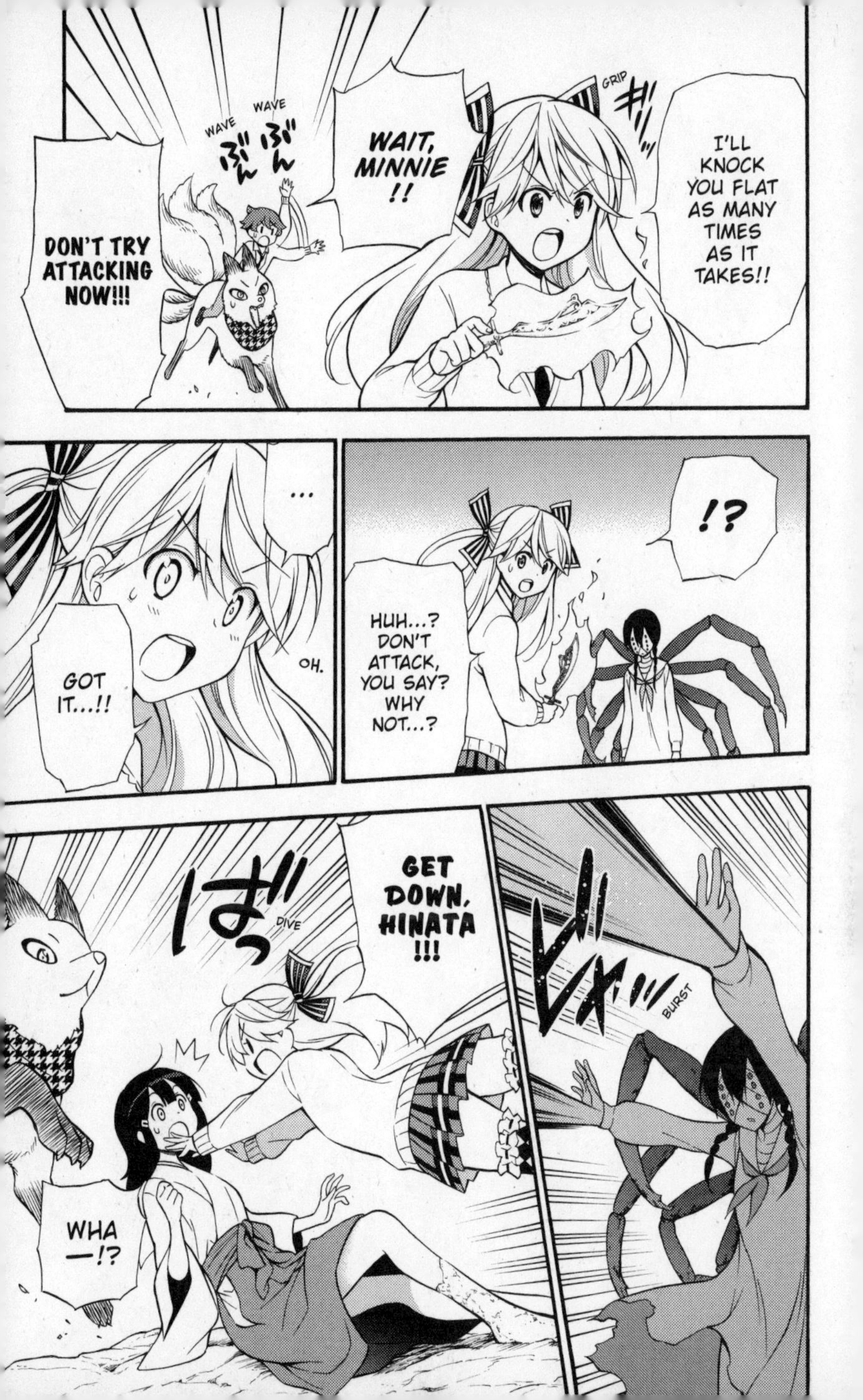
I'LL KNOCK YOU FLAT AS MANY TIMES AS IT TAKES!!
GRIP
WAIT, MINNIE!!
WAVE WAVE
ぶんぶん
DON'T TRY ATTACKING NOW!!!
!?
HUH...? DON'T ATTACK, YOU SAY? WHY NOT...?
...
OH.
GOT IT...!!
BURST
GET DOWN, HINATA!!!
ばっ
DIVE
WHA—!?

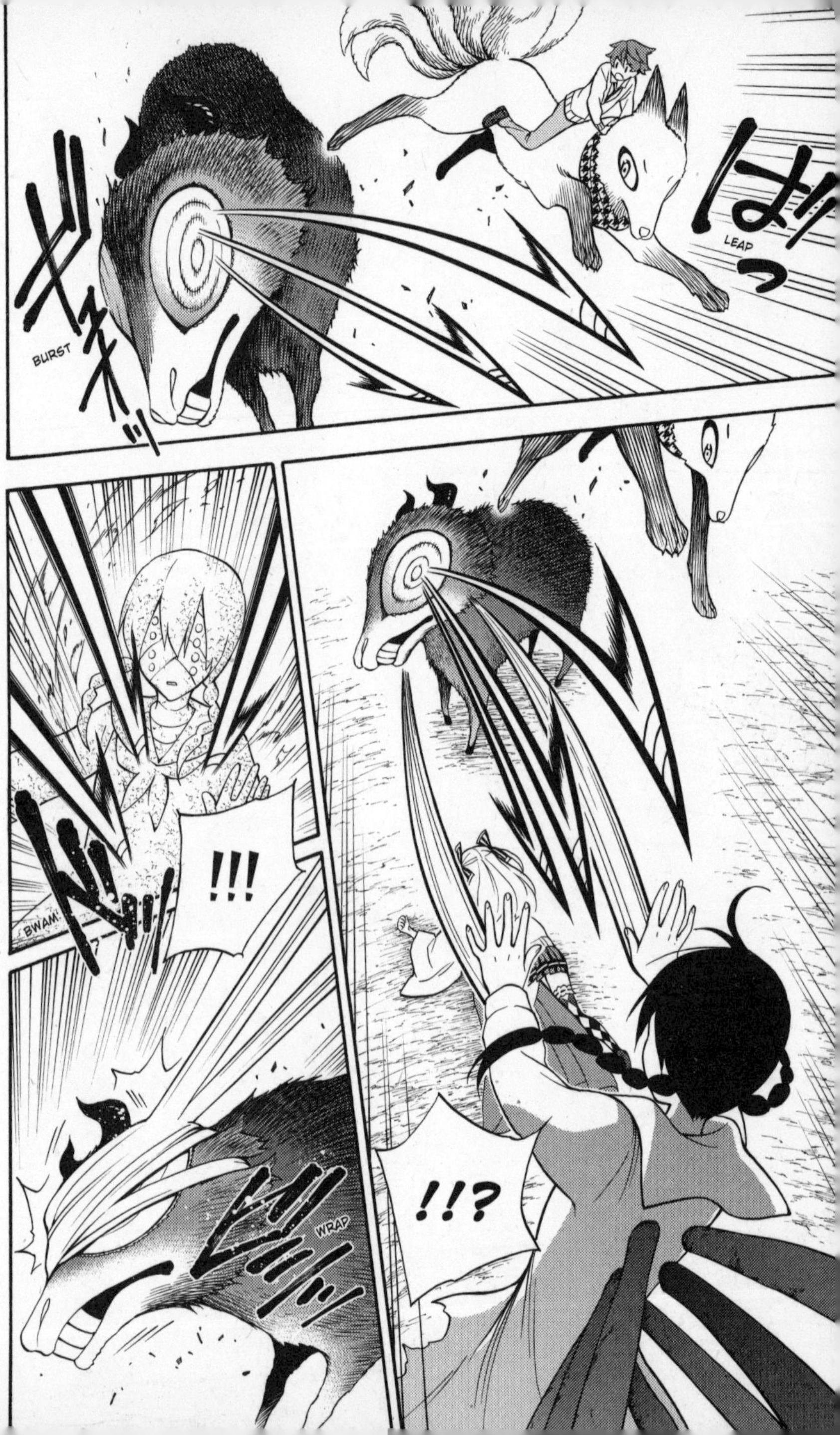
はっ
LEAP
BURST
!!?
!!!
BWAM
WRAP

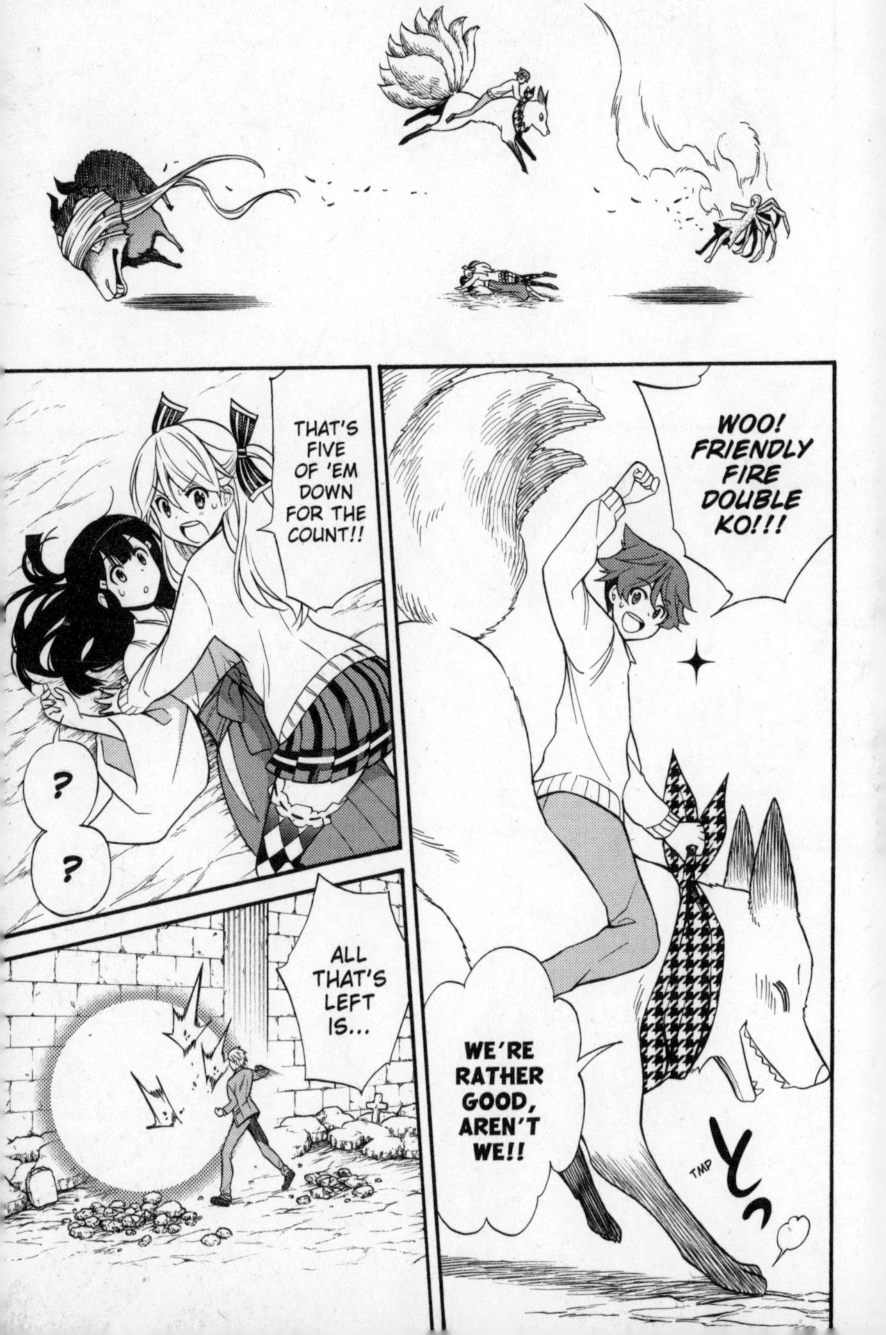
WOO! FRIENDLY FIRE DOUBLE KO!!!
WE'RE RATHER GOOD, AREN'T WE!!
TMP
THAT'S FIVE OF 'EM DOWN FOR THE COUNT!!
?
?
ALL THAT'S LEFT IS...

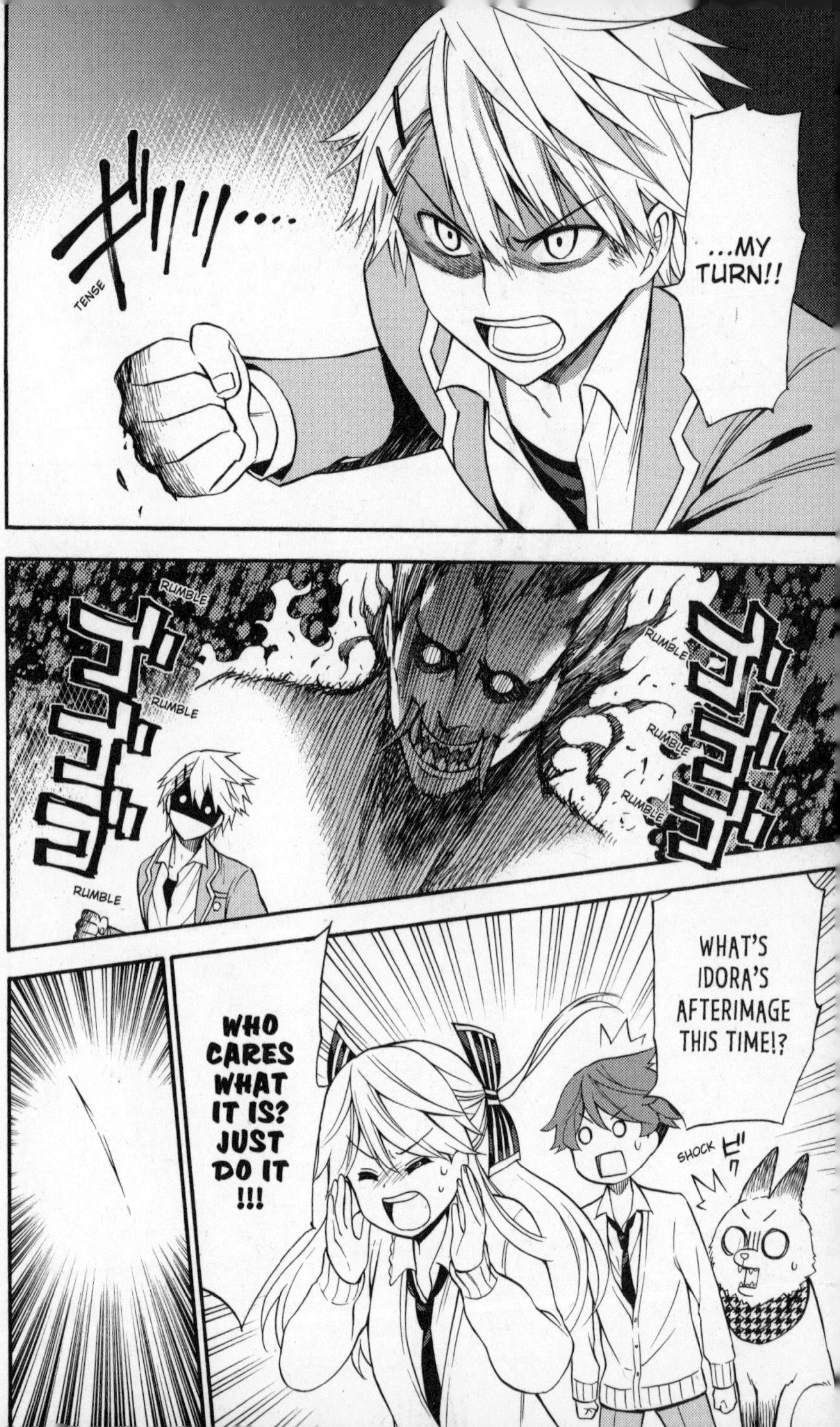
TENSE
...MY TURN!!
RUMBLE
RUMBLE
RUMBLE
RUMBLE
RUMBLE
RUMBLE
WHAT'S IDORA'S AFTERIMAGE THIS TIME!?
SHOCK
WHO CARES WHAT IT IS? JUST DO IT!!!

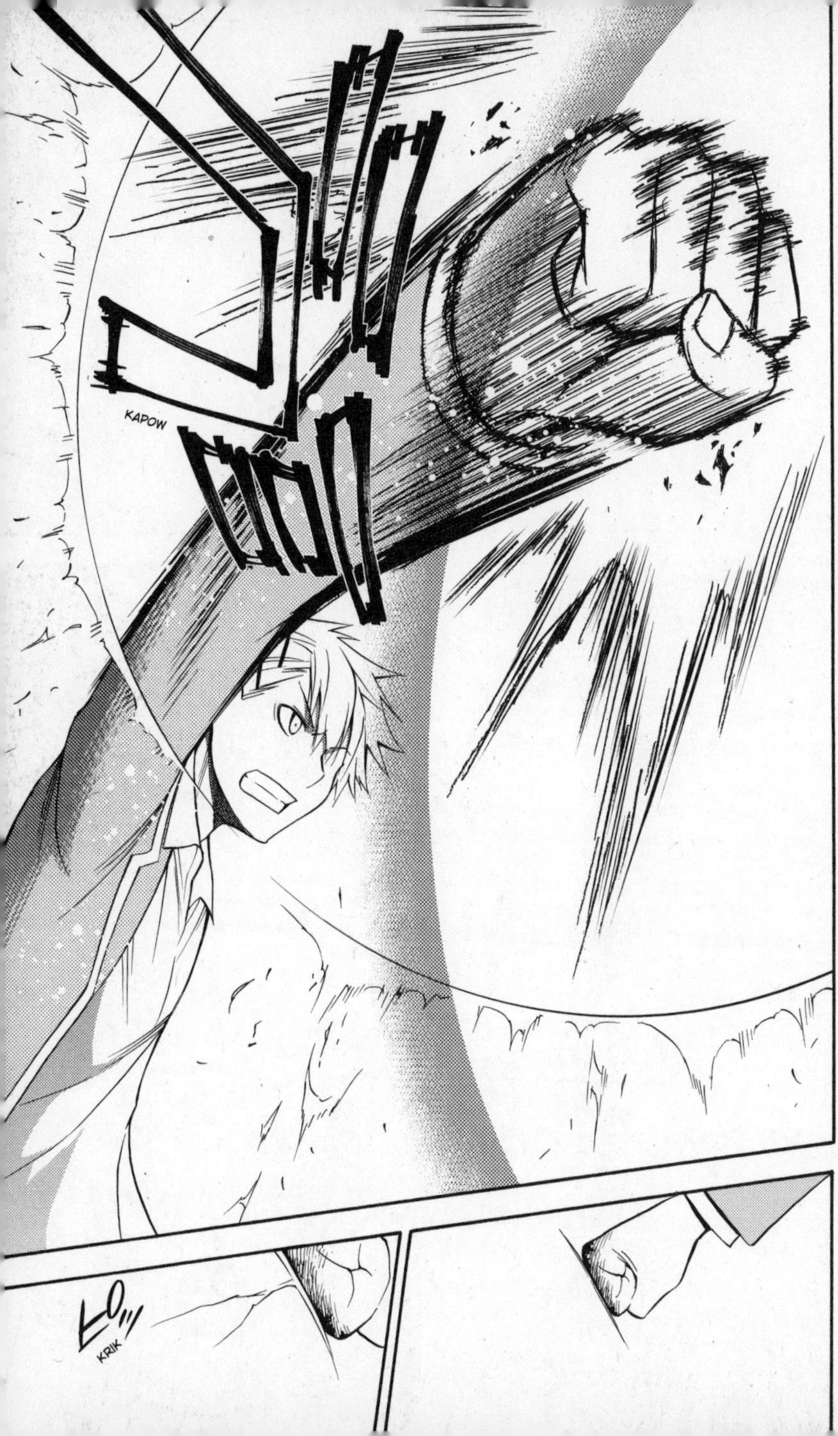
KAPOW
KRIK

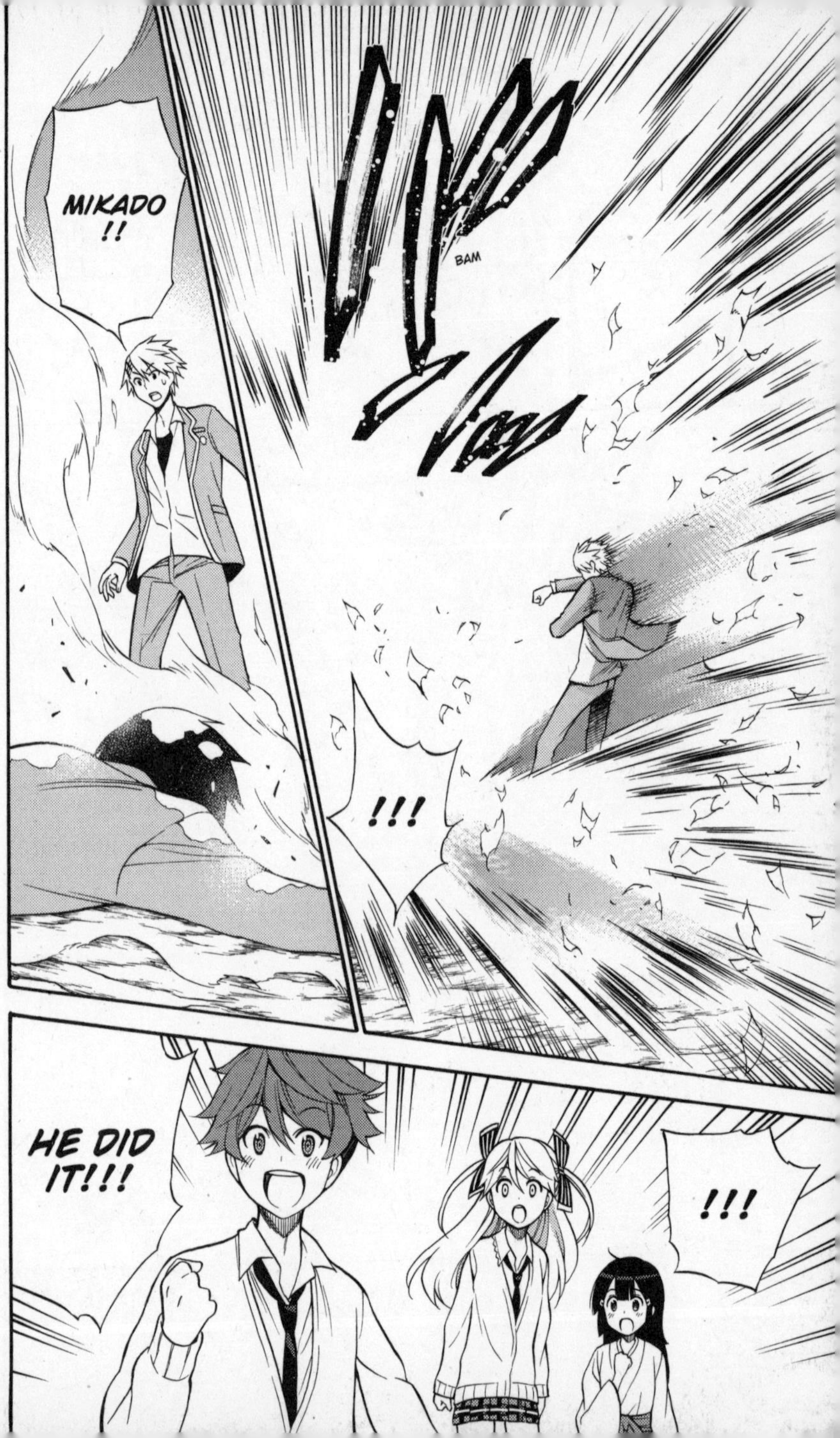
BAM
!!!
MIKADO !!
!!!
HE DID IT!!!

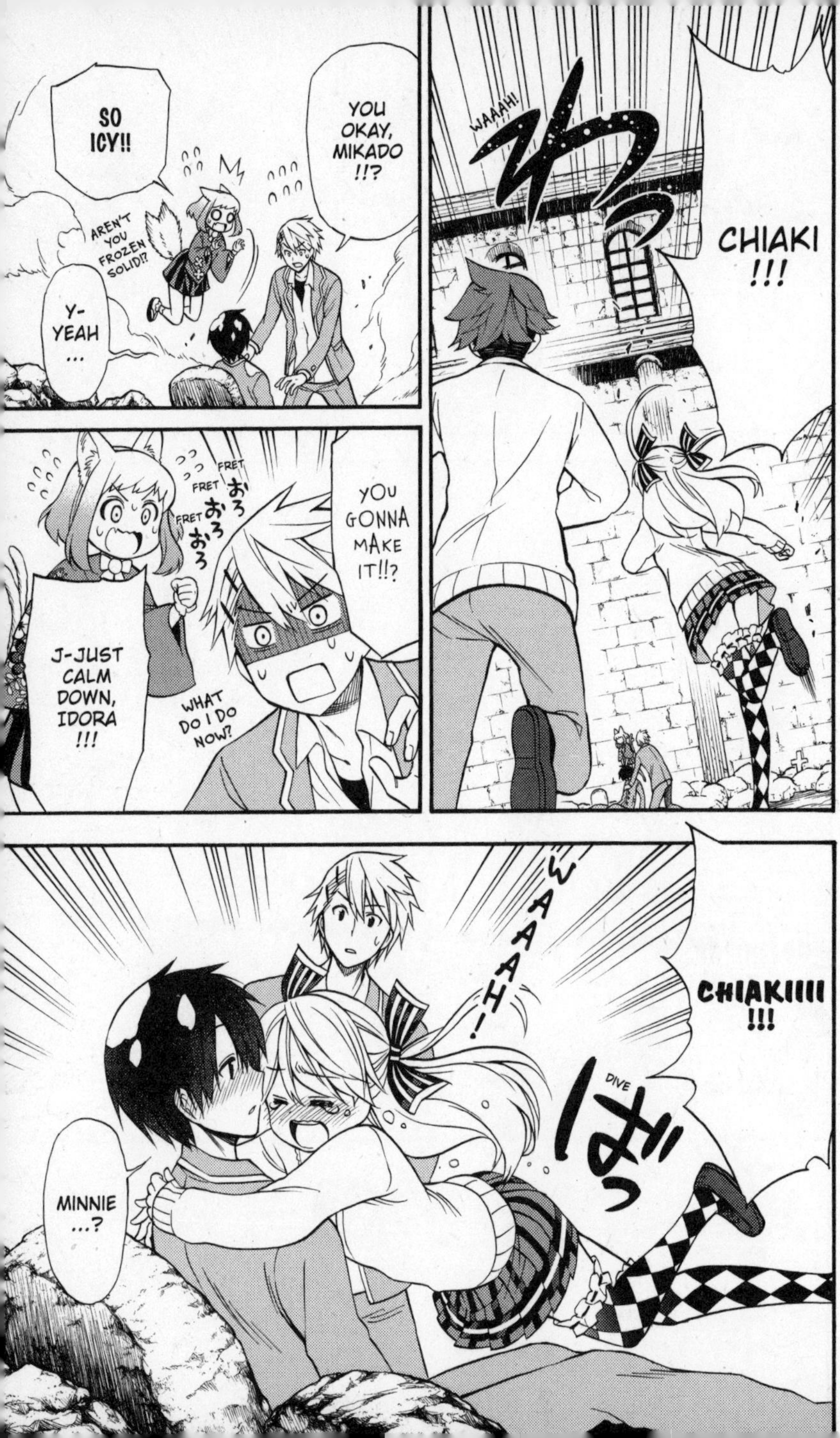
WAAAH!
わっ
CHIAKI!!!
YOU OKAY, MIKADO!!?
SO ICY!!
AREN'T YOU FROZEN SOLID!?
Y-YEAH...
YOU GONNA MAKE IT!!?
FRET FRET FRET
おろおろおろ
WHAT DO I DO NOW?
J-JUST CALM DOWN, IDORA!!!
CHIAKIIIII!!!
WAAAAAH!
DIVE
ばっ
MINNIE...?

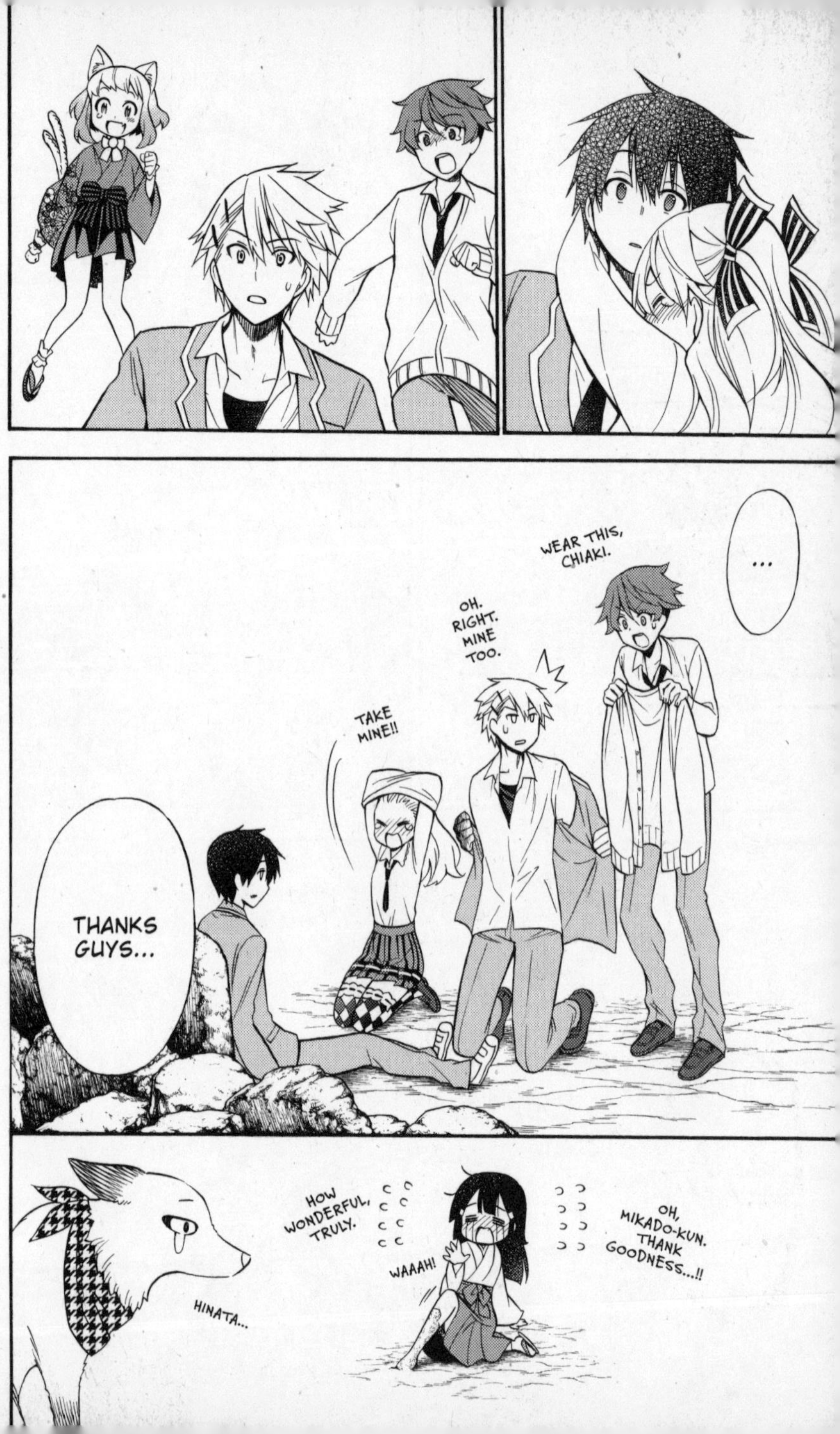
...
WEAR THIS, CHIAKI.
OH. RIGHT. MINE TOO.
TAKE MINE!!
THANKS GUYS...
OH, MIKADO-KUN. THANK GOODNESS...!!
WAAAH!
HOW WONDERFUL, TRULY.
HINATA...

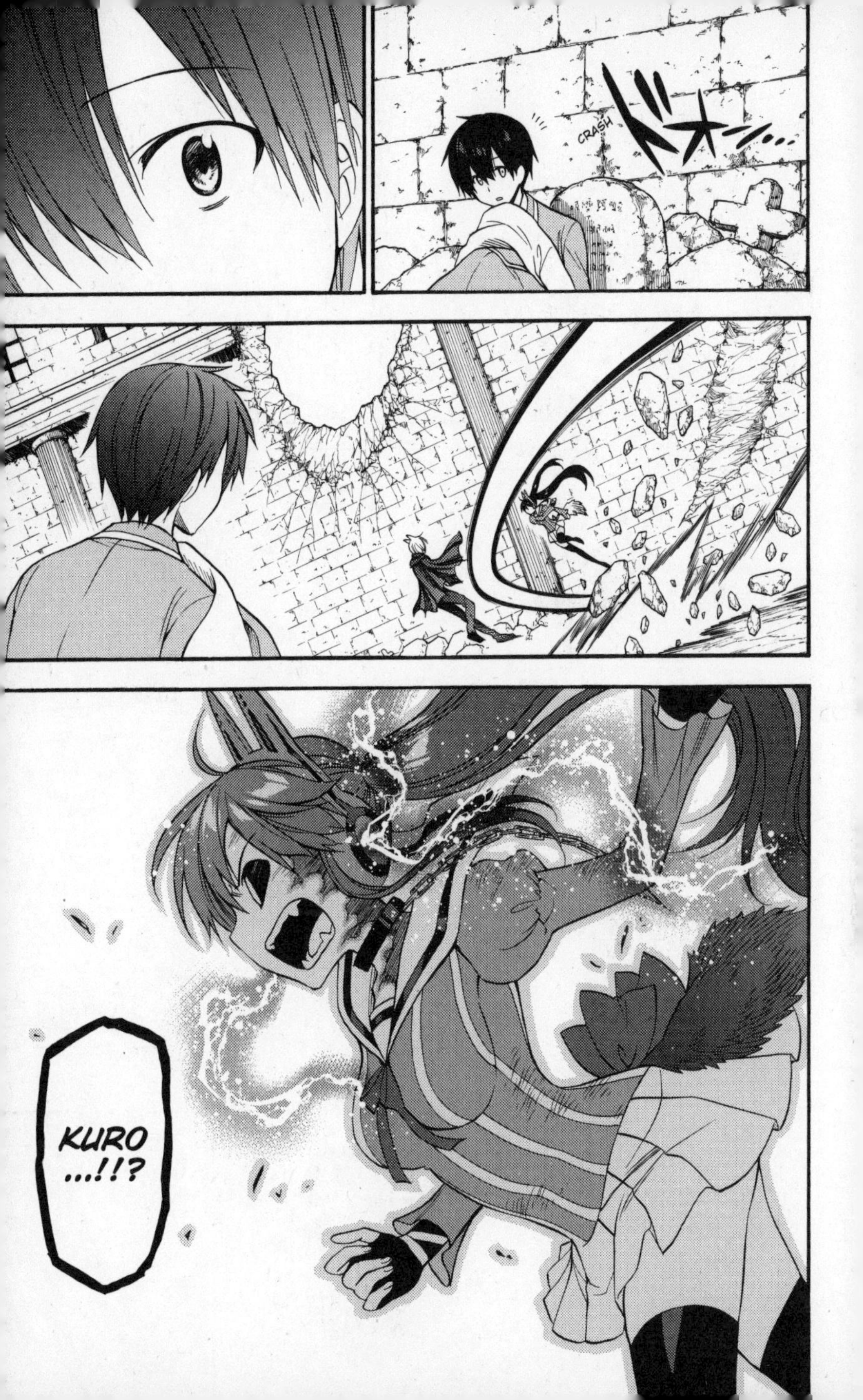
ドオン…
CRASH
KURO ...!!?

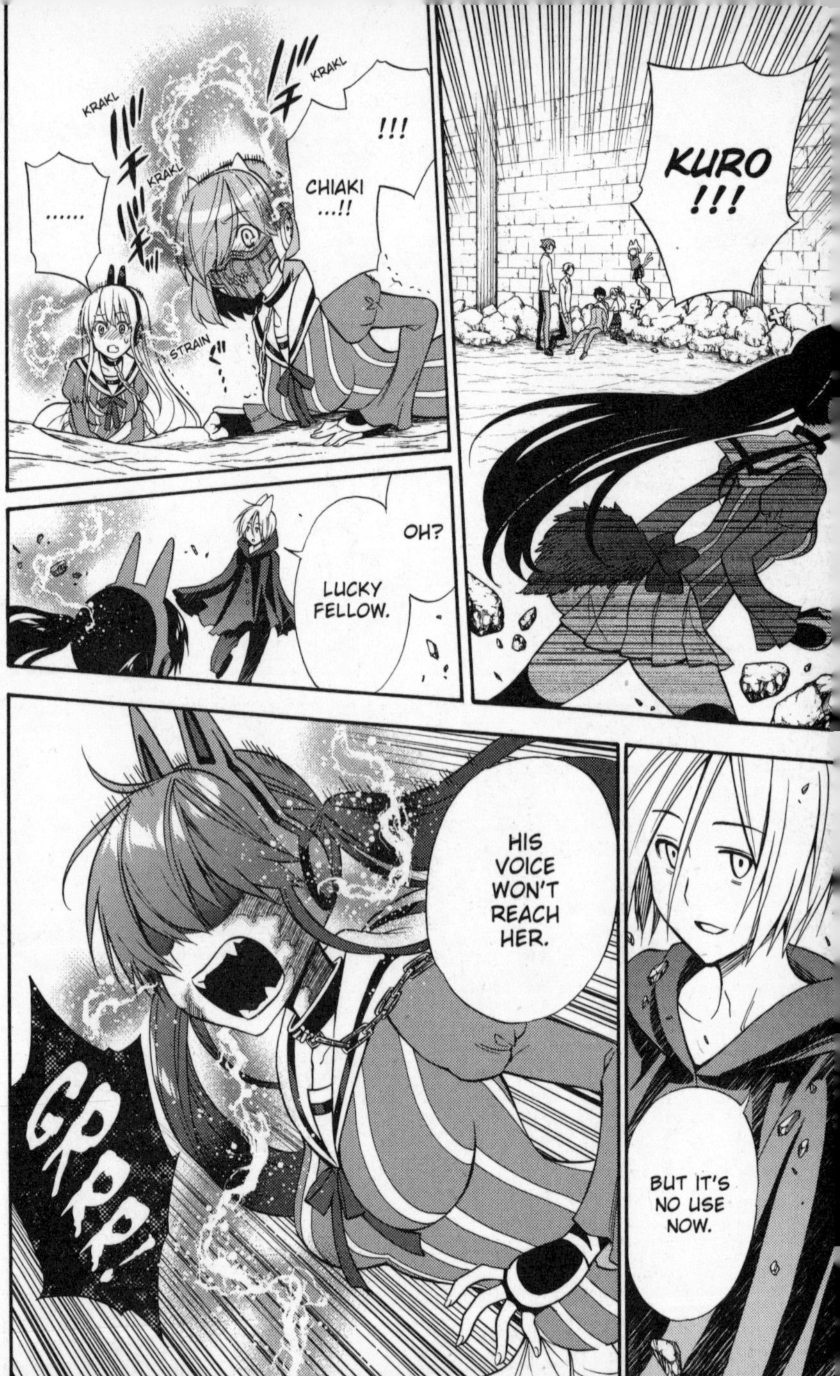
KURO !!!
KRAKL
!!!
CHIAKI ...!!
KRAKL
KRAKL
......
STRAIN
OH?
LUCKY FELLOW.
BUT IT'S NO USE NOW.
HIS VOICE WON'T REACH HER.
GRRR!

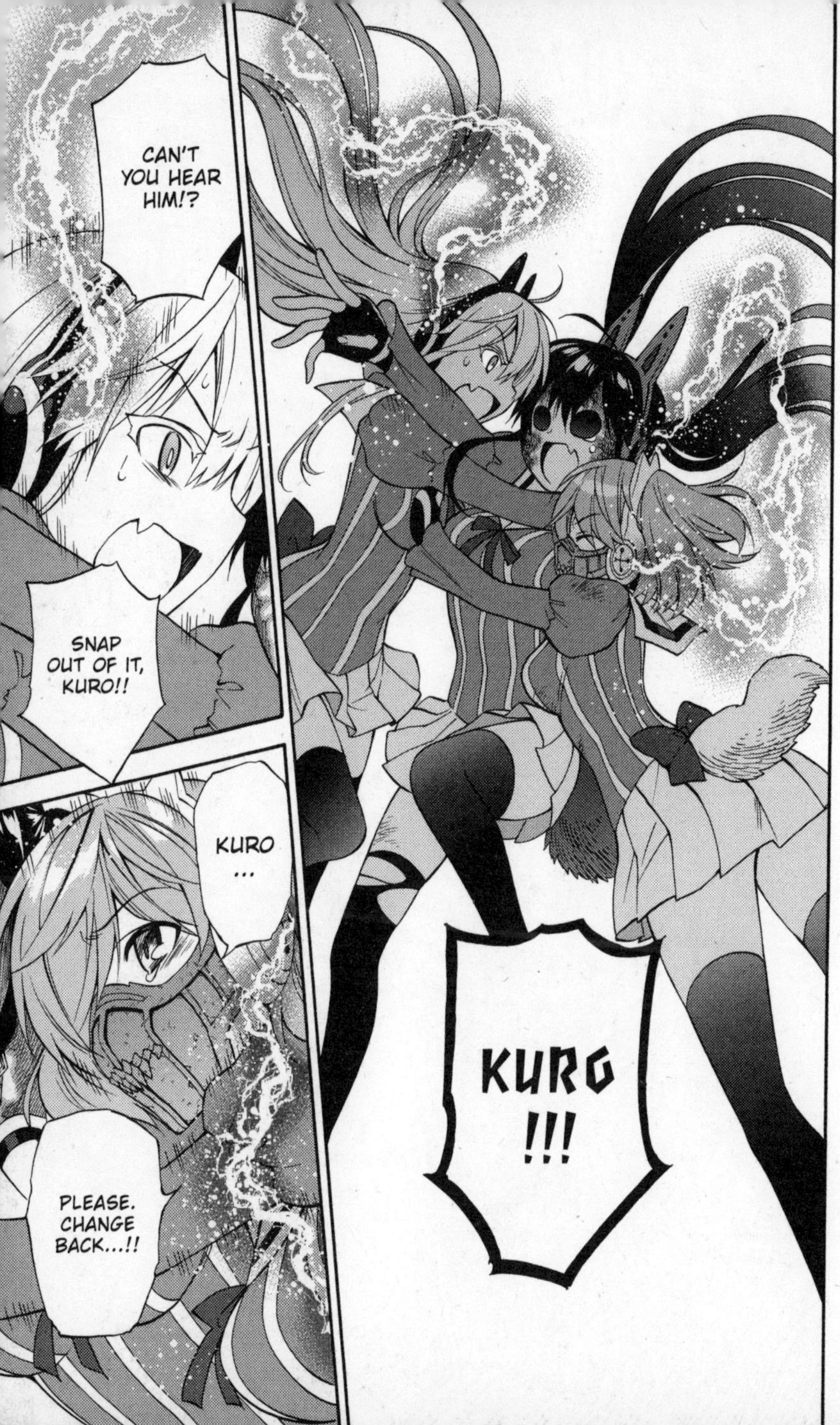
KURO !!!
CAN'T YOU HEAR HIM!?
SNAP OUT OF IT, KURO!!
KURO ...
PLEASE. CHANGE BACK...!!

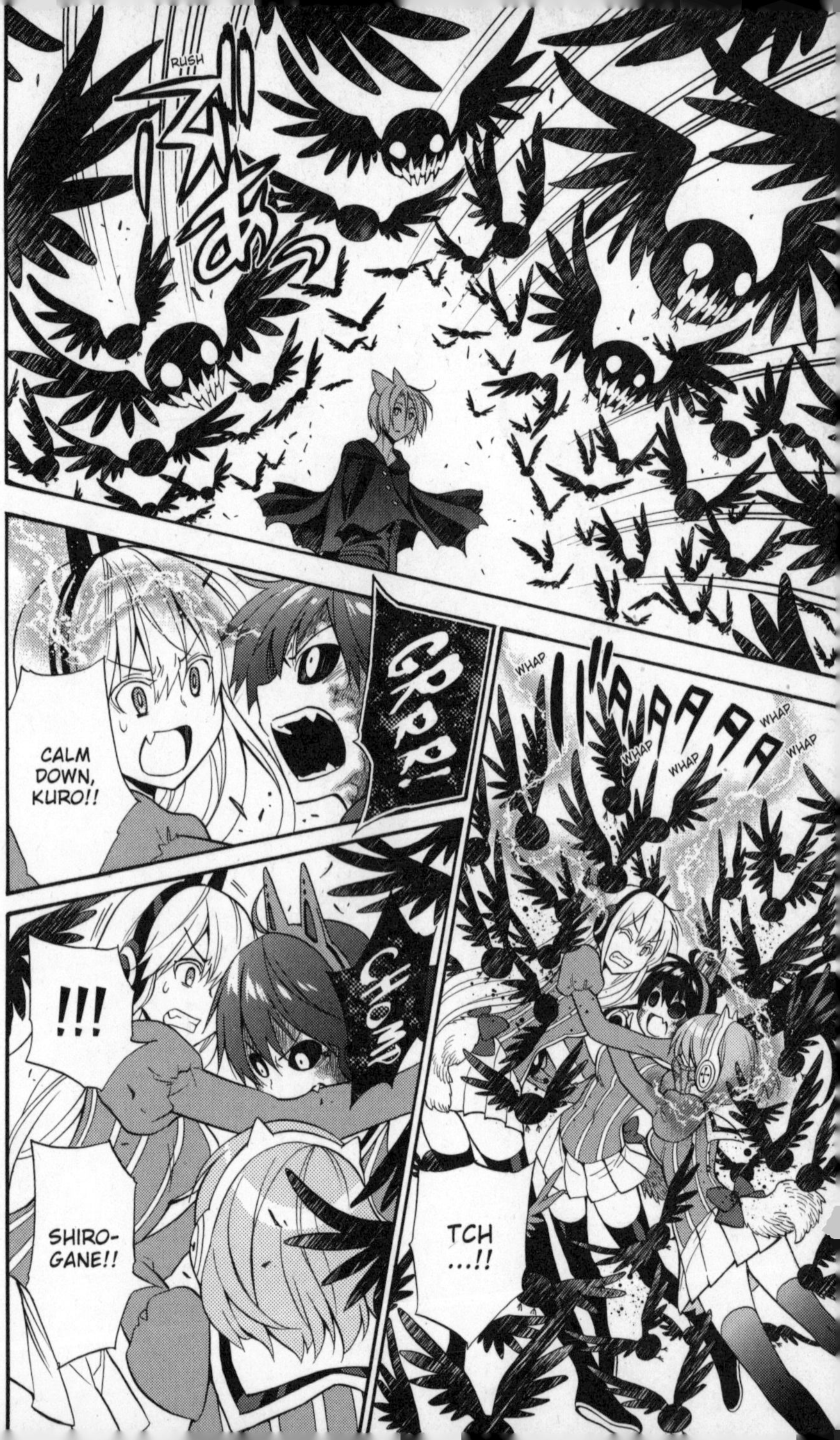
RUSH
WHAP
AAAAA
WHAP
WHAP
WHAP
WHAP
TCH ...!!
CALM DOWN, KURO!!
GRRR!
!!!
CHOMP
SHIRO-GANE!!

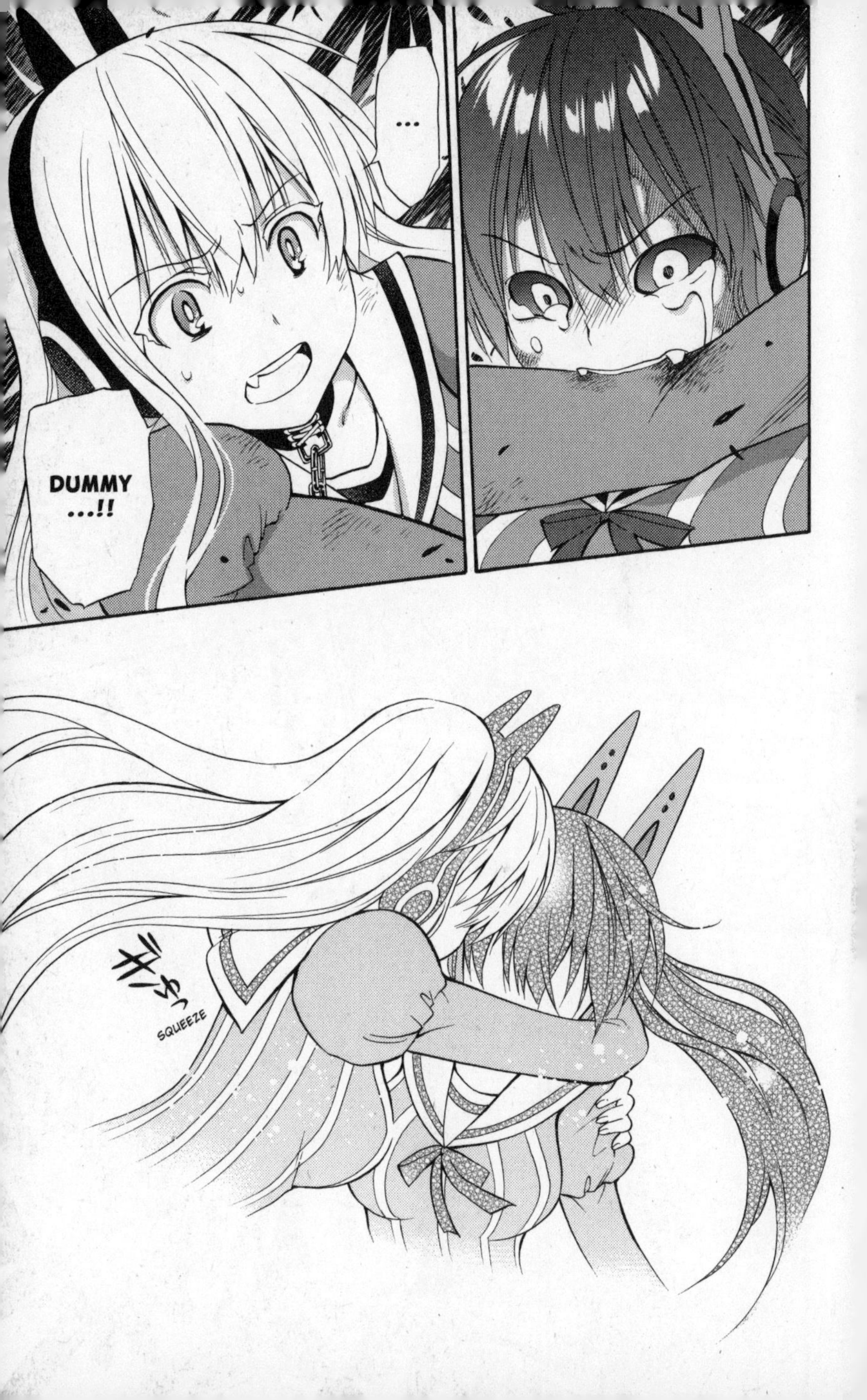
...
DUMMY ...!!
ギゅっ
SQUEEZE

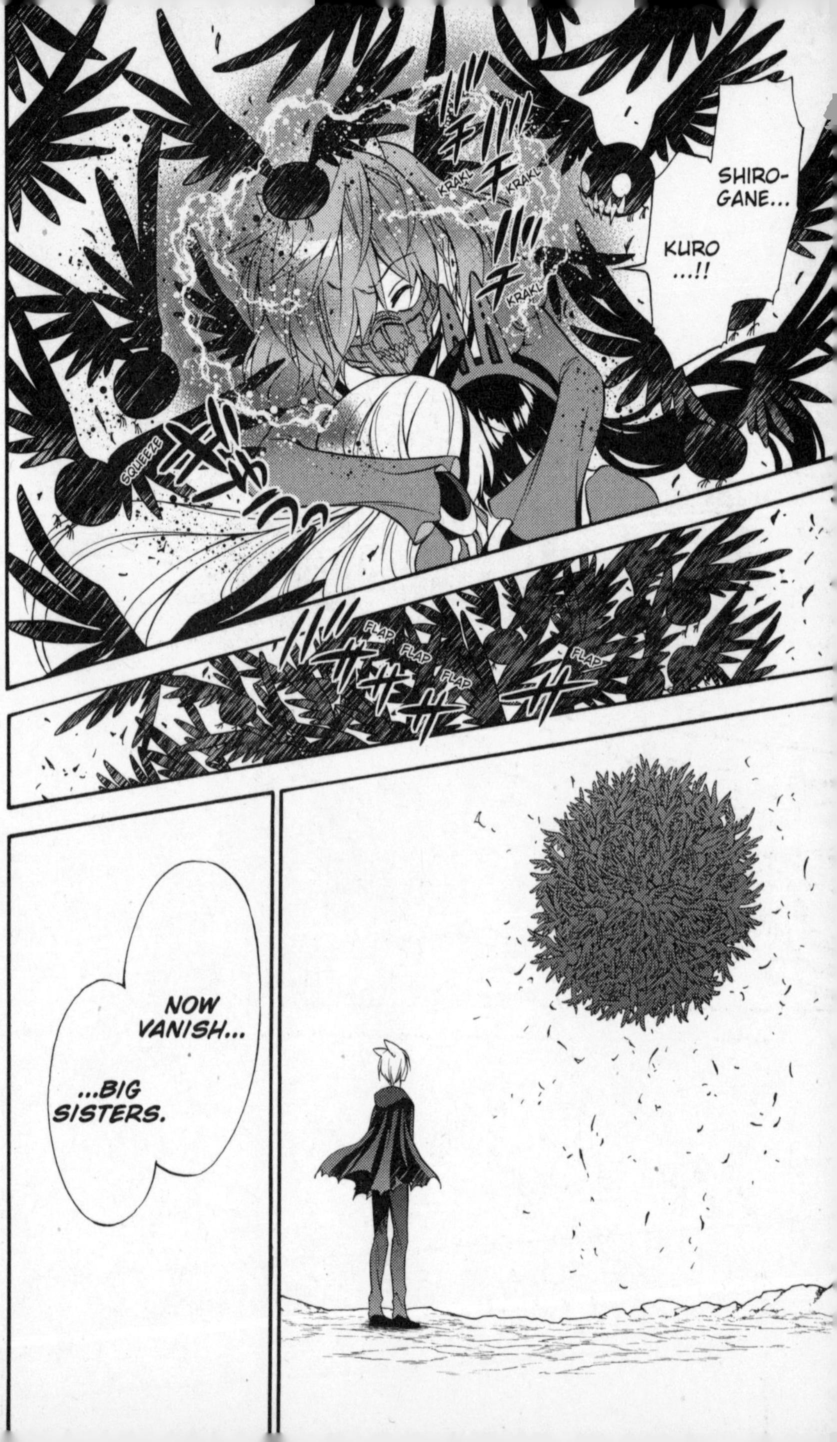
SHIRO-GANE...
KURO ...!!
KRAKL
KRAKL
KRAKL
SQUEEZE
FLAP
FLAP
FLAP
FLAP
NOW VANISH...
...BIG SISTERS.

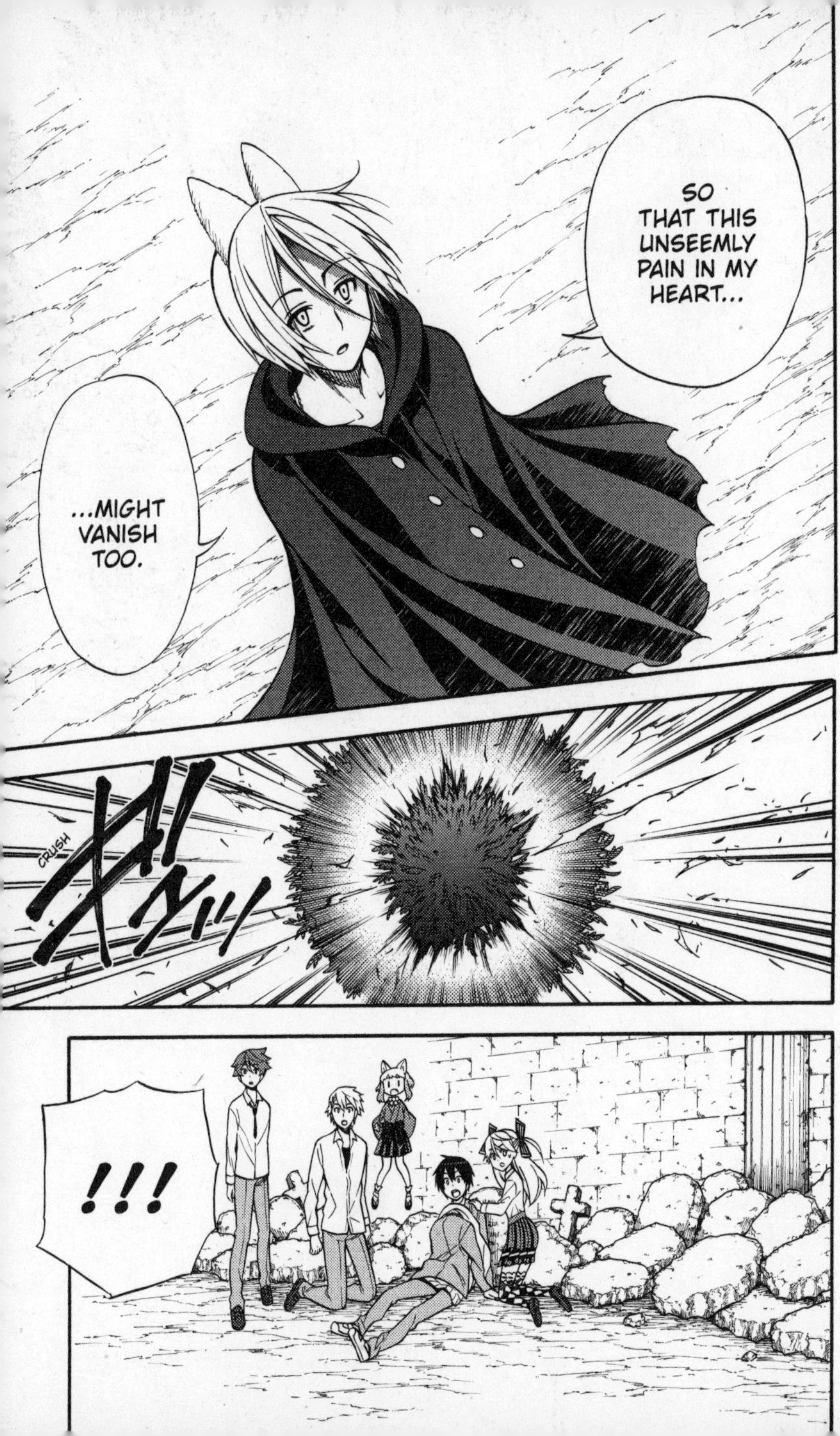
SO THAT THIS UNSEEMLY PAIN IN MY HEART...
...MIGHT VANISH TOO.
CRUSH
!!!

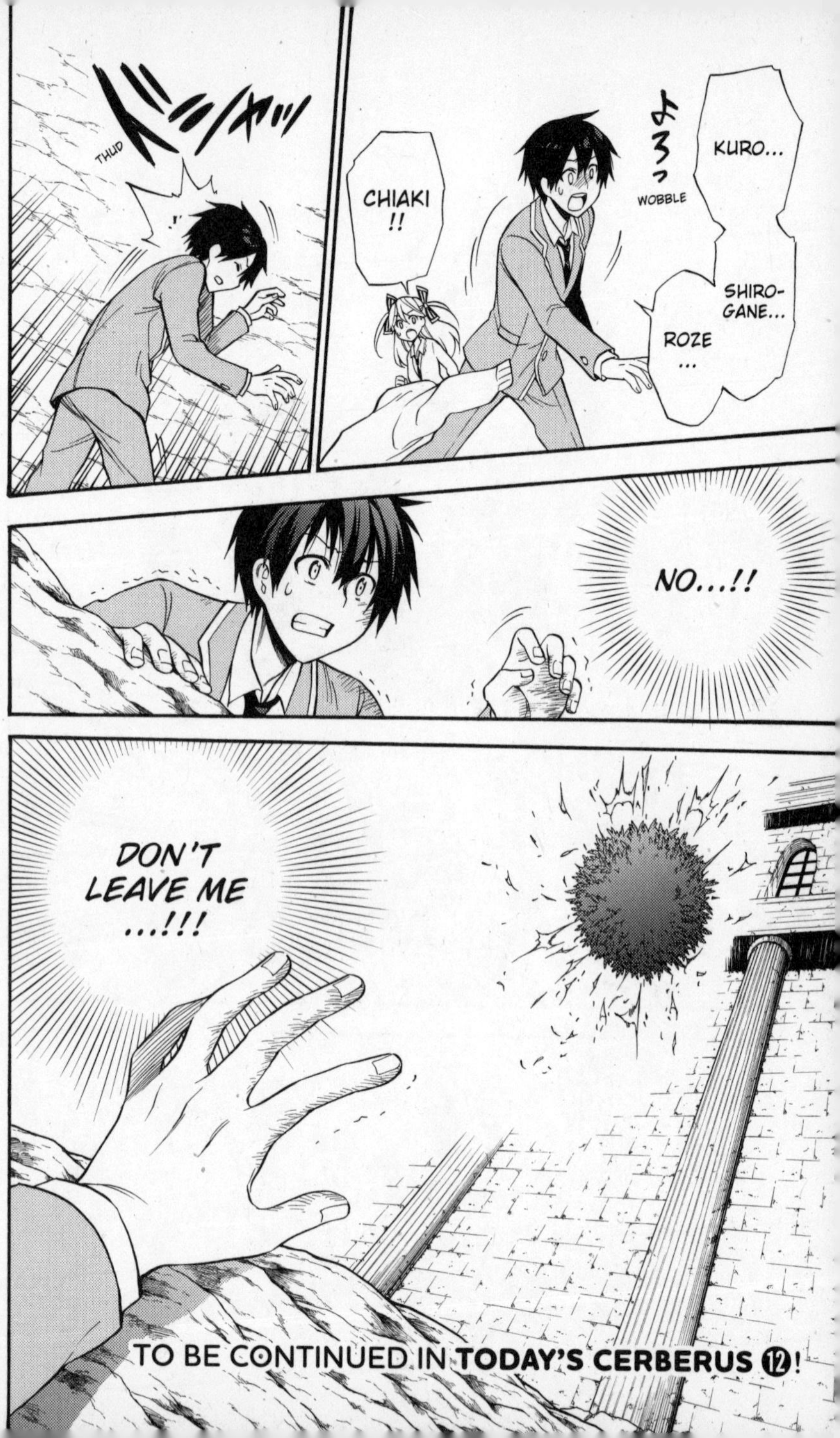
KURO...
よろっ
WOBBLE
SHIRO-GANE...
ROZE...
CHIAKI!!
ドシャッ
THUD
!'
NO...!!
DON'T LEAVE ME...!!!
TO BE CONTINUED IN TODAY'S CERBERUS 12!

TODAY'S CERBERUS

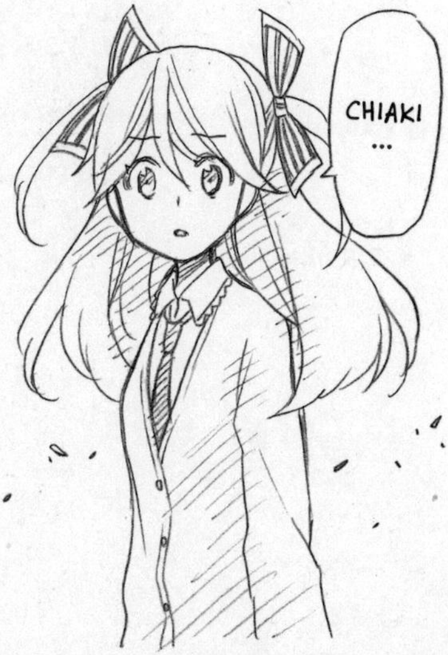
CHIAKI
...

TODAY'S CERBERUS

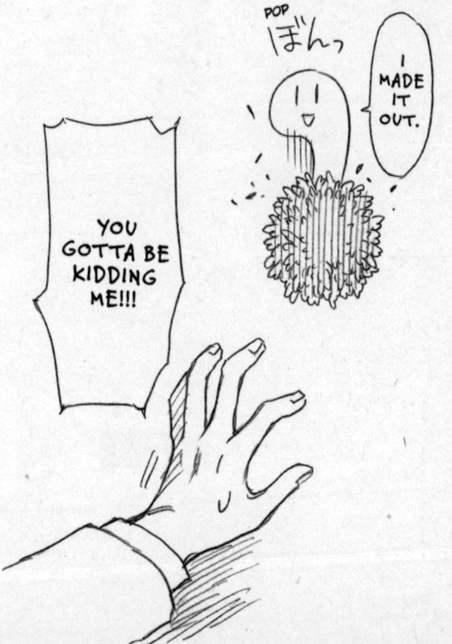
POP
ぼんっ
I MADE IT OUT.
YOU GOTTA BE KIDDING ME!!!

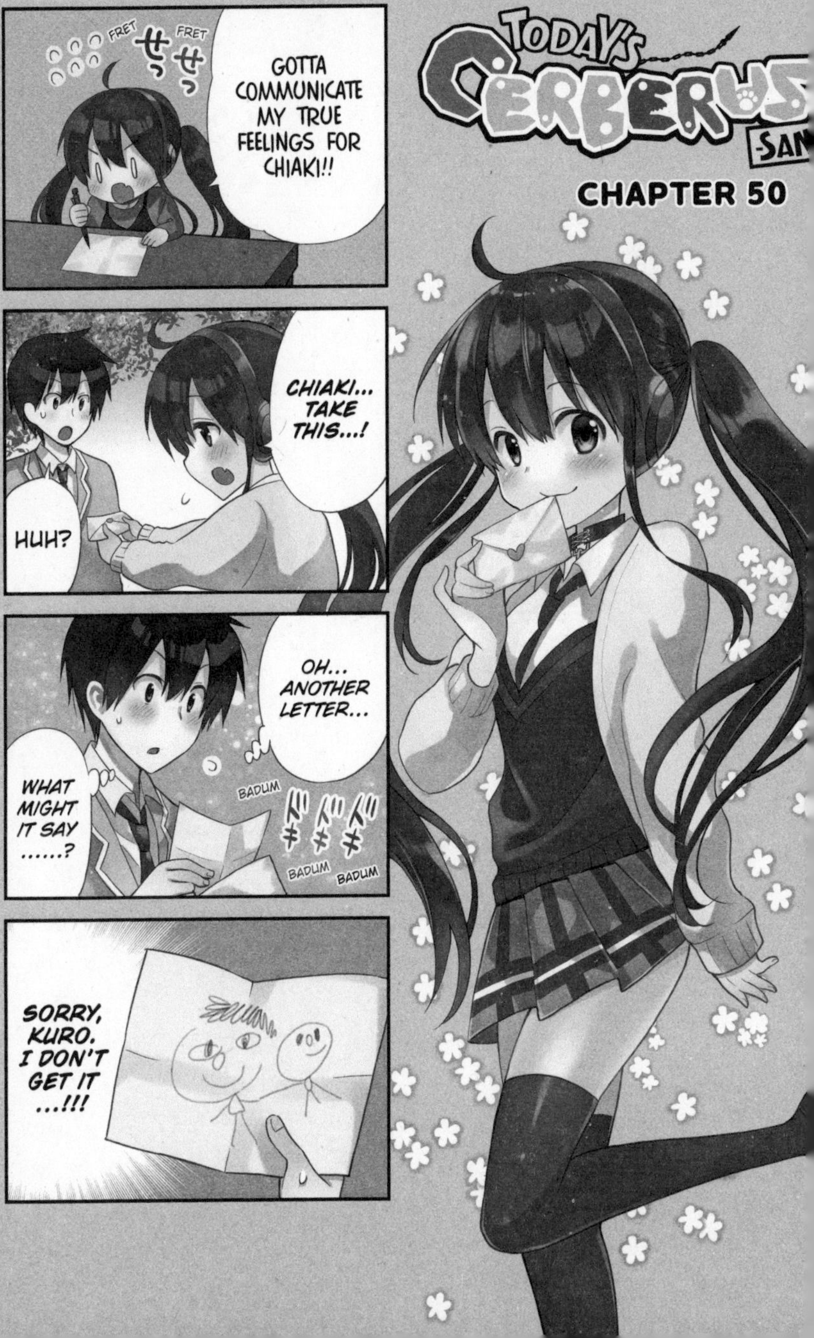
TODAY'S CERBERUS-SAN
CHAPTER 50
FRET FRET
せっせっ
GOTTA COMMUNICATE MY TRUE FEELINGS FOR CHIAKI!!
CHIAKI... TAKE THIS...!
HUH?
OH... ANOTHER LETTER...
BADUM BADUM BADUM
WHAT MIGHT IT SAY ......?
SORRY, KURO. I DON'T GET IT ...!!!

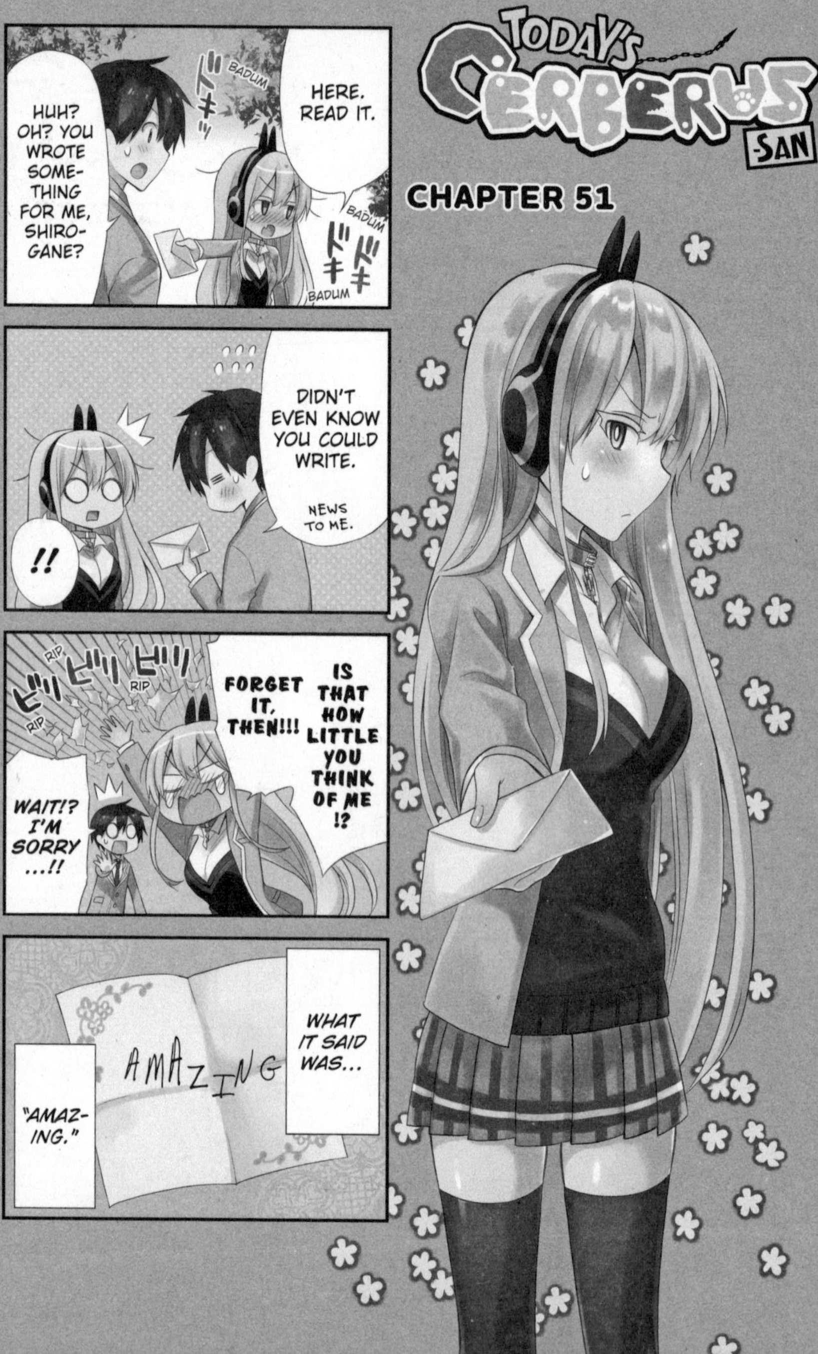
TODAY'S CERBERUS -SAN
CHAPTER 51
HERE. READ IT.
BADUM ドキ BADUM ドキ BADUM
ドキッ BADUM
HUH? OH? YOU WROTE SOME-THING FOR ME, SHIRO-GANE?
DIDN'T EVEN KNOW YOU COULD WRITE.
NEWS TO ME.
!!
IS THAT HOW LITTLE YOU THINK OF ME !?
FORGET IT, THEN!!!
ビリ RIP ビリ RIP ビリ RIP
WAIT!? I'M SORRY ...!!
WHAT IT SAID WAS...
AMAZING
"AMAZ-ING."

TODAY'S CERBERUS -SAN

CHAPTER 52

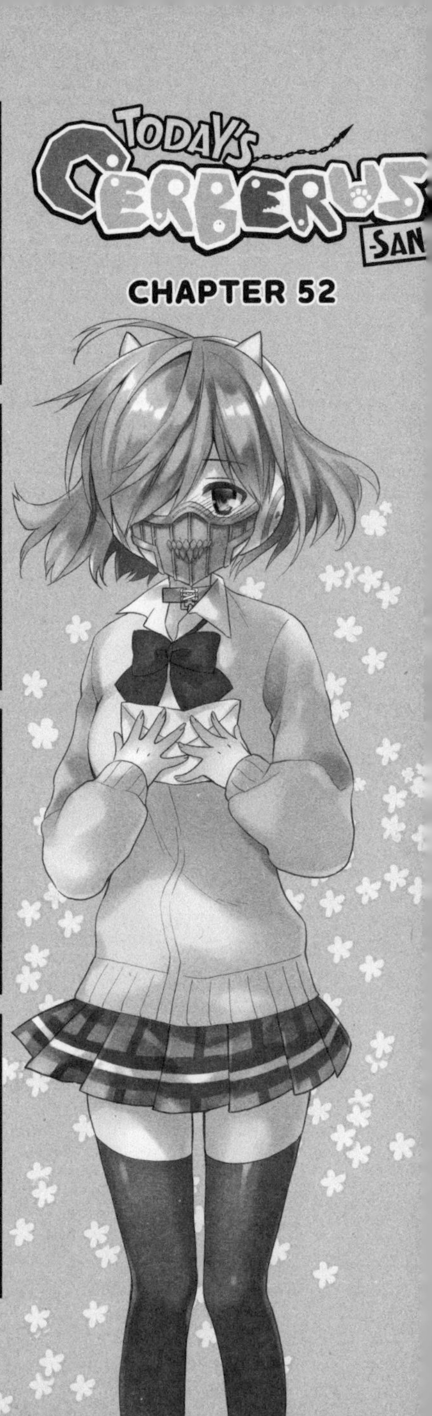

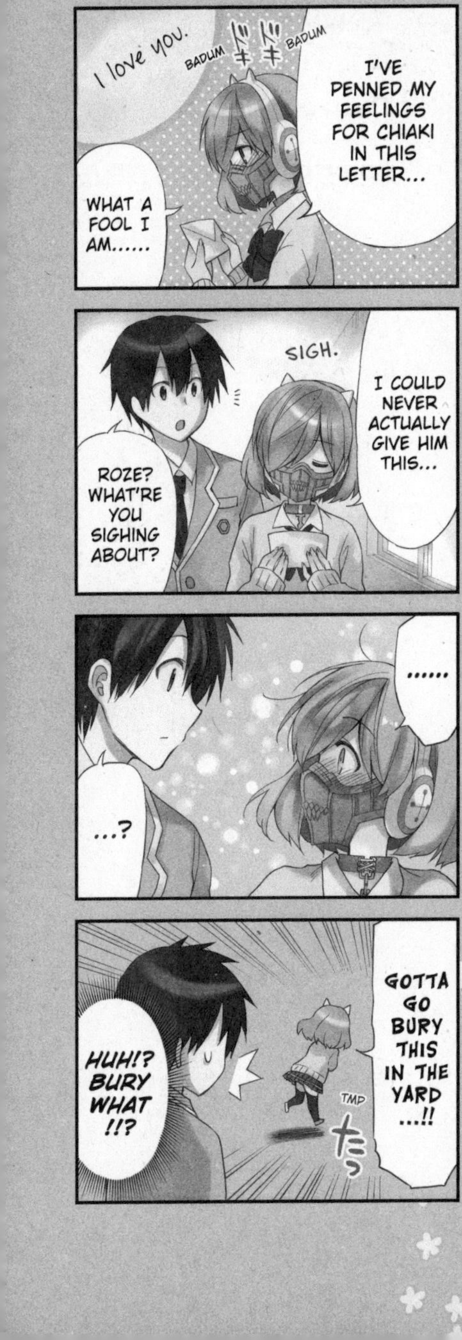

I'VE PENNED MY FEELINGS FOR CHIAKI IN THIS LETTER...
BADUM ドキドキ BADUM
I love you.
WHAT A FOOL I AM......
I COULD NEVER ACTUALLY GIVE HIM THIS...
SIGH.
ROZE? WHAT'RE YOU SIGHING ABOUT?
......
...?
GOTTA GO BURY THIS IN THE YARD ...!!
TMP たっ
HUH!? BURY WHAT !!?

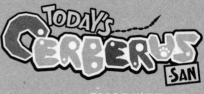

TODAY'S CERBERUS-SAN

CHAPTER 53

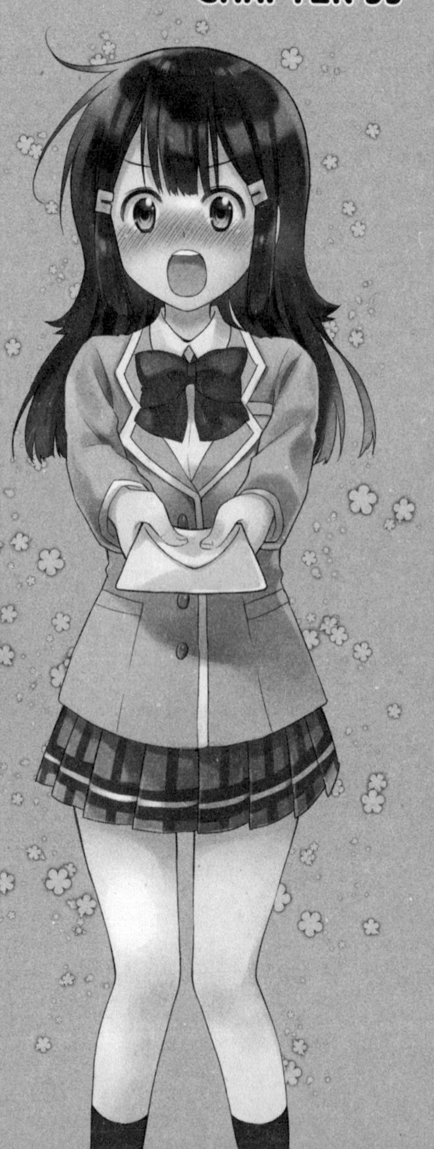

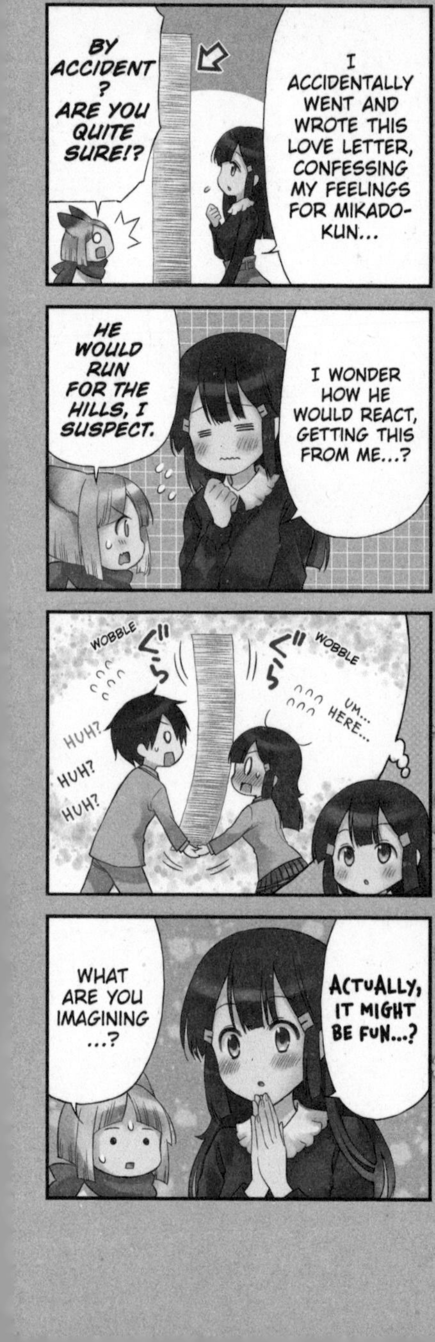
I ACCIDENTALLY WENT AND WROTE THIS LOVE LETTER, CONFESSING MY FEELINGS FOR MIKADO-KUN...
BY ACCIDENT? ARE YOU QUITE SURE!?
I WONDER HOW HE WOULD REACT, GETTING THIS FROM ME...?
HE WOULD RUN FOR THE HILLS, I SUSPECT.
ぐら WOBBLE
UM... HERE...
HUH? HUH? HUH?
ぐら WOBBLE
ACTUALLY, IT MIGHT BE FUN...?
WHAT ARE YOU IMAGINING...?

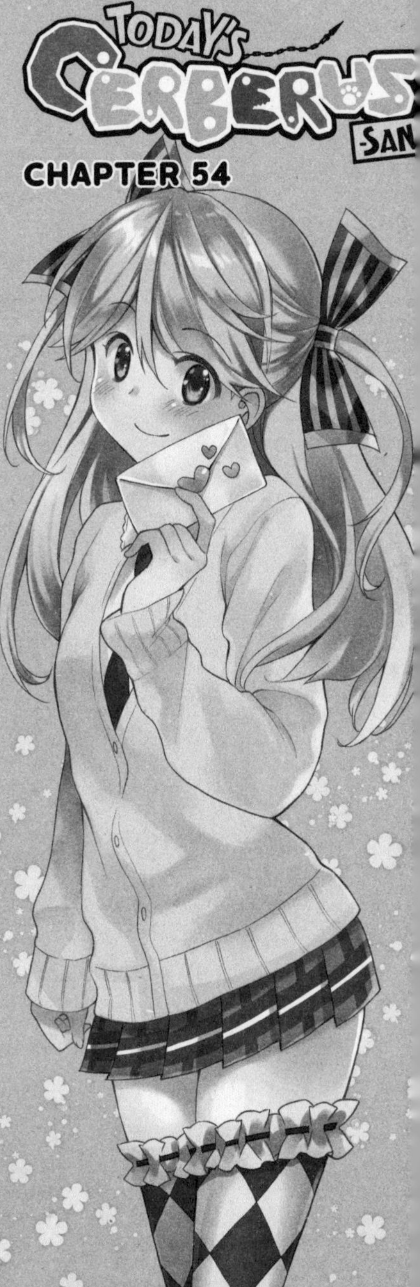
TODAY'S CERBERUS -SAN
CHAPTER 54

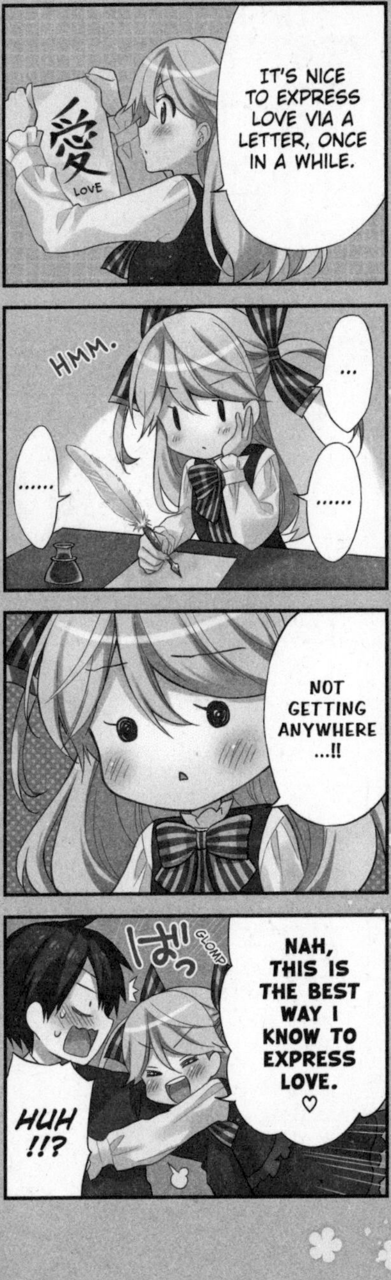
IT'S NICE TO EXPRESS LOVE VIA A LETTER, ONCE IN A WHILE.
愛
LOVE
...
HMM.
......
......
NOT GETTING ANYWHERE ...!!
NAH, THIS IS THE BEST WAY I KNOW TO EXPRESS LOVE. ♡
GLOMP
HUH !!?

MI-KUN'S SITUATION

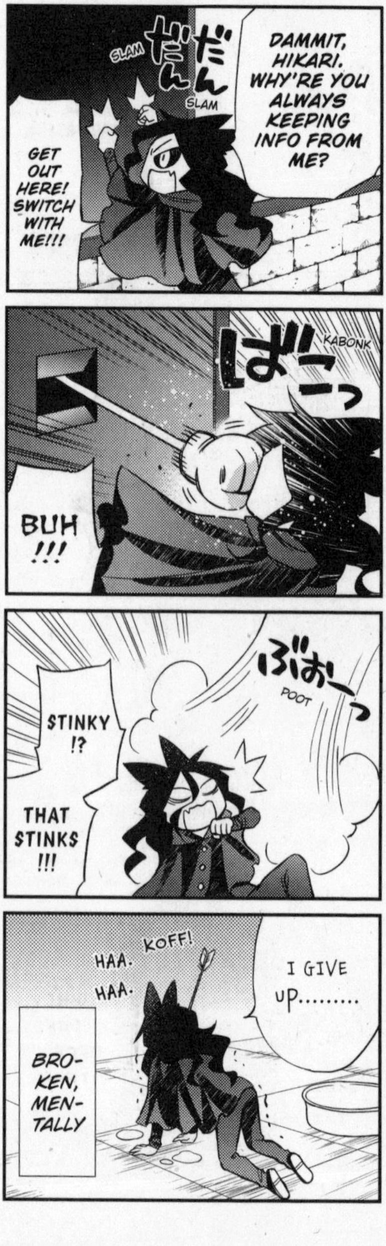
DAMMIT, HIKARI. WHY'RE YOU ALWAYS KEEPING INFO FROM ME?
だん SLAM
だん SLAM
GET OUT HERE! SWITCH WITH ME!!!
ばこーっ KABONK
BUH!!!
ぶおーっ POOT
STINKY!?
THAT STINKS!!!
I GIVE UP.........
KOFF!
HAA. HAA.
BROKEN, MENTALLY

ALMIGHTY VESSEL

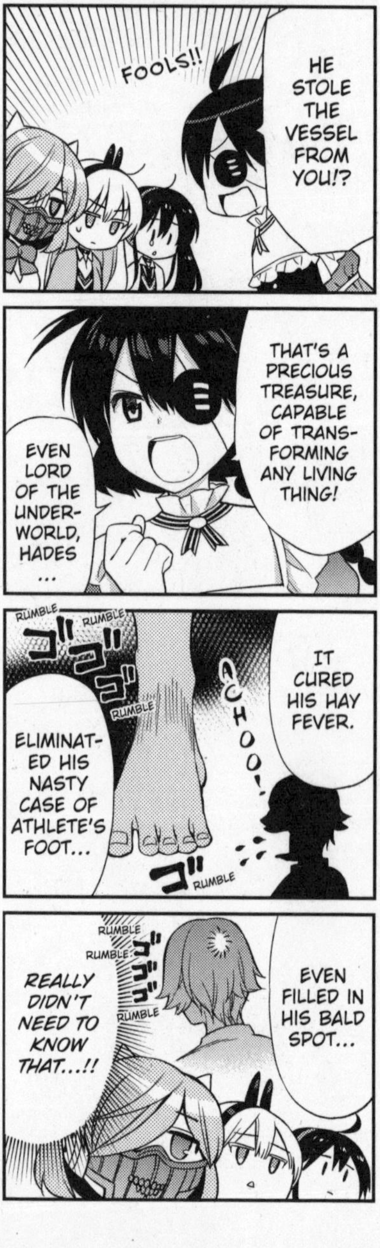
HE STOLE THE VESSEL FROM YOU!?
FOOLS!!
THAT'S A PRECIOUS TREASURE, CAPABLE OF TRANSFORMING ANY LIVING THING!
EVEN LORD OF THE UNDERWORLD, HADES...
IT CURED HIS HAY FEVER.
ACHOOO!
ゴゴゴ RUMBLE RUMBLE RUMBLE
ELIMINATED HIS NASTY CASE OF ATHLETE'S FOOT...
ゴ RUMBLE
EVEN FILLED IN HIS BALD SPOT...
ゴゴゴ RUMBLE RUMBLE RUMBLE
REALLY DIDN'T NEED TO KNOW THAT...!!

TRUE NATURE OF THE TRAP

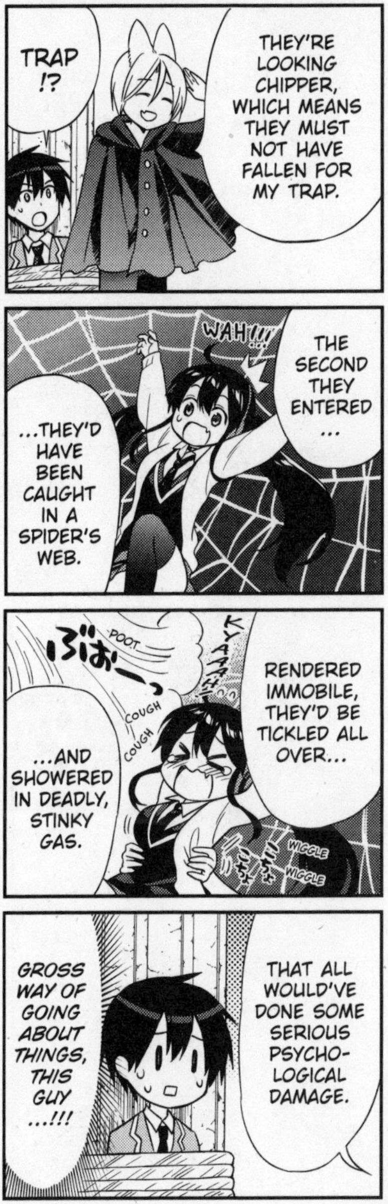
THEY'RE LOOKING CHIPPER, WHICH MEANS THEY MUST NOT HAVE FALLEN FOR MY TRAP.
TRAP !?
WAH!!!
THE SECOND THEY ENTERED ...
...THEY'D HAVE BEEN CAUGHT IN A SPIDER'S WEB.
RENDERED IMMOBILE, THEY'D BE TICKLED ALL OVER...
KYAAAH!
POOT
COUGH
COUGH
...AND SHOWERED IN DEADLY, STINKY GAS.
WIGGLE
WIGGLE
THAT ALL WOULD'VE DONE SOME SERIOUS PSYCHO-LOGICAL DAMAGE.
GROSS WAY OF GOING ABOUT THINGS, THIS GUY ...!!!

POWER-UP

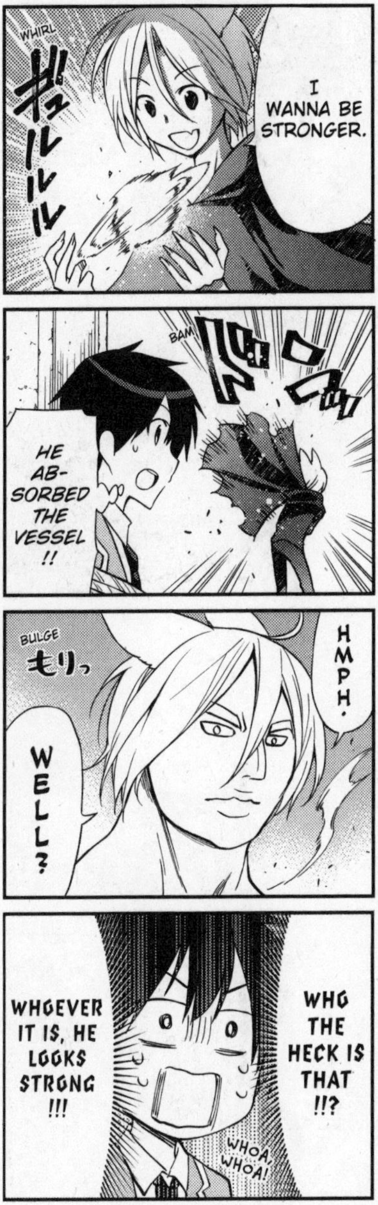
I WANNA BE STRONGER.
WHIRL
BAM
HE AB-SORBED THE VESSEL !!
HMPH.
BULGE
もりっ
WELL?
WHO THE HECK IS THAT !!?
WHOEVER IT IS, HE LOOKS STRONG !!!
WHOA, WHOA!

PROVACATION, TAMA-STYLE

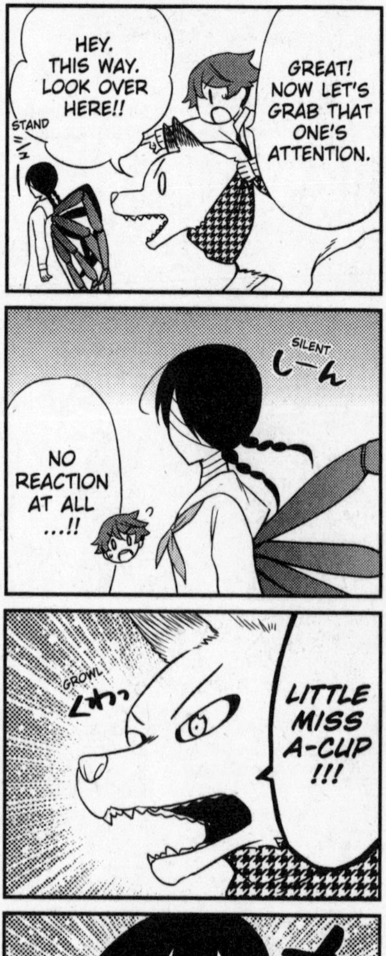
GREAT! NOW LET'S GRAB THAT ONE'S ATTENTION.
HEY. THIS WAY. LOOK OVER HERE!!
STAND
SILENT
NO REACTION AT ALL ...!!
LITTLE MISS A-CUP !!!
GROWL
FWIP

SLEEP

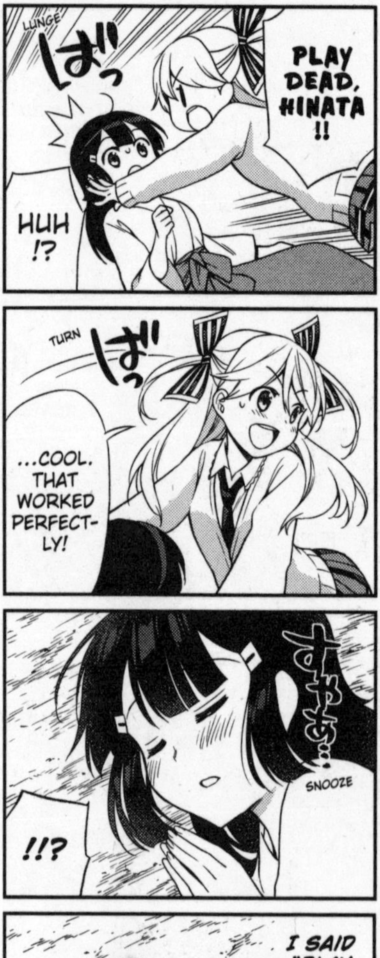
PLAY DEAD, HINATA !!
LUNGE
HUH !?
TURN
...COOL. THAT WORKED PERFECT-LY!
SNOOZE
!!?
I SAID "PLAY DEAD"...
...NOT "LAY IN BED"!!!

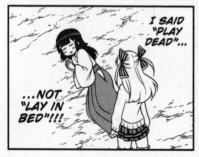

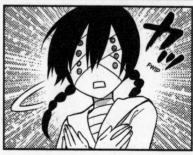

MONSTER GIRL INSECURITIES

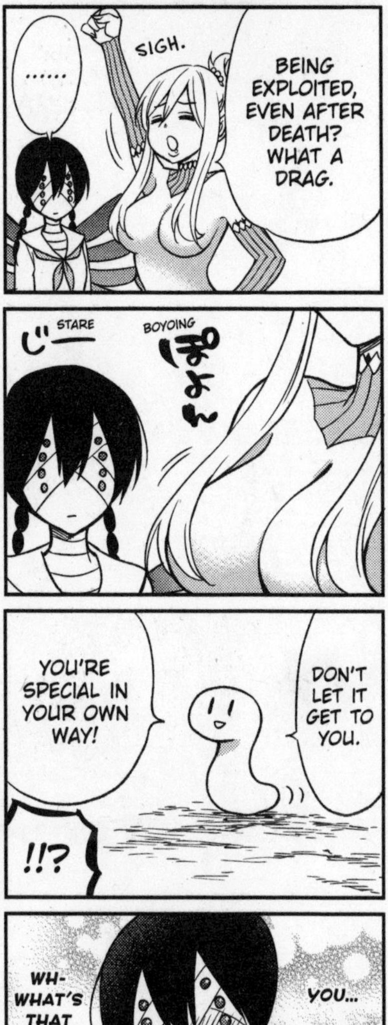
BEING EXPLOITED, EVEN AFTER DEATH? WHAT A DRAG.
SIGH.
......
BOYOING
ぽよん
STARE
じー
DON'T LET IT GET TO YOU.
YOU'RE SPECIAL IN YOUR OWN WAY!
!!?
YOU...
WH-WHAT'S THAT EVEN MEAN ...!?

MY FAVORITE

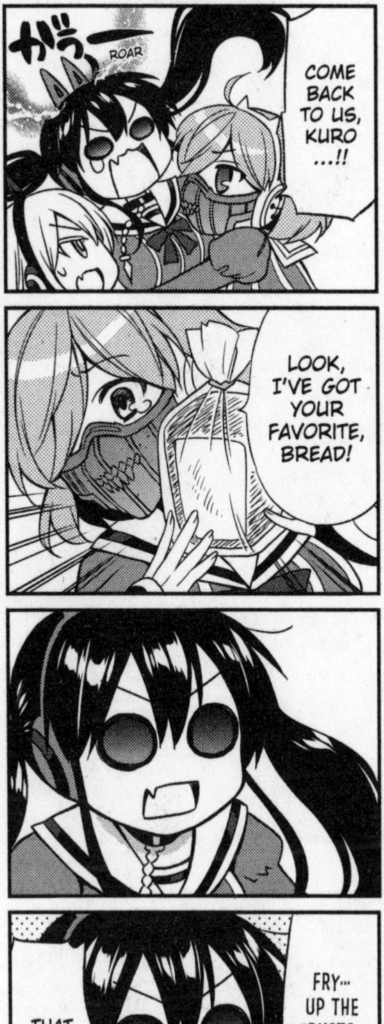
COME BACK TO US, KURO ...!!
がうー
ROAR
LOOK, I'VE GOT YOUR FAVORITE, BREAD!
FRY... UP THE CRUSTS... SPRINKLE WITH SUGAR... YUM.
THAT REACHED HER !!?

STAFF ANALOG-> MORI, YUU JUNA, TAKAYUKI MURAYAMA, HORIGUCHI
DIGITAL-> YOSHII
COLOR LAYERING-> TSUBASA FUKUCHI

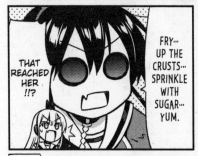

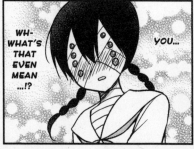

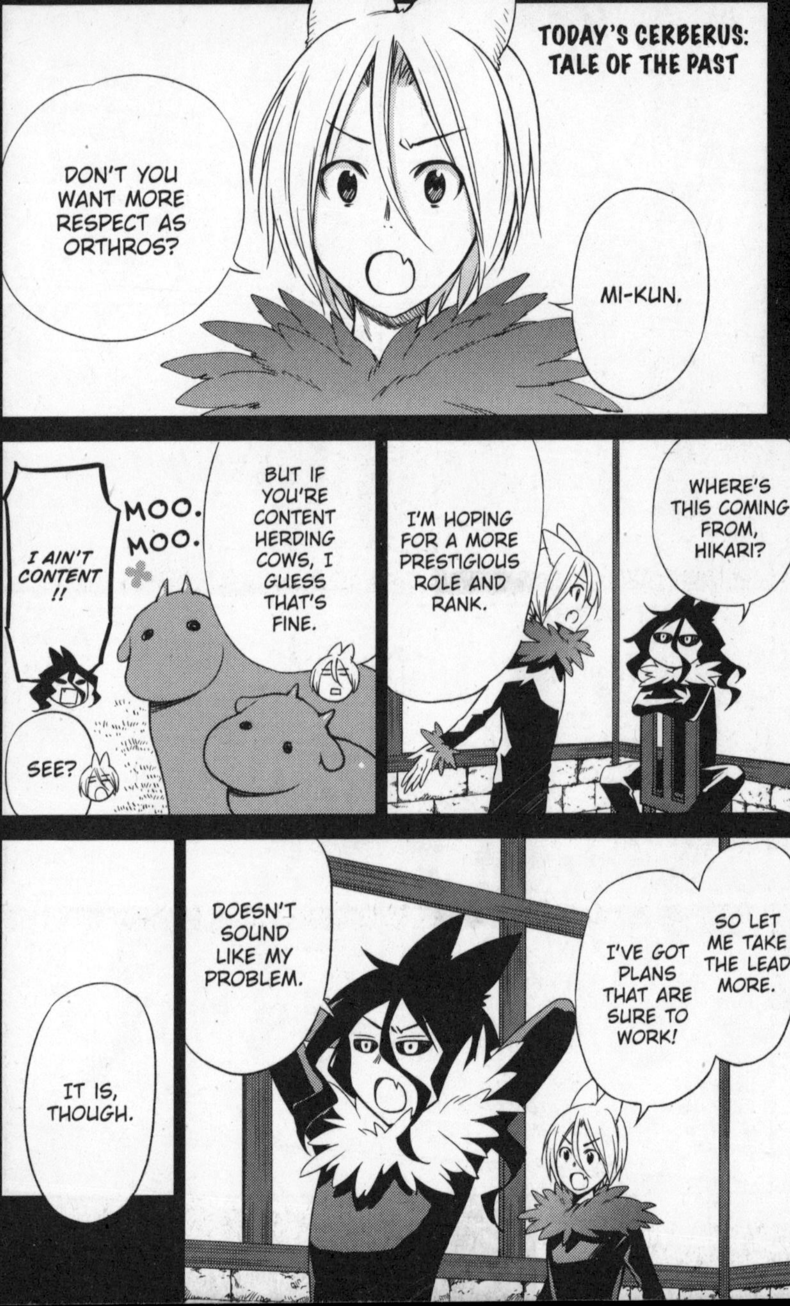
TODAY'S CERBERUS: TALE OF THE PAST
MI-KUN.
DON'T YOU WANT MORE RESPECT AS ORTHROS?
WHERE'S THIS COMING FROM, HIKARI?
I'M HOPING FOR A MORE PRESTIGIOUS ROLE AND RANK.
BUT IF YOU'RE CONTENT HERDING COWS, I GUESS THAT'S FINE.
MOO. MOO.
I AIN'T CONTENT !!
SEE?
SO LET ME TAKE THE LEAD MORE.
I'VE GOT PLANS THAT ARE SURE TO WORK!
DOESN'T SOUND LIKE MY PROBLEM.
IT IS, THOUGH.

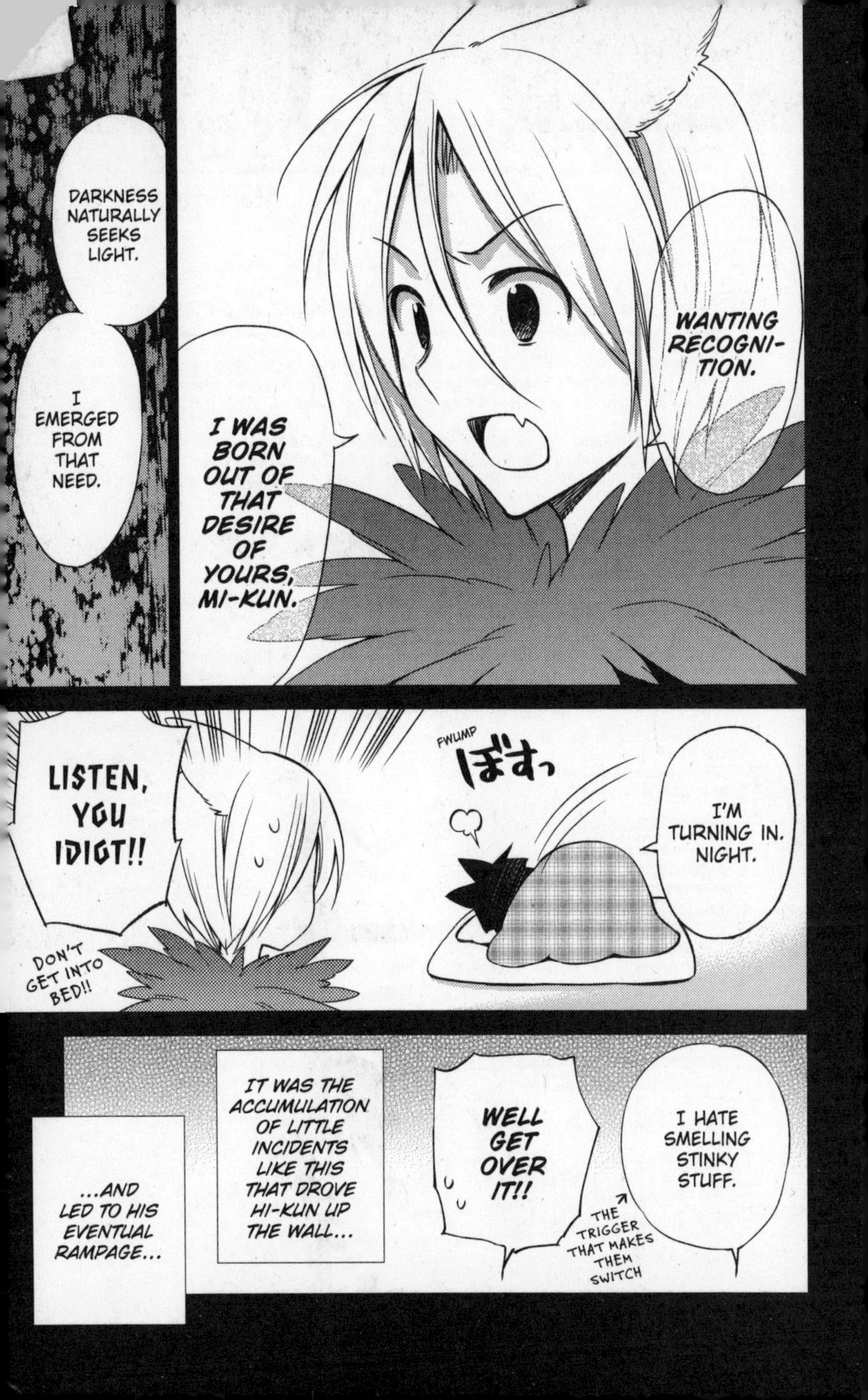
WANTING RECOGNITION.
I WAS BORN OUT OF THAT DESIRE OF YOURS, MI-KUN.
DARKNESS NATURALLY SEEKS LIGHT.
I EMERGED FROM THAT NEED.
FWUMP
ぼすっ
I'M TURNING IN. NIGHT.
LISTEN, YOU IDIOT!!
DON'T GET INTO BED!!
I HATE SMELLING STINKY STUFF.
THE TRIGGER THAT MAKES THEM SWITCH
WELL GET OVER IT!!
IT WAS THE ACCUMULATION OF LITTLE INCIDENTS LIKE THIS THAT DROVE HI-KUN UP THE WALL...
...AND LED TO HIS EVENTUAL RAMPAGE...

TODAY'S CERBERUS ⑪

Ato Sakurai

Translation: Caleb D. Cook • **Lettering: Bianca Pistillo**

TODAY'S KERBEROS Vol. 11 ©2018 Ato Sakurai/SQUARE ENIX CO., LTD. First published in Japan in 2018 by SQUARE ENIX CO., LTD. English translation rights arranged with SQUARE ENIX CO., LTD. and Yen Press, LLC through Tuttle-Mori Agency, Inc.

English translation ©2019 by SQUARE ENIX CO., LTD.

Yen Press
1290 Avenue of the Americas
New York, NY 10104

Visit us at yenpress.com
facebook.com/yenpress
twitter.com/yenpress
yenpress.tumblr.com
instagram.com/yenpress

First Yen Press Edition: January 2019
The chapters in this volume were originally published as ebooks by Yen Press.

Yen Press is an imprint of Yen Press, LLC.
The Yen Press name and logo are trademarks of Yen Press, LLC.

The publisher is not responsible for websites (or their content) that are not owned by the publisher.

Library of Congress Control Number: 2016946072

ISBNs: 978-1-9753-8374-9 (paperback)
978-1-9753-8375-6 (ebook)

10 9 8 7 6 5 4 3 2 1

WOR

Printed in the United States of America